GERMAN NAVY
HANDBOOK
1939–1945

JAK P. MALLMANN SHOWELL

SUTTON PUBLISHING

First published in 1999 by
Sutton Publishing Limited · Phoenix Mill
Thrupp · Stroud · Gloucestershire · GL5 2BU

This paperback edition first published in 2002

British Library Cataloguing in Publication Data
A catalogue record for this book is available from the British Library

ISBN 0 7509 3205 8

Typeset in 10/13pt Baskerville.
Typesetting and origination by
Sutton Publishing Limited.
Printed in Great Britain by
J.H. Haynes & Co. Ltd, Sparkford.

CONTENTS

ACKNOWLEDGEMENTS

If this book needs a dedication, then let it remember those historians who have searched for the truth and the people who have helped by providing information. Sadly, a good number of these characters are no longer around to enrich our lives.

This project has been ongoing for over thirty years and it would be difficult to list all the people who have helped. Therefore I thank everybody and hope that this book will do their efforts justice.

The following have been especially helpful and I am grateful for their assistance in supplying help, materials, information or photographs: Professor Heinfried Ahl of *Kormoran*; Ivar Berntsen; Heinrich Böhm and Maria; Jan Bos; Horst Bredow and the German U-boat Archive in Cuxhaven; Professor Gus Britton, MBE; the staff of the Military Section in the Bundesarchiv in Freiburg; Cdr Richard Compton-Hall, MBE, RN (Retd), and the Royal Navy Submarine Museum; Trevor Cox; Kpt.z.S. Hans Dehnert; Kurt Fritz Dennin; Ralph Erskine; Ursula Kähler von Friedeburg; 'Jumbo' Gerke; Cpt Otto Giese who served aboard *Columbus, Anneliese Essberger* and several U-boats; Hans Karl Hemmer of *Pinguin, Adjutant* and *Komet*; Wolfgang Hirschfeld; Peter Huckstepp from New Zealand; Geoff Jones; Friedrich Kiemle of *Köln*; Dr Joachim Kindler of *Widder*; Fritz Köhl; Kpt.z.S. Otto and Dr Erika Köhler; David Lees of the German Naval Interest Group of the World Ship Society; Kevin Mathews; Dr Ulrich Mohr of *Atlantis*; Heinrich Mueller; Eva Meisel whose husband was captain of *Admiral Hipper*; Gerd Neubacher; Axel Niestle; Fregkpt. Karl-Heinz Nitschke and his wife Ilse; Fregkpt. Albert Nitzschke and the Deutscher Marinebund; Military History Department of the National Defence College in Tokyo; Ian Millar; Hermann and Elsa Patzke; Paul Preuss; Ray Priddey; Admiral Bernhard Rogge; Richard Russon (United States Coast Guard Auxiliary of Florida); the Walter Schöppe Collection in U-Boot-ARCHIV, Cuxhaven; Franz Selinger; Knut Sivertsen and the Trondheim Defence Museum; Roger Suiters; Heinz Tischer from *Thor*; Irmy Wenneker whose husband was captain of *Deutschland* and later naval attaché in Tokyo; Gordon Williamson and Dave Wooley.

The German naval ensign fluttering in a light breeze. The Germans used the Beaufort scale, invented by the English admiral who died in 1857, for measuring wind strength. The flag would suggest that this is a force 2 or 3.

CHRONOLOGY

1870

France declared war on Prussia, the largest of the German-speaking kingdoms, hoping the Catholic south would help suppress the Protestants in the North.

1871

The German-speaking countries united under the King of Prussia and defeated France. The German nation was founded in the palace at Versailles and the King of Prussia became emperor. The Imperial Navy was founded.

1914

Outbreak of the First World War.

1918

11 November. The First World War ended with Germany's defeat and the abdication of the Emperor (*Kaiser*). The guns officially fell silent at 1100 hr on the 11th day of the 11th month. The Kaiser had left Germany the day before.

21 November. The remains of the German fleet surrendered.

1919

12 January. A communist uprising in Berlin was crushed.

9 February. The first non-stop air service between London and Paris came into being. Civil flying was still prohibited, so only military passengers could be carried. Flying time was three and a half hours.

31 March. Admiral Adolf von Trotha became the Supreme Commander-in-Chief of the Navy.

21 June. Seventy ships of the German fleet interned at Scapa Flow in the Orkneys and with only skeleton crews on board hoisted their war ensigns as an indication that the process of scuttling them had started. The British fleet was at sea, but a few tugs and picket boats managed to tow some ships into shallow waters before the majority of them sank.

28 June. Germany agreed to the ultimatum from the Allies and signed the Diktat of Versailles, although having to pay such heavy war reparations meant there would be still more famine throughout Germany.

1920

7 April. A French army of occupation marched into the industrial heartland of Germany because war reparations had slowed down. Much of what was being produced in Germany had to be handed over to the Allies, and the workers, suffering from severe shortages of food and other essentials, couldn't see the point of working as slaves for foreigners.

8 August. Foundation of the National Socialists' Workers Party (*Nationalsozialistische Deutsche Arbeiter Partei* – NSDAP). At this time socialists were nicknamed 'Sozis' hence the new party became 'Nazis'.

30 August. Admiral Paul Behncke became Supreme Commander-in-Chief of the Navy.

1921

1 January. The Imperial Navy (*Kaiserliche Marine*) was renamed *Reichsmarine*.

11 April. The new flag of the Reichsmarine was hoisted for the first time.

21 July. Senior officers of the United States Navy were shocked when in a demonstration the ex-German battleship *Ostfriesland* was sunk by six bombs dropped from aircraft. So far the navies of the world had maintained that battleships could only be sunk by heavy

A minesweeper flotilla at sea. The photograph was taken from *M133*.

artillery. This success against a substantial target brought about new naval thinking.

3 August. The NSDAP founded its own private army, the *Sturm Abteilung* or SA, which was also known as the Brownshirts.

13 December. The Washington Treaty was signed.

31 December. The ensign of the Imperial Navy was officially lowered for the last time by naval units. However, it was hoisted again on 31 May of each year in remembrance of the men who had died during the First World War.

1922

The black, white and red flag with a large iron cross in the middle and a small black, red and gold jack inset – the ensign of the Reichsmarine – was hoisted for the first time by naval units.

1923

22 June. The German economy and its currency collapsed when the Mark had been devalued to the rate of more than 600,000 Marks to the British Pound. Passive resistance had further slowed industrial and agricultural output because the workers were living in poverty while the results of their labours had to be paid as war reparations. Britain and the United States were also suffering from industrial unrest with widespread poverty and unemployment.

8–9 November. The NSDAP attempted to overthrow the Bavarian government by force.

23 November. The NSDAP was banned.

1924

January. The light cruiser *Berlin*, under command of Paul Wülfing von Ditten, left Kiel for a two month tour to the Azores, Canaries, Madeira and Spain. Apart from cruises to countries around the Baltic, this was the first postwar cadet training cruise.

October. Admiral Hans Zenker succeeded Paul Behncke as Supreme Commander-in-Chief of the Navy.

A squadron of battleships visited Spain and *Berlin* embarked on her second cruise to foreign waters.

1925

7 January. The light cruiser *Emden*, the first major warship built in Germany after the First World War, was launched in Wilhelmshaven.

27 February. The NSDAP was refounded.

26 April. General Paul von Hindenburg (1847–1934) who defeated the Russians at Tannenberg in 1914 and later became the Supreme Commander-in-Chief of the General Army Staff, was elected as President of Germany. He wanted to restore the German monarchy. The large number of votes from women had been crucial in his success. In Britain women were still not allowed to vote.

April. Admiral Konrad Mommsen was appointed to the position of Fleet Commander. Such a post had not existed since the end of the First World War. The survey ship *Meteor*, under the command of Fregkpt. Fritz Spiess, left for the famous Atlantic Expedition. She surveyed the South Atlantic and did not return until May 1927.

This shows the second naval ensign after the end of the First World War. The stripes were black, white and red at the bottom. Earlier flags also had a small black, red and gold striped jack in the top left hand corner.

August. The light cruiser *Hamburg*, under Fregkpt. Groos, left Wilhelmshaven for the first German postwar naval circumnavigation of the Earth.

September. The light cruiser *Berlin*, under Kpt.z.S. Ernst Junkermann, embarked upon a more ambitious cadet training voyage around South America.

9 November. The *Schutz Staffel* or SS was founded by the NSDAP.

1926

5 May. Beginning of the First General Strike in Britain.

14 November. The new light cruiser *Emden*, under Kpt.z.S. Richard Foerster, left for a world tour for cadet training.

1927

December. The light cruiser *Berlin,* under Kpt.z.S. Carl Kolbe, left for a training cruise to the Far East and Australia.

1928

29 March. Women in Britain were given the vote.

1 October. Admiral Erich Raeder became Commander-in-Chief of the Navy. Major naval administrative reshuffles and reorganisation usually took place in October and coincided with the publication of a new *Rangliste* (Rank list).

December. The light cruiser *Emden* departed for a world cruise under the command of Lothar von Arnauld de la Periere, a holder of the *Pour le Merite* from the First World War.

1929

13 May. The light cruiser *Emden* returned from a training cruise to the West Indies and the entire contingent of cadets stepped over to the newly commissioned cruiser *Karlsruhe*, under Kpt.z.S. Eugen Lindau, for a shakedown cruise through the Mediterranean and around Southern Africa.

1930

The NSDAP increased their seats in the government from 12 to 107, making them the second largest party after the Socialists – whence Germany was dominated by Sozis and Nazis.

December. The light cruiser *Emden* sailed to Africa and the Far East under command of Fregkpt. Robert Witthoeft-Emden, who later became naval attaché in Washington. All the men who served aboard the legendary light cruiser *Emden* during the First World War were awarded that name as part of their surname by the Kaiser in recognition of their extraordinary service. This happened around the time of the abdication, when the Kaiser was no longer in a position to bestow military awards.

1931

19 May. Pocket battleship *Deutschland* was launched.

November. The light cruiser *Karlsruhe*, under command of Kpt.z.S. Erwin Wassner, embarked upon a cadet training cruise to South America and Alaska.

1932

25 February. Adolf Hitler became a German citizen. He was born in Austria.

March and April. President Hindenburg defeated Hitler in two stages of what became tight-run presidential elections. At first Hindenburg dismissed Hitler as 'a Bavarian corporal', but during the humiliating second elections between the two, Hitler's vote was increased by almost 40 per cent, making him a powerful force in German politics.

30 October. Battles were fought in London between the police and unemployed hunger marchers demanding a better deal for the starving poor.

6 November. The NSDAP lost thirty-four seats in the governmental elections. Shortly before this Hindenburg refused to appoint Hitler as chancellor.

1933

January. The German embassies in Washington, London and Paris opened offices for naval attachés. This is the first time since before the First World War that there had been such positions.

The light cruiser *Karlsruhe* on a pre-war training cruise for officer cadets. The ship aroused a great deal of interest wherever it called as can be seen here by the numerous cars and the crowds on the quay. The flag flying on the bows is the naval ensign of the old Weimar Republic.

30 January. Hindenburg appointed Hitler as chancellor.

5 March. The last multi-party governmental elections. The NSDAP gained about 40 per cent of the votes.

14 March. The black, red and gold striped jack inset in the naval flag was removed by order of the Reich's president, Paul von Hindenburg.

1 April. Jewish shops were boycotted by the NSDAP.

2 May. Trade unions were banned by the NSDAP.

1934

3 June. Pocket battleship *Admiral Graf Spee* was launched.

24 October. The National Labour Front was introduced by the NSDAP.

1935

16 March. Hitler repudiated the Diktat of Versailles and re-introduced national conscription.

21 May. The *Reichsmarine* was renamed *Kriegsmarine*.

18 June. The German-Anglo Naval Agreement was signed.

29 June. U1, the first new submarine since the First World War, was commissioned.

27 September. Karl Dönitz was appointed Chief of the first U-boat Flotilla, named after the First World War commander Otto Weddigen.

7 November. The new naval ensign with swastika was officially hoisted for the first time.

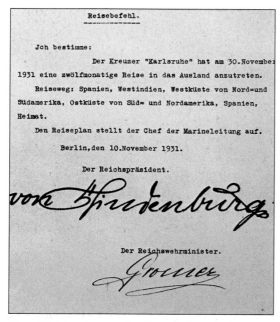

The official written order from Reichspresident Paul von Hindenburg, authorising a twelve-month-long voyage along America's west coast.

1936

7 March. The Rhineland, which had been demilitarised by the Versailles Diktat, was re-occupied by German forces.

30 May. The first phase of the Naval Memorial at Laboe near Kiel was officially opened and Hitler laid the first wreath in the Hall of Commemoration.

18 July. The Spanish Civil War began.

3 October. Battleship *Scharnhorst* was launched.

1937

6 February. The heavy cruiser *Admiral Hipper* was launched.

8 June. The heavy cruiser *Blücher* was launched.

1938

4 February. Hitler appointed himself Supreme Commander-in-Chief of all Germany's armed forces and servicemen swore an oath of allegiance to him personally.

13 March. Austria was made part of Germany.

28 March. The Spanish Civil War ended.

21 May. Battleship *Gneisenau* was launched.

22 August. The heavy cruiser *Prinz Eugen* was launched.

September. The 'Z-Plan' was formulated.

29 September. The Munich Agreement was signed. The British prime minister returned home waving a piece of paper and saying, 'Peace in our Time'.

8 December. The aircraft carrier *Graf Zeppelin* was launched.

1939

27 January. Hitler officially approved the 'Z-Plan'.

9 February. The British government prepared for war by distributing bomb shelters to people living in likely target areas.

14 February. Battleship *Bismarck* was launched.

15 March. German troops marched into Bohemia and Moravia (both districts of Czechoslovakia).

1 April. Battleship *Tirpitz* was launched and the head of the Navy, Erich Raeder, was promoted to Admiral of the Fleet (Grand Admiral), a position which had not existed since the end of the First World War.

28 April. Hitler renounced the Anglo-German Naval Agreement.

22 May. A military agreement for mutual support was signed between Germany and Italy.

18 August. The German Naval High Command ordered the emergency War Programme to come into force.

19 August. The first U-boats left German ports to take up waiting positions in the North Atlantic.

21 August. Pocket battleship *Graf Spee* left Germany to take up a waiting position in the South Atlantic.

22 August. A non-aggression pact was signed by Germany and the Soviet Union.

24 August. Pocket battleship *Deutschland* left Germany to take up a waiting position in the North Atlantic.

1 September. German troops reoccupied territories which had been taken away from Germany after the First World War to become the Polish Republic.

3 September. Britain sent an ultimatum to Germany saying that a state of war would exist between the two countries unless troops were withdrawn from Poland. Subsequently Britain and France declared war.

13 September. The U-boat War Badge was re-introduced with a modern design incorporating a swastika instead of the imperial crown. *U47* penetrated into the British anchorage at Scapa Flow and torpedoed the battleship *Royal Oak*.

17 September. The Russians invaded the eastern regions of Poland, but Britain did not seem to object to the Russian attack.

23 November. The auxiliary cruiser *Rawalpindi* was sunk by *Scharnhorst*.

13–17 December. The Battle of the River Plate and the scuttling of pocket battleship *Admiral Graf Spee*.

1940

31 March. The first auxiliary cruiser, *Atlantis*, under Kpt.z.S. Bernhard Rogge, left German waters for what was to become the longest cruise (622 days) of the Second World War.

6 April. The second auxiliary cruiser, *Orion*, under Kpt.z.S. Kurt Weyher, left German waters.

9 April. Germany invaded Denmark and Norway. The heavy cruiser *Blücher* was sunk in Oslo Fjord.

10 April. The light cruiser *Königsberg* was sunk by bombs in Bergen harbour (Norway).

10 May. Germany invaded Holland, Belgium, Luxembourg and France.

15 May. Dutch forces capitulated.

27 May–4 June. The British Expeditionary Force on the continent was evacuated from the beaches at Dunkirk.

4 June. The War Badge for Destroyers was introduced.

7 June. Britain awarded the first Victoria

The naval ensign drawn by the author's father aboard *U377*.

Cross of the Second World War, its highest military decoration for bravery, to Cpt Bernard Warburton-Lee of the destroyer HMS *Hardy*.

10 June. Italy declared war on France and Britain. The last remnants of British forces in Norway were withdrawn.

17 June. The first U-boats refuelled in French Atlantic ports.

22 June. An armistice was signed by French and German leaders in the same railway carriage in Compiegne where the Armistice had been signed ending the First World War.

27 June. The British government announced a blockade of the European continent.

30 June. A German aircraft landed near St Peter Port to mark the beginning of the German occupation of the Channel Islands.

17 August. Germany announced a total blockade of the British Isles and allowed U-boats to conduct unrestricted sea warfare, where they could sink ships without warning.

24 August. Battleship *Bismarck* was commissioned.

30 August. Plans for an invasion of Great Britain were postponed.

31 August. The War Badge for Minesweepers,

The stern of *U53* or *U52* with the naval ensign of the Third Reich.

Security Forces and Submarine Hunters was introduced.

August. Britain swapped bases for fifty old American ships, many of them small warships suitable for convoy escorts.

16–20 October. The most successful U-boat group attack took place against convoys SC7 and HX79.

1941

25 February. Battleship *Tirpitz* was commissioned.

17 March. U99 (Kptlt. Otto Kretschmer) and U100 (Kptlt. Joachim Schepke) were sunk by destroyers after they had been detected by Type 286 radar. This was the first sinking where radar played a vital role.

1 April. The War Badge for Blockade Breakers was introduced.

24 April. The War Badge for Auxiliary Cruisers was introduced.

30 April. The Fleet War Badge was introduced. Auxiliary cruiser *Thor* (Kpt.z.S. Otto Kähler) made fast in Hamburg after a successful voyage lasting 329 days.

8 May. Pinguin (Kpt.z.S. Ernst-Felix Krüder), the auxiliary cruiser which had sunk or captured most shipping, was sunk by the cruiser HMS *Cornwall.*

9 May. U110 (Kptlt. Fritz-Julius Lemp) was captured by British forces without German survivors having been aware that their boat had fallen into British hands. The booty included an Engima code writer, set up with the code of the day and a book with details on how to operate it during the next few weeks.

18 May. Battleship *Bismarck* and the heavy cruiser *Prinz Eugen* left Gotenhafen.

24 May. The British battlecruiser *Hood* was sunk by *Bismarck.*

27 May. Bismarck was sunk following extensive attacks by British forces.

30 May. The Motor Torpedo Boat War Badge was introduced.

4 June. Emperor Wilhelm II and ex-King of Prussia died in Holland where he had been living since leaving Germany at the end of the First World War.

22 June. Germany invaded the Soviet Union.

24 June. The War Badge for Naval Artillery was introduced.

23 August. Auxiliary cruiser *Orion* (Kpt.z.S. Kurt Weyer) arrived in French waters following a successful voyage of 511 days.

28 August. U570 (Kptlt. Hans Rahmlow) surrendered to an aircraft in mid-Atlantic.

15 November. U459, the first purpose-built supply U-boat, was commissioned by Korvkpt. Georg von Wilamowitz-Möllendorf, one of the oldest submarine commanders.

22 November. Auxiliary cruiser *Atlantis* (Kpt.z.S. Bernhard Rogge) was scuttled after 622 days at sea while under attack from the British cruiser *Devonshire.*

29 November. Auxiliary cruiser *Kormoran* (Kpt.z.S. Theodor Detmers) was sunk on its 350th day at sea, following a battle with the Australian cruiser *Sydney*.

30 November. Auxiliary cruiser *Komet* (Konteradmiral Robert Eyssen) arrived in Hamburg after a voyage of 516 days.

7 December. Japanese forces attacked the United States Pacific Fleet at Pearl Harbor.

11 December. Germany declared war against the United States of America.

1942

14 January. Auxiliary cruiser *Thor* sails from the Gironde Estuary in France for her second operational voyage.

12/13 February. The Channel Dash – when *Scharnhorst*, *Gneisenau* and *Prinz Eugen* plus an escort of smaller ships, all under command of the Fleet Commander Admiral Otto Cilliax, dashed from France to Northern Europe.

26/27 February. *Gneisenau* was put out of action as a result of bomb hits received during a raid on Kiel.

13/14 March. Auxiliary cruiser *Michel* successfully broke through the English Channel for the start of her first voyage.

27 March. A British commando raid on St Nazaire (France) among other things put out of action the only dry dock large enough to accommodate the big German battleships.

20 April. Motor Torpedo Boats were given their own autonomous command under Kpt.z.S. Rudolf Petersen.

9 May. Auxiliary cruiser *Stier* left Germany.

12 September. The *Laconia* Incident – when *U156* (Kptlt. Werner Hartenstein) sank the passenger liner and afterwards mounted a rescue operation because it was discovered that there were Italian prisoners of war on board. (Italy was fighting the war on Germany's side at this time.)

27 September. Auxiliary cruiser *Stier* had to be scuttled following damage by the American auxiliary cruiser *Stephen Hopkins*.

4 November. End of the Battle of El Alamein and the beginning of the German retreat in North Africa.

1943

14 January. The Allied leaders met for the Casablanca Conference.

January. Hitler made his famous proposal to scrap the surface fleet.

30 January. Grand Admiral Erich Raeder resigned. He was succeeded by Karl Dönitz as Supreme Commander-in-Chief of the Navy.

2 February. Field Marshal Friedrich Paulus surrendered, marking the end of the Battle for Stalingrad which had lasted since a Russian counter-attack on 19 November 1942. This German defeat is often taken as the turning point of the war.

March. The sixth consecutive month in which Germany had over a hundred U-boats in the North Atlantic, but thus far it had not come to a large-scale convoy battle.

16–19 March. U-boat attacked a mass of merchant ships just after the fast convoy HX229 of 40 ships caught up with 54 ships of the slower SC122, making this the biggest convoy battle of the war.

23 March–8 April. Convoy HX231 succeeded in crossing from Canada without loss after throwing off every attacking U-boat, although the 'Air Gap' in the Atlantic was still almost 800 km wide.

May. Over 40 U-boats were lost which has prompted many historians to label this as the turning point of the U-boat war. However, Dönitz never recognised it as such and said it was only a temporary setback.

25 July. The end of Mussolini's reign of power in Italy.

3 September. Allied forces landed in Italy.

8 September. Italy surrendered and changed sides to fight against Germany.

22 September. British X-craft attacked battleship *Tirpitz* in Norway.

17 October. *Michel*, the last operational auxiliary cruiser, was sunk by US Submarine *Tarpon* thus ending cruiser warfare on the high seas.

26 December. The Battle of North Cape and the sinking of *Scharnhorst* by British forces.

1944

5 April. British forces mounted a large-scale attack against battleship *Tirpitz* in Norway.

13 May. The Clasp for the Roll of Honour of the German Navy was instituted.

15 May. The U-boat Clasp was instituted.

May. Schnorkels, enabling U-boats to run their diesel engines without surfacing, came into widespread use.

6 June. The Allied invasion of France at Normandy.

11 June. U490, the last remaining supply U-boat, was sunk.

12 June. U2321 (Type XXIII) the first electro-submarine was commissioned.

27 June. U2501 (Type XXI) the first large electro-submarine was commissioned.

July. An experimental command was founded under Admiral Helmuth Heye to develop new midget craft.

12 November. *Tirpitz* was sunk in Norway.

13 November. The War Badge for Midget Weapons was introduced in seven grades.

1945

30 January. The passenger liner *Wilhelm Gustloff* was sunk in the Baltic. Over 5,000 refugees were killed.

10 February. The passenger liner *General von Steuben* was sunk, killing 2,700 people.

13 February. Allied air forces attacked the City of Dresden, killing more than 130,000 people. More civilians were killed during this one raid than during the entire bombing war against Britain. The atom bombs dropped later on Japan also killed fewer people.

16 April. The passenger liner *Goya* was sunk, killing over 6,000 refugees.

30 April. Hitler committed suicide in his command bunker in Berlin and Grand Admiral Karl Dönitz became Head of State.

3 May. The passenger liner *Cap Arkona* was sunk, killing several thousand people. Other passenger liners bombed around this time also resulted in heavy loss of life.

4 May. At 1830 hrs the German delegation signed the Instrument of Surrender at Field Marshal Montgomery's headquarters south of Hamburg.

5 May. At 0800 hrs cessation of all hostilities on land, on sea and in the air by German forces came into effect.

AFTER THE FIRST WORLD WAR – NEW BEGINNINGS

The first German Navy, the so-called Federal Fleet, was founded in 1848 and renamed Royal Prussian Fleet in 1852. In 1867 it became The Fleet of the North German Federation. Four years later, shortly after the unification of the German States, Emperor Wilhelm I changed this core into the Imperial Navy (*Kaiserliche Marine*). After the First World War, the name was changed to *Reichsmarine* and in 1935 it became the *Kriegsmarine*. The Federal German Navy (*Bundesmarine*) was founded in 1954 in the west, while the eastern German Democratic Republic founded the *Volksmarine* in 1960.

During the Battle of Jutland in the First World War, a British destroyer used the cover of darkness to launch two torpedoes against the battleship *Pommern*. Only the two end sections remained afloat long enough for witnesses to gasp as the heart of a massive steel fortress disintegrated, taking over 800 men to their deaths. *Pommern* had been laid down during the last days of 1905, when underwater warfare was still relegated to the realms of science fiction and torpedoes were novel curiosities. Yet, only a decade later, this last event in a chain of catastrophic losses made German sailors realise that the horrors of new technology had arrived with a vengeance. Consequently similarly vulnerable ships, without armoured protection below the waterline, were banished to secondary duties, such as serving as harbour defence batteries or accommodation ships.

About two years later, in 1919, the Versailles Diktat demanded that these antiquated potential disasters be brought back for front line service to form the backbone of Germany's postwar navy. The incompetence displayed by the war-time military command of all nationalities was now taken over by politicians. Turning their hateful propaganda into short sighted revenge, the Allies found the audacity to call their ultimatum for a peace 'a treaty', despite negotiations having played no role in its composition. Many Germans called it '*Verat* of Versailles' meaning 'Treachery or Betrayal' instead of *Vertrag* (Treaty). This ill-conceived document was no more than a smokescreen to cover their own shortcomings among the chaos which still surrounded them. Instead of seriously looking towards peace, the politicians not only unwittingly created a vehicle for leading Europe into the next large-scale war, but they also provided a ladder for allowing the unscrupulous access to Germany's power vacuum.

Allied leaders hardly had time to rest on their laurels, hoping the immense problems in Europe would remain hidden under their thin veneer of harsh jurisdiction, when the world's attention focused on the Far East. A hive of activity in Japan saw the foundation of what could quickly become the most powerful navy in the Pacific. America was more than perturbed because the economic depression prevented even a country as mighty as the United States from keeping

M145 having been hauled up a slipway for routine maintenance. The photograph was taken in Cuxhaven long before the war, showing the Sanftleben Shipyard which was later renamed Beckmann Shipyard.

pace with such an arms race. The big powers had no alternative other than to attempt some persuasive intimidation to slow down the Japanese expansion. This led the major maritime nations to convene a conference, which concluded with the signing of the so-called Washington Treaty of 1922.

German naval aspirations, left rotting in the shallow waters of the continental lowlands, did not feature in Washington. Yet, the agreement had a most pronounced affect upon the small navy struggling for survival in Wilhelmshaven. The Washington Treaty limited battleships to 35,000 tons with 16-in guns and cruisers to 10,000 tons with 8-in guns. The vast area between these two types became a prohibited zone which could

only be encroached by aircraft carriers. The interesting point, seemingly overlooked by the politicians and their fleet of naval advisers, was that the Versailles Diktat allowed Germany to build battleships up to 10,000 tons with 11-in guns. This offered the *Reichsmarine* an opportunity of creating a ship which would be too fast for the massive Allied battleships but powerful enough to blast every Washington Treaty cruiser out of the water without even coming within range of its guns. Thus, in an instant, Germany acquired the linchpin for rolling her puny Versailles Diktat navy into battle.

However, the building of new ships presented problems of immense proportions because much of the heavy production plants had been dismantled, destroyed or taken abroad. This craze of stripping German industry went as far as planning the removal of oak panelling in the main hall of the naval officers' school. It resulted in the liquidation of the naval shipyard in Danzig, and facilities in Kiel being downgraded to mere maintenance operations. Only the old imperial yard in Wilhelmshaven remained under full military control, but there the facilities looked like a scrap merchant's depot which had had its stock stolen. Not only were the yards empty and in a deplorable mechanical state, but the skilled labour had also vanished, and this dilapidation stretched far into the industrial heartland, making supplies an unknown quantity. The first step in the redevelopment plans had to be the re-establishment of industrial and commercial facilities. Once this was under way, the light cruiser *Emden* became the first ship to be laid down in Wilhelmshaven as a test to see whether the postwar system could still produce goods of the required quality.

This period of time saw some astonishing happenings, many of which have been buried under a cloak of misleading concepts. Visions of economic depression, mass unemployment, uncertainties within Germany's leadership and miserable living conditions have helped in derailing historians' thinking. The years immediately after the First World War witnessed some of the most astounding technical innovations of the century, making the world recoil under the pressure of new contrivances. This point cannot be overemphasised, because these years saw the beginning of a process in which world leaders should have responded to fantastic opportunities offered by new technology. Instead they led the masses down a slippery path of self destruction to incredible suffering, where no-one, not even the winners, gained any benefit.

To give just two examples of the enormous contribution made by technology towards the building of ships. Krupp, the steel giant, invented new types of steel. Known as Wotan Hard and Wotan Soft, the metal could be given two distinctively different properties. The hard variety was ideal for areas where projectiles needed to be deflected while the other could absorb impacts without patches shearing off. An additional bonus came when Krupp found a way of welding the steels together, without losing their unique properties. This opened up completely new opportunities, making it unnecessary to attach armour to the outside of a ship. Instead the entire hull could be constructed from a gigantic armoured box. Another major advance, of possibly even greater potential, was in the field of propulsion. The majority of blind avenues, such as sodium hydroxide engines, had been abandoned early in the First World War and production had focused on refining conventional principles. After the war, German firms looked into the possibility of enlarging Rudolf Diesel's internal combustion engine to fit into large ships. The first diesel endurance run from Kiel to Wilhelmshaven via Skagen, the northern tip of Denmark, had taken place only a few years before the war, illustrating that this powerplant was still very much in its infancy. Despite its simplicity and development potential, there were considerable problems when enlarging the principle for huge marine engines. Eventually, the most promising design, developed by MAN of Augsburg, was tested in the artillery training ship *Bremse* and later similar engines were installed in the light cruiser *Leipzig* as supplementary cruising power. ('Bremse' is usually translated as meaning 'brake', but it is also a 'horsefly' – a tiny insect with a vicious bite.)

The early MAN diesel engines not only produced satisfactory power, but, as a side

3

A minesweeper flotilla at speed, with *M145* on the left and *M98* on the right. Keeping such tight formation required considerable concentration and some of the minesweeping manoeuvres involved considerable risk.

M133 at sea. The flotilla leader's pennant flies from the top of the main mast.

effect, provided an incredibly long range. Consuming fuel in such small quantities made it possible to develop ships for operations in the South Atlantic without tanker support. This unexpected turn of events gave rise to two contrasting opinions within the naval high command. The conventional side had followed the idea of developing a fleet of small monitor type of battleships for harbour defence duties. Now, the new diesel engines made the more ambitious turn their attention to far-off seas and to a new strategy – commerce raiding.

Powerful nations possessed the means of mounting close blockades of enemy harbours to bring the flow of commercial traffic to a halt. Weaker nations, on the other hand, had to adopt a strategy of sinking merchant ships where they could not be caught by more powerful warships. Such hit-and-run commerce raiding or *guerre de course* had already been perfected by the French during the era of sailing ships, and when the Germans adopted the idea during the First World War they called it *Kreuzerkrieg*, meaning 'cruiser war'. The naval command never had any illusions of winning a war with commerce raiders, but the ability to mount such a campaign posed a significant threat to the increasing quantities of imports flowing into Europe. These goods were no longer luxuries, but essential raw materials for feeding industrial giants. The German admirals argued that the threat of cutting these supply routes would almost certainly result in the Allies wanting to discuss different terms than those imposed by the Versailles Diktat.

The main problems of commerce raiding were outlined by Erich Raeder (who later became Supreme Commander-in-Chief of the Navy) in an official account of the war at sea (*Der Kreuzerkrieg in den ausländischen Gewässern, Vol.1*), for which he was awarded an honorary doctorate by the University of Kiel, whence the letters 'h.c.' in his title.

Modern trends in sea traffic and the development of efficient communications systems are making the conduct of cruiser war more difficult. Steaming along the shortest route between two ports makes it easier for raiders to locate their quarry, but it also enables the enemy to protect those well-defined sea lanes. The increasing use of radio will also make raider operations more arduous because the enemy can instantly broadcast positions and deploy resources accordingly. Therefore large scale raider activity will force the enemy to sail its merchant men in convoys with warship support, meaning raiders will also have to hunt in packs and sooner or later two cruiser squadrons will meet on the high seas.

The outcome of such an eventuality had already been voiced before the First World War by Grand Admiral Alfred von Tirpitz, who said, 'The nation with the strongest battle fleet in support will win the day.'

In 1927, Admiral Hans Zenker (Commander-in-Chief of the Navy) spelt out the advantages in a letter to Admiral Erich Raeder saying,

We could build either small heavily armoured battleships for harbour defences or we can think further about the tasks we might have to face in the future. Monitors cannot operate outside our own coastal waters and we need more modern concepts to challenge the might of the French navy and, at the same time, be powerful enough to cope with Washington Treaty cruisers. None of our existing ships could tackle either of these two tasks. So what choice have we?

The Zenker administration chose commerce raiding in far distant waters and invented a new variety of ship known as *Panzerschiff* or pocket battleship. *Deutschland*, the first of this type, was admired by foreign navies. Although British admirals did not get unduly flustered, the French responded by designing faster and better armoured ships (such as

A minesweeper at sea.

Dunkerque and *Strasbourg*). The advantages of commerce raiding seemed to have outweighed the negative views expressed earlier by Erich Raeder, because when he became Commander-in-Chief of the Navy in 1928, he further directed naval policy towards the southern oceans. The 'Overseas Cruiser' listed in the famous Z-Plan, for example, was conceived with commerce raiding in mind, while the Z-Plan battleship was intended to protect such raiders in far distant waters.

One of the major snags with commerce raiding in southern waters was the crossing of the relatively narrow North Atlantic. There was no way German ships could avoid coming uncomfortably close to their old enemy – France. And Great Britain threatened to be an even bigger thorn in the flesh, capable of presenting significant intimidation especially to damaged, homeward-bound ships. So, to overcome this problem, Germany required a fleet of escort battleships specially for these potentially dangerous waters. These did not require terribly long ranges and thus could be built along more conventional lines. Therefore the ships listed in the Z-Plan were divided into two distinct types. One futuristic version for commerce raiding, and a set of conventional ships for operations in North Atlantic and European waters. Commerce raiding battleships were never built, but

Bismarck and *Tirpitz* were examples of the escort type.

Hitler's coming to power and the rise of National Socialism is usually cited as being the main trigger of Germany's re-armament plan. Yet Hitler's highly negative influence on the navy and on naval research has hardly been recognised. The first point to consider is that Hitler has often been called a dictator, but he was hardly in a position to dictate. By the time he came to power, the National Socialists had already created two private armies: the SA and the SS, and this incredible fragmentation, with powerful commanders running their own shows, penetrated into many aspects of the German war machine. Just to give one example, during the first few months of the war Hitler ordered an increase in submarine construction, but the system did not supply the necessary steel because it was siphoned off for other uses.

Hitler's rise to power and the German-Anglo Naval Agreement of 1935 had a considerable negative effect on naval development inasmuch as the combination brought innovation to a standstill. When Hitler became chancellor, he was supported by less than a quarter of the total vote. The National Socialists (the NSDAP) knew they urgently needed to consolidate their shaky foundations. So they looked for prestige and chose quantity rather than quality. Consequently they turned towards the mass production of First World War technology instead of continuing the *Reichsmarine*'s

Pocket battleship *Deutschland* with a red, white and black identification stripe over the forward turret, suggesting this photograph was taken around the time of the Spanish Civil War. The position of the main optical rangefinder at the top of the main control tower shows just how huge these devices were. The quality of the lenses was superb.

M18, one of the more modern minesweepers. Although some photographs of minesweepers cruising past the setting sun look rather idyllic, life was not always quite that comfortable, as the following sequence shows. Life on board could get pretty rough and rather damp.

M18, soaking the lookouts on the open deck.

M18, struggling through the North Sea.

efforts in the field of innovation. For example, the deadly technology which put together electro-submarines of Type XXI towards the end of the war, was available in 1935 but then there was no incentive to develop such revolutionary weapons systems. Germany chose cheaper hardware which could be quickly assembled with less effort and without innovation.

Naval development under Hitler was so rapid and chaotic that the entire system toppled the moment Britain and France declared war. This is best illustrated by the massive reorganisation programme carried out shortly after the beginning of the conflict. Not only was it necessary for the navy to change its administrative system, but the entire method of working and supplying

ships had to be changed as well. This should not be taken as criticism of the naval leadership because higher commanders frequently worked without definite direction. However, it is important to bear in mind that much of the naval hardware was just as unsuitable for fighting a war against Britain and France as the administration system had been, but changing the machinery was considerably more difficult than modifying a bureaucratic system.

When Britain and France declared war, German naval leadership was never under the illusion that they could win a war at sea. On hearing the declaration, Admiral Raeder, the Supreme Commander-in-Chief, spurred his staff into action by saying, 'We can only show the world how to die with dignity.'

TREATIES, AGREEMENTS, ULTIMATUMS AND PLANS

THE DIKTAT OF VERSAILLES

This ultimatum of 440 clauses was imposed on Germany by the victorious Allies as a condition for ending the First World War. In many history books it is still disguised under the name of 'Treaty of Versailles' although negotiations played no part in its composition. Even David Lloyd George, the British prime minister from 1916 to 1922, was dismayed by the severity of the terms and said that they could only lead to another war having to be fought at three times the cost of the last. The American Senate voted against its ratification, but despite widespread opposition to the concentration of hate and injustices in the 200 pages, the diktat was still forced upon the defeated German nation.

The signing of the document created considerable unrest and turmoil inside the country, making it plain that the majority of people despised their leaders for having agreed to the harsh conditions. The general clause whereby they had to recognise that Germany and Germany alone was responsible for starting the war caused widespread resentment.

The following main clauses affected the post-First World War navy:

• The entire navy, including shore-based personnel, will consist of not more than 15,000 men. Not more than 1,500 of these may be officers and Germany may not maintain a naval reserve. The armed forces will consist of only volunteers, with officers committing themselves to serve for a minimum of 25 years and other ranks for a minimum of 12 years. People leaving the navy may not undertake military training nor serve in any other branch of the armed forces. Officers who were in the navy during the war and remain in the armed forces must commit themselves to serve until they are 45 years old unless there is some acceptable reason for early retirement, such as medical grounds.

• The size of Germany's post-war navy will be limited to 6 battleships of the *Lothringen* or *Deutschland* classes, 6 small cruisers, 12 destroyers and 12 torpedo boats. Germany must also maintain and keep operational minesweepers as specified by the Allies.

• All ships not in German ports will cease to be German property and ships in neutral ports will be handed over to the Allies.

• Eight specified battleships, 42 modern destroyers and 50 modern torpedo boats will be disarmed, but their artillery must remain on board and these vessels must be delivered to ports specified by the Allies.

• All warships under construction at the end of the war will be destroyed and materials scrapped.

A quick-firing gun on the bows of *T157*. These weapons were fitted for training purposes and were often shared by passing them from one boat to another.

• All U-boats, salvage vessels and mobile docks, including submarine pressure docks, will be handed over to the Allies and delivered at Germany's expense to specified ports.

• All objects, machines and materials which are decommissioned as a result of the above clauses may be used only for commercial or trade purposes.

• Germany may not build or acquire warships, except to replaces losses. The sizes of such replacements shall be limited to: 10,000 tons for battleships; 6,000 tons for small cruisers; 800 tons for destroyers and 200 tons for torpedo boats. Battleships and cruisers must be at least 20 years old, and destroyers and torpedo boats need to be 15 years old before new ones may be built, unless they are replacing a lost ship.

• Germany may not build or own submarines, including submarines for commercial uses and all military aircraft are prohibited as well. Existing aircraft must either be handed over to the Allies or scrapped.

• All ammunition, including torpedoes and mines, is to be handed over to the Allies and warships may only carry quantities of ammunition specified by the Allies. Germany may not produce munitions for export.

• Germany will be responsible for clearing mines in specified areas along the continental coasts.

• Germany must provide free access to the Baltic and may not erect guns or fortifications in coastal areas. Fortifications still in place must be destroyed. In addition to this Germany must hand over charts and other navigational information about shipping channels in her waters.

• Powerful radio stations such as the transmitters in Berlin, near Hannover and at Nauen [near Berlin] may not transmit military or political information and the exact nature of their transmission is to be controlled by the Allies. New transmitters may not be built in Germany nor by Germany in foreign countries.

• All information about ships and their equipment, as well as port facilities, is to be made available to the Allied Control Commission. This includes plans, specifications, munitions details and training manuals.

In addition to the above mentioned points, there was a detailed list of war reparations, which amounted to a large labour force seeing itself working as slaves for the Allies. The resulting poverty and famine created an ideal climate for germinating the extreme policies presented by the NSDAP, and after ten years of starvation and unemployment, people were more than happy to take their chances with the prospects offered by Hitler's provocative proclamations. The pathetic point about this massive core of discontent was that the limitation of radio and

newspapers made the majority of Germans unaware that the rest of Europe, and indeed also the United States, found itself in a similar social predicament. Therefore the people following Hitler were hardly aware of the fact that a large proportion of their poverty did not stem directly from the imposition of the Versailles Diktat, but from the general economic climate within the world. The victorious Allies went to extraordinary lengths to suppress such depressing news, making the problems even worse. When looking at Europe's social history with that wonderful illuminator called 'hindsight', one wonders whether Britain's decision to declare war on Germany in 1939 was a desperate attempt at using 'fright of the enemy without' as a means of controlling the rebellious working classes within its own flagging economy.

THE WASHINGTON TREATY

The United States president, Warren Harding, opened a naval disarmament conference in Washington on 12 November 1921 which eventually led to the signing of a treaty early in 1922. At first only Japan, France and Britain had been invited, but later they were joined by China, Italy, Holland, Belgium and Portugal. The main aim had been an attempt to slow down the massive naval development gripping Japan, and consequently Japan came out as the major loser. The size of fleets was laid down in the following proportions: Britain and the USA: Japan: France and Italy with a ratio of 20 : 12 : 7. In addition to these ratios, the treaty specified the maximum size of ships and armaments as follows: battleships 35,000 tons with 406-mm guns; aircraft carriers 27,000 tons with 10 guns of up to 203-mm; cruisers 10,000 tons with 203 mm guns.

The conference also decided that in future, ship displacement was going to be

Battleship *Gneisenau*'s main artillery (280 mm) in action.

37-mm quick-firing guns in action against aircraft. In this case barrels had to be loaded manually, but the anti-aircraft gun version of this calibre had a hopper for holding a number of shells for more rapid fire.

A quick-firing gun aboard *U123*, although it looks as if the ship in the distance has been hit by a torpedo. Generally there were two large calibres on U-boats: the wide deck here indicates that *U123* was a Type IX, which was usually fitted with a 105-mm gun while the smaller Type VII had an 88-mm weapon.

measured with the United States ton rather than the metric ton, benefiting Germany because this also affected the Diktat of Versailles. A metric ton is 1,000 kg while the US ton is 1,016 kg, meaning Germany could slightly increase the size of her ships.

THE LONDON NAVAL AGREEMENT OF 1922

This was an attempt at supplementing the shortcomings of the Washington Naval Treaty and to conciliate the dissatisfaction generated by the conference. However, France and Italy could not agree with the points brought up in London and Japan resigned from the protocol in 1934.

THE LONDON SUBMARINE AGREEMENT OF 1930

Germany signed this agreement in 1936, shortly after Hitler's renunciation of the Versailles Diktat and his reintroduction of national conscription. The aim of the agreement had been to prevent surprise attacks against merchant ships by forcing submarines to stop their quarry and inspect it. The ship was only allowed to be sunk if it was carrying war supplies and then only after the submarine had seen to the safety of the crew. How this was to be done was not specified, yet this agreement was ratified by the German government and became the basis of the navy's new Prize Ordinance

Regulations which specified stop and search procedures for enemy merchant ships.

THE ANGLO-GERMAN NAVAL AGREEMENT

Germany gained more than Britain, so this should really be called the German-Anglo Agreement. It was signed on 18 May 1935, a few months after Hitler had repudiated the Versailles Diktat and made his famous proclamation about the reintroduction of national conscription together with new armaments laws. By signing the agreement, Germany volunteered to restrict the size of her fleet to 35 per cent of the Royal Navy, except submarines which were allowed to be built up to 45 per cent. It even permitted more U-boats to be built in future, but then Germany would have to give due notice and sacrifice tonnage in other categories. These limitations applied to the total size of the fleet and to the number of ships within each class.

Britain was happy with this arrangement because she still did not have an effective armaments agreement with Japan and it was thought that this treaty would at least prevent an arms race in Europe. Admiral Erich Raeder told his staff that the day Hitler signed it was the happiest of his life because Germany could not have hoped for better naval conditions during the coming years. Later he went as far as prohibiting war games where Britain was the enemy. The agreement was cancelled by Hitler in April 1939.

THE 'Z-PLAN'

The Z-Plan was the name of the naval development programme formulated in 1938 for the following ten years. It came about as a result of Hitler revising his opinions and telling Grand Admiral Erich Raeder that the navy should consider the possibility of having

to face the British Royal Navy in battle. However, he emphasised that this would not be until 1948 at the earliest. This was indeed a drastic change of mind because just a few months earlier Raeder had been assured that there were no possibilities of having to go to war against Britain.

Following initial discussions, the Naval High Command decided to build a fleet of long-range ships based on the pocket battleship concept, with a view to using them to intercept merchant convoys on the high seas of far distant waters. Such warfare would force Britain to escort ships with powerful warships and thus tie up the Royal Navy's resources. At the same time, Germany would attack shipping nearer home with more conventional battleship types such as *Bismarck* and *Tirpitz*. The job of committing these thoughts to paper was given to Kpt.z.S. Werner Fuchs, who soon discovered that the requirements burst the system far beyond the agreed limitations imposed by various international agreements. Calling his initial list 'Plan X', for the lack of a better name, he and his fellow officers whittled the demands down to a manageable size before presenting the result to the Supreme Naval Command as 'Plan Y'. The third modification, then identified as 'Plan Z', was laid before Hitler for authorisation. The exact details of what was included in the document are somewhat irrelevant because it was approved early in 1939 and scrapped a few weeks after the outbreak of the war. Thus it hardly influenced the ship building programme. The important point was that the 'Z-Plan' reflected the thinking within the Supreme Naval Command of a powerful fleet of surface ships. When the war started Germany slowly adopted a navy centred on submarines and other small craft. However, this was not an instantaneous switch and it was 1943 before Hitler announced that the surface fleet should be thrown into the dustbin.

Wilhelmshaven after an air raid in 1944.

Then the U-boat Chief, Karl Dönitz, who had been promoted to Grand Admiral, advised him against such a move because vast enemy resources would be unleashed against the German homeland once the Allies realised the fleet was no longer a threat. The decision to build a powerful submarine fleet was made so late after the beginning of the war that the vast majority of U-boats never came within shooting distance of the enemy.

THE CASABLANCA CONFERENCE

American and British leaders met at Casablanca (in Morocco, North Africa) during January 1943, where they agreed to give the war against U-boats top priority and also to make the total destruction of Germany and the German people their main aim. Although the Russian leader, Joseph Stalin, did not attend due to the ferocity of the war on his home front, he did later consent that the Allies must insist on the unconditional surrender of Germany and that no other end of the war in Europe should be considered. As several influential British and American leaders said, 'this closed the door against negotiations tighter than Napoleon had done at the height of his reign of terror throughout Europe.'

This dreadful imposition seems to have been conveniently forgotten by several influential postwar historians, yet it played a vital role in prolonging the war in Europe. German leaders understood the demands of 'Unconditional Surrender' to mean that the war would continue until there was nothing left in Germany. It was no longer a war against Hitler or against the Nazi Party, but against the ordinary German people. It meant that German industry would be totally destroyed and the country reduced to farmland. The only certain result of such action was that millions of Germans would starve to death. At the same time Russia would claim millions of

men to work as slaves in the Soviet Union while German women filled its brothels. In addition to this, what was left in the area which had been Germany was to pay a heavy debt of war reparations. There would be no German government and no one to speak for the people because all internal affairs would be regulated by the victors.

This Allied demand made it not only impractical but also impossible for military leaders to dispose of Hitler or to call for an early end to the war, and gave them no alternative other than to fight on until the bitter end. Although the exact meaning of the term 'Unconditional Surrender' is left open to interpretation and after the war Allied leaders attempted to dilute the severity of its significance, the view expressed above is how Grand Admiral Karl Dönitz and

Kiel. Air raids became increasingly disruptive as the war progressed and direct hits like this curtailed a number of naval operations; consequently essential services were placed under concrete.

The Scharnhorst bunker in Kiel accommodated the headquarters of the 5th U-boat Flotilla. This flotilla was important because it specialised in providing essential stores for all new submarines leaving for their first missions.

other German leaders saw the situation at the time, which explains why none of them could agree to an early surrender. As Dönitz said, 'had any of the leaders given up, then they would have been branded the traitors of the people whom they were serving.' This view was further strengthened by the mass slaughter of millions of German civilians, mainly women, children and old people, who died horrific deaths at the hands of the Allied air forces, while their homes were reduced to rubble. There were several attacks where the German losses during a single night were greater than the total British bombing losses of the whole war. After the war, this opinion was further supported by the continued mass destruction of port facilities, dry docks, cranes, industrial plants and water defences protecting the lowlands.

THE ORGANISATION OF THE KRIEGSMARINE, NOVEMBER 1938

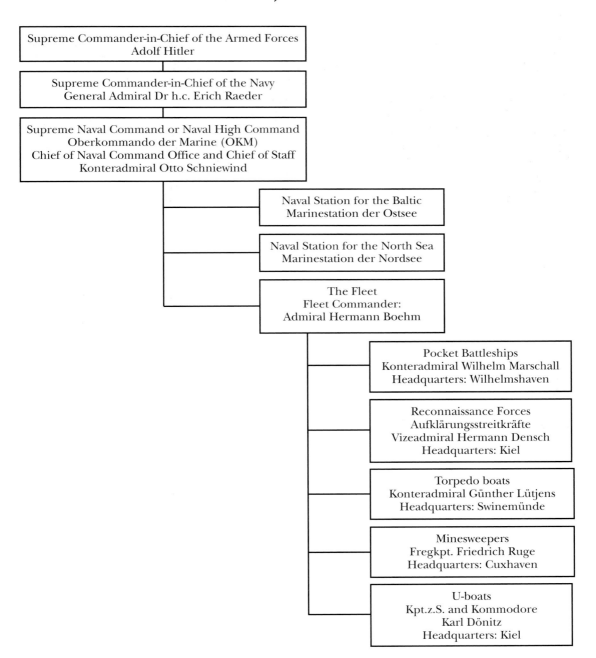

Supreme Commander-in-Chief of the Armed Forces
Adolf Hitler

Supreme Commander-in-Chief of the Navy
General Admiral Dr h.c. Erich Raeder

Supreme Naval Command or Naval High Command
Oberkommando der Marine (OKM)
Chief of Naval Command Office and Chief of Staff
Konteradmiral Otto Schniewind

Naval Station for the Baltic
Marinestation der Ostsee

Naval Station for the North Sea
Marinestation der Nordsee

The Fleet
Fleet Commander:
Admiral Hermann Boehm

Pocket Battleships
Konteradmiral Wilhelm Marschall
Headquarters: Wilhelmshaven

Reconnaissance Forces
Aufklärungsstreitkräfte
Vizeadmiral Hermann Densch
Headquarters: Kiel

Torpedo boats
Konteradmiral Günther Lütjens
Headquarters: Swinemünde

Minesweepers
Fregkpt. Friedrich Ruge
Headquarters: Cuxhaven

U-boats
Kpt.z.S. and Kommodore
Karl Dönitz
Headquarters: Kiel

OPERATION ORDERS

The following is a generalised synopsis of the type of instructions issued to commanders of surface raiders towards the end of 1940.

MAIN OBJECTIVES

Your main objectives are to conduct cruiser war in foreign waters, to lay mines and to assist U-boat operations. The most important aim of these activities will be to tie-up enemy shipping and naval forces in distant waters to relieve pressure in Europe. Therefore it is more important to remain at sea for the longest possible period than to run up high sinking figures. It is far more vital to damage the enemy in the following ways than run the risk of being sunk: force the enemy to delay sailing schedules; force the enemy to redirect shipping along the longest possible routes; force the enemy to adopt the convoy system in as many areas as possible and force the enemy to employ warships to guard these groups of merchant ships; discourage neutral countries from helping Britain and thus make the acquisition of war materials difficult.

ADVICE

The disguise of your ship and your method of attack should be changed frequently so that the enemy cannot get a clear picture of your appearance and cannot determine exactly how many raiders there are operating on the high seas. Create the maximum disruption with a sudden appearance and try to prevent your quarry from using its radio; by so doing you will make it difficult for the enemy to determine your position. Make it impossible for the enemy to anticipate your next move. Leave the operations area as soon as you suspect that your position has become known. Under no circumstances move to a new area and start offensive action the moment you arrive. It will be far more effective to withdraw from the scene completely. That way enemy forces are left to search your known operations area and they will not be diverted to follow you.

Elusiveness is the most important weapon of any raider. Avoid conflict with warships, even if their armament appears to be inferior, and under no circumstances run the risk of being damaged. Should it become impossible to avoid warships, then use your disguise until the last possible moment and engage every weapon at your disposal. Such a desperate course of action might still result in a favourable conclusion, but use this only as a means of last defence after all else has failed. Great attention must be paid to small details of disguise, including the behaviour of people on deck. It would help to give the impression of having women and children on board.

Should it prove impossible to continue with your operations, then return home. Should that option also be impossible then consider the following points. You are free to decide what you do with your ship, with your weapons and your crew. You may opt to make for Italian bases and offer assistance; use the ship to inflict maximum damage on the enemy. As a last resort make for a neutral port and sink the ship in deep water outside the territorial limits.

Shooting the midday sun aboard auxiliary cruiser *Thor*. Getting the navigation correct was vital. Most measurements were taken by a number of men so that they could compare results and possibly eliminate mistakes. The long shadows suggest that the boat is a considerable way from the equator.

A naval radio room. The typewriter in the bottom left corner, by the man's hand, is a naval version of the famous Enigma code writer. Originally these held three wheels above the keyboard, as can be seen here,

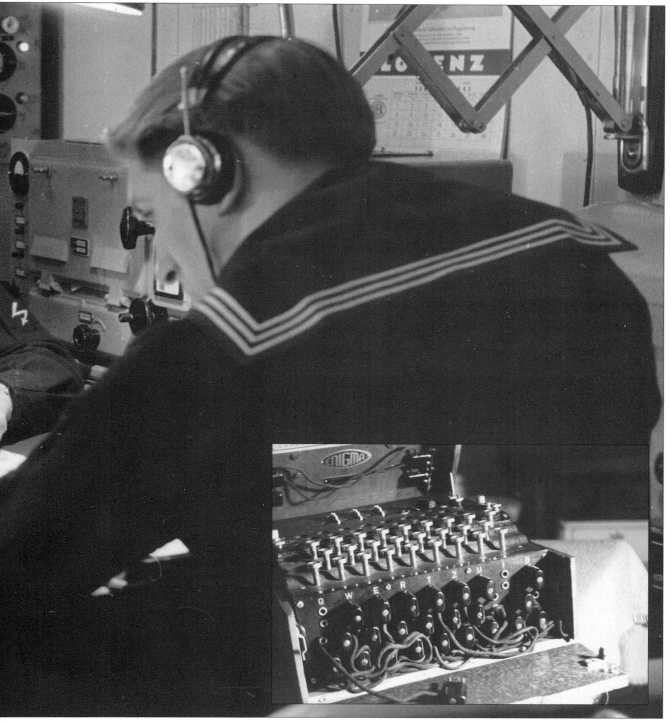

but later the discs were made thinner so that four could be fitted into the same slot. Radio rooms usually also had at least half a dozen different wheels to choose from. Inset: Enigma code writer.

SUPPLIES

Supplies will be provided on request, but every effort must be made to use cargoes from captured ships. Should you require special items, please remember it will take a while before they reach you and *delivery cannot be guaranteed.*

USE OF RADIO

Observe radio silence at sea. Should your position become known to the enemy as a result of an engagement, then make every effort to transmit at least the following: your position, brief report regarding your successes, your plans for the future, your fuel situation, the state of your supplies and any news which might help other raiders. You are free to transmit short signals whenever you feel it necessary. (The Germans were under the impression that Britain could not determine the positions of short signals which were made up of a code of very few Morse letters.)

THE POLITICAL SITUATION

You should keep up to date with political developments by listening to German, neutral and enemy broadcasts, but you must treat foreign news with caution because this will obviously portray Germany in a negative light. Lies and half-truths are common features of enemy propaganda. There could well be a danger of you getting the wrong impression, especially as you will be on your own for a long time. It is important for you to remember the justice of the German cause and to keep your faith in your weapons, in the Führer and in Germany's ultimate victory.

The following countries are to be treated as hostile: Great Britain and all her colonies, Australia, Canada, South Africa, New Zealand, Egypt and Iraq, all Belgian colonies and all French colonies. The United States of America, Spain, the Soviet Union and the Republic of Ireland are to be treated as neutral. Every effort must be made to avoid incidents with these neutral nations, since some of them are seeking an excuse to join the war against Germany.

Only Japan and Italy are to be treated as friendly nations. The latter's territories in the east are of no use as raider bases because they lack modern facilities, but they could turn out to be suitable as places of refuge. There is a friendship pact between Japan and Germany, meaning that there are several ports which could be approached in times of difficulties.

THE GENERAL SITUATION REGARDING THE ENEMY

Britain cannot protect all her ships, nor has she the resources to run all of them in convoys. Therefore it should be possible to find unprotected merchant ships on the high seas. Coastal waters, including those belonging to neutral countries, are often patrolled by reconnaissance aircraft and great care must be exercised in such locations.

COOPERATION WITH U-BOATS

You will have loaded sufficient resources to act as supply ship for two U-boats. The idea is that submarines should fight their way into southern waters to meet you and then to return to France. Once you have made contact with these submarines, you will cease all raider activity and concentrate on keeping the U-boats operational for as long as possible.

THE FLEET COMMAND AND LARGE SURFACE SHIPS AT WAR

OPENING MOVES

In the event of war, Germany expected the Royal Navy to establish a blockade of her ports and therefore prepared to move larger ships out to sea before their escape could be prevented. Such action was considered important because the two large blockade-buster battleships, *Bismarck* and *Tirpitz*, were still under construction and Germany had no way of breaking such a siege. Although the naval administration classed *Scharnhorst* and *Gneisenau* as battleships, both of them were technically battlecruisers with a main armament of nine 280-mm guns. *Bismarck* and *Tirpitz* had eight much more powerful 380-mm guns. The difference in performance can be better illustrated with the secondary armament: all four ships were fitted with 150-mm weapons. The older guns on the battlecruisers had a maximum range of 12 km while *Bismarck* and *Tirpitz* could reach targets slightly more than 20 km away.

Ironically, the Royal Navy was in no position to impose such a blockade and when the war started Germany had only three ship

The lightship *Elbe 2. Elbe 1* was the lightship furthest out and *Elbe 3* the one nearest to land. These guides were essential for finding the deep water channel funnelling into the approaches to Cuxhaven and Hamburg.

Pocket battleship *Admiral Graf Spee* during 1937 with a radar aerial already fitted on the turret of the main optical rangefinder. *Graf Spee* looked very similar to *Admiral Scheer*. The four rectangular windows of the admiral's bridge are a good distinguishing feature: there are four of them, one for every letter of the word 'Spee'. *Admiral Scheer* had three windows on the admiral's bridge, and the large rectangular name plate with 'Coronel' was also missing. (Coronel was the name of a major battle won by Admiral Graf Spee in 1914 off Chile in South America.) Just to confuse the issue, *Scheer* later had this typical triangular box-like command tower replaced by a smaller, tubular structure, and the single searchlight seen here at the front of the tower was later replaced by two platforms, one on each side of the tower.

for operations in far-off waters. One of these, pocket battleship *Admiral Scheer* (Kpt.z.S. Hans-Heinrich Wurmbach), was lying off Wilhelmshaven with much of her internal machinery dismantled for a refit. Consequently she remained out of action for some time. The other two pocket battleships, *Admiral Graf Spee* (Kpt.z.S. Hans Langsdorff) and *Deutschland* (Kpt.z.S. Paul Wenneker), were also due in dock for routine maintenance, but this was postponed and both of them left German waters on 21 and 24 August respectively, to take up pre-planned waiting positions at designated locations in lonely parts of the Atlantic. *Graf Spee* made for the south while *Deutschland* remained closer to home in the north.

Deutschland's supply ship, *Westerwald* (Fregkpt. Peter Grau), left Germany at about the same time and *Altmark* (Korvkpt. Heinrich Dau), the other purpose-built fleet supply ship, was refuelled in Texas before joining *Graf Spee*.

On hearing the British and French declaration of war on 3 September 1939 the Supreme Naval Command of the Kriegsmarine sent a signal to all units at sea telling them to start aggressive action, but emphasised that Prize Ordinance Regulations had to be obeyed. This meant that merchant ships could not be sunk by surprise. They had to be stopped, perhaps even searched, and then they were allowed to be sunk only if they were carrying contraband. At the same time

Pocket battleship *Deutschland* passing the swing bridge in Wilhelmshaven harbour with men in parade position on deck.

the attackers had to see to the safety of the crew. Hitler still believed that peace would be resumed after the Polish campaign had been brought to a satisfactory conclusion and did not want to jeopardise this aim by aggravating the British government. On 5 September, as

The scuttling of *Admiral Graf Spee* (above and opposite). The funnel shows the two main diesel exhaust pipes. While the design was still on the drawing board, it was thought that diesel engines would make it possible to dispense with funnels and build a vessel with a flat superstructure resembling a modern aircraft carrier. However, low diesel exhausts would have presented quite a problem because the heavy oil burnt in huge marine engines produces a brown, oily residue which collects on the first cool surface it meets. Thus a funnel-less superstructure would have become coated in black grime. Note that the all important, and at that time highly secret, radar aerial has been left on the superstructure. This was salvaged by British agents and gave the Royal Navy an insight into the performance of German radar.

further concession to this strategy, *Deutschland* and *Graf Spee* were ordered to cease all offensive action and to withdraw from their operations areas. That day also saw one other significant event: the US President, Franklin D. Roosevelt, forestalled any attempt at drawing forces of combatant nations into the western Atlantic, by declaring the so-called 'Pan-American Neutrality Zone', which was to be patrolled by US warships. This move was possibly more detrimental to the Royal Navy than the Kriegsmarine, because Germany had only few ships capable of operating so far from home. Hitler was anxious that the United States should not side against him and, as negotiations were in progress between the two countries, German forces were not only under strict instructions to obey Prize Ordinance Regulations but also told to avoid conflict with the United States at all cost.

The two pocket battleships reached their waiting areas undetected, with the Royal Navy having no idea of their whereabouts. This process had not been uneventful. *Graf Spee*, for example, had narrowly escaped being sighted by the cruiser *Cumberland*, on passage from Rio de Janeiro to Freetown. *Graf Spee*'s reconnaissance aircraft spotted the approaching cruiser and signalled the pocket battleship and *Altmark* to alter course. *Deutschland* and *Graf Spee* were eventually given permission to start their raiding activities during the night 25/26 September, by which time each ship had used one quarter of its fuel and provisions, and the need to complete the postponed overhauls had become more pressing. The Royal Navy had guessed that there was at least one raider at sea, but did not get confirmation until late October when survivors from *Graf Spee*'s first victim, the British freighter *Clement*, reached South America. The presence of a second raider was not definitely established until much later, on evidence of survivors from the Norwegian freighter *Lorentz W. Hansen*.

The British and French Navies responded by forming hunting groups with which to bring the raiders to battle. These were: Force 'F' (the cruisers *Berwick* and *York*), covering the waters between North America and the West Indies; Force 'G' (the cruisers *Exeter*, *Cumberland*, *Ajax* and *Achilles*), along the east coast of South America; Force 'H' (the cruisers *Sussex* and *Shropshire*), around the Cape of Good Hope; Force 'I' (the cruisers *Cornwall*, *Dorsetshire* and the aircraft carrier *Eagle*), in the southern Indian Ocean; Force 'K'

(the battleship *Renown* and the aircraft carrier *Ark Royal*), off the north-east coast of Brazil; Force 'L' (the battleship *Dunkerque*, the aircraft carrier *Bearn* and the cruisers *Georges Leygues*, *Gloire* and *Montcalm*), operating in the Atlantic from Brest; Force 'M' (the cruisers *Dupleix* and *Foch*), in West African waters, from Dakar; and Force 'N' (the aircraft carrier *Hermes*, the cruiser *Neptune* and the battleship *Strasbourg*), in the West Indies. The establishment of these forces shows that Germany had successfully achieved its objective of tying up enemy forces.

It is hardly surprising that the initial efforts of these groups brought little reward. The only success was the light cruiser *Caradoc*'s sinking of the 4,327 ton supply ship *Emmy Friedrichs*, while she was on her way to meet *Graf Spee*. There was hardly any hope of the raiders being found in such a vast area. The Royal Navy desperately needed some clues, and such information could only be gleaned from radio messages transmitted by victims. The composition of distress calls was changed from the standard SOS to more specific codes that identified the type of attacker. 'RRR' was introduced first for surface raiders, followed later by 'QQQ', meaning disguised merchant ship and 'SSS' was used to signify attack by submarine. Initially the letters were transmitted three times, but later in the war they were repeated four times. Using such distress messages, Commodore Harwood was able to predict that *Graf Spee* was heading towards South America, and it was there that he intended to intercept her with his Force 'G'. Harwood's brilliant piece of deduction led to the famous battle in the estuary of the River Plate (La Plata) and to the scuttling of *Admiral Graf Spee* near Montevideo on 17 December 1939.

Meanwhile *Deutschland* was recalled after sinking just two ships. She had been in Gotenhafen for about four weeks before the Royal Navy discovered her whereabouts. The two elusive sisters, the battleships *Scharnhorst* (Kpt.z.S. Kurt Caesar Hoffmann) and *Gneisenau* (Kpt.z.S. Harald Netzbandt), slipped out of Germany at the same time as *Deutschland* was making for home, with the intention of testing the Royal Navy's vigilance by striking at blockading British cruisers. The Germans were unaware that such forces did not exist and the mere success of reaching the open waters of the North Atlantic was already regarded as a victory in itself. Admiral Wilhelm Marschall (Fleet Commander aboard *Gneisenau*) had orders not to take any risks. So he sailed into mid-Atlantic before feigning a break-out southwards, but in reality he turned north to head back into home waters. His attempt to mislead the enemy was wasted on this occasion because Britain was not aware of the squadron's movements. In fact, when *Scharnhorst* was spotted by the armed merchant cruiser *Rawalpindi*, she was wrongly identified as the pocket battleship *Deutschland*, whose presence had been reported earlier.

By the end of 1939, all German surface raiders were back in port and the year closed with a definite lull. The success of the big ships in terms of tonnage sunk appears meagre when compared with the results achieved by a handful of tiny U-boats, mines or aircraft, but sinking ships was not the primary objective. It was considered far more important that the large ships should disrupt and stretch disproportionally large elements of the enemy's shipping. When evaluating tonnage sunk, it must also be remembered that German capital ships were constantly plagued by orders to sink as many ships as possible but to avoid taking any risks.

Successful operations in the Atlantic without interference from the Royal Navy were made possible by the B-Dienst (*Funkbeobachtungsdienst*) under the leadership of Heinz Bonatz. A radio monitoring and intelligence service had been established as

This should be *Scharnhorst*, although having identified it as such probably means that it is the sister ship *Gneisenau* because they were so alike. The flimsy extension to the navigation bridge, which can be seen on the port (right hand in the photograph) side suggests that the ship is close to port, because these structures were removed at sea. The rectangular box above the 10-metre-long optical rangefinder is of special interest because a radar aerial has been fitted on the right hand side.

early as May 1915 to survey enemy radio traffic and evaluate the information collected. In 1939 the Royal Navy was still using an outdated cipher system, which helped the Germans to break into British networks. The B-Dienst had its shortcomings, and some admirals complained that its information came too late to act upon, but the service was small and could not evaluate all the radio traffic. The strength of the system lay in its ability to keep tabs on the enemy once an operation was in progress. During the Norwegian campaign in April 1940, for example, the B-Dienst often determined convoy sailing times, although tracking them was impossible because ships maintained radio silence once they were under way. The B-Dienst was also kept informed of British fleet dispositions by sending reconnaissance aircraft over the main anchorages, thus enabling officers to build up an accurate picture of which enemy ships were likely to be confronted. During the first two years of war, Germany had the upper hand in respect of naval intelligence. By comparison, British naval forces had no or few clues as to the whereabouts of German ships.

The supply ship *Tannenfels*.

DISGUISED MERCHANT SHIPS BREAK OUT

The first auxiliary cruisers were ready to leave Germany in March 1940, just a few weeks before the invasion of Norway. The commanders of these ships were free to decide which of the two practical routes they should follow into the southern oceans. They could either sail around the Faeroe Islands and then head south-west to pass between Britain and Iceland, or they could go farther north to try their luck through the Denmark Strait between Iceland and Greenland. (From the first wave, only *Komet* took a different route. She reached the Pacific by heading east along the Siberian Sea Passage. The second wave was bold enough to sail through the English Channel.) The Denmark Strait was difficult on account of icebergs, but it did offer two distinct advantages. First, fog tended to collect in the area and could be used to conceal the movement of raiders; and, secondly, it was easier to find suitable hiding places in the remote waters north of Iceland, where raiders could wait for suitable conditions without excessive fear of being detected. The fact that apart from *Bismarck* every one of the German warships got through without trouble shows how well the natural elements shielded ships in the days before radar.

The pocket battleship *Deutschland* had been renamed *Lützow* and had completed her overhaul ready to sail with this first wave of disguised merchant ships, but the Naval High Command ordered her to remain in Europe until after the invasion of Norway. Her days as merchant raider ended abruptly on 11 April 1940 when she was hit by a torpedo from the British submarine *Spearfish*. *Lützow* (Kpt.z.S. August Thiele) was due to have rendezvoused with her supply ship *Nordmark*, whose commander, Fregkpt. Peter Grau, was somewhat frustrated by the delay and requested permission to raid merchant shipping on his own. *Nordmark*'s three 150-mm quick-firing guns were adequate armament and her speed sufficient for the task, but the Naval High Command refused on the grounds that her large cargo of fuel was too valuable to risk in battle. In addition to this, it was thought that she would become a sitting target once her description had been circulated because her typical tanker silhouette could not be disguised. (Just to complicate the issue, *Nordmark* had also been renamed. A few months earlier, at the beginning of the war she was called *Westerwald*.)

FIRST ACTIONS AGAINST RAIDERS

The first auxiliary (or 'ghost') cruisers operated for some four months without the British being aware of their presence, and it was mid-July 1940 before definite news of the ships' existence reached the Admiralty. The Royal Navy immediately cancelled independent sailings and re-routed shipping, but the chances of bringing the raiders to battle were slim. There were too few of them, Britain had no idea of their whereabouts and the forces which had been assembled earlier to hunt *Graf Spee* and *Deutschland* were now engaged in other duties.

Despite the odds of finding auxiliary cruisers being slim, the British armed merchant cruiser (AMC) *Alcantara* ran into *Thor*, the second echelon of the first wave of ghost cruisers. The battle that ensued was quick and decisive, with *Thor* damaging *Alcantara* so severely that the British ship was forced to withdraw. This brief action made it clear that not only were raiders present, but that they could also mount an impressive punch. Two British cruisers (*Cumberland* from Simonstown and *Dorsetshire* from Freetown) were dispatched from Africa to hunt *Thor*, but their mission was futile as the action had taken place a long way away, on the other side of the Atlantic.

The confirmation that raiders were at large prompted the Operational Intelligence Centre at the Admiralty to set up a special sub-section to deal exclusively with ghost cruisers. The initial measures and resources necessary to deal effectively with the problem were limited to the point of being useless. However, the men appointed for this work collected data in an attempt to build up a picture of the enemy and to deploy the ships at their disposal as effectively as possible.

Auxiliary cruiser *Thor* still with her pre-war name displayed on the bows. *Thor* was commanded by Kpt.z.S. Otto Kähler for her first cruise and by Kpt.z.S. Günther Gumprich for her second. Ursula von Friedeburg, the wife of Admiral Hans-Georg von Friedeburg, married Otto Kähler after her first husband committed suicide at the end of the war.

Light cruiser *Köln* behaving badly in moderate seas. These ships were thought to have had exceptionally good sea-keeping qualities, so one wonders what it must have been like on other ships.

Light cruiser *Köln*. Manning the upper posts was quite an art during rough weather and climbing up to such positions demanded considerable acrobatic skills. Perhaps it is no wonder that the Navy was so keen to promote gymnastics and keeping fit. The lenses of a rangefinder can just be seen above the protective wall.

CRUISER WAR AT ITS PEAK

Ghost cruisers enjoyed an active and highly successful hunting season throughout the summer of 1940, virtually unhindered by interference from enemy warships. The long hours of daylight and the seasonal good weather of the summer months were unfavourable for mounting further break-out attempts from Germany. In addition to this, a number of ships ready for action were kept in port in readiness for the planned invasion of the British Isles, and were not released for autonomous naval operations until the final postponement of Operation 'Sealion' in the autumn.

The instructions given to the next major wave of purpose-built warships differed from those that had been issued a year earlier. The German High Command had learned that although lone merchantmen were easy targets, their distress calls resulted in all other commercial traffic scattering and thus making the raider's task more difficult. In future the primary target for purpose-built raiders was going to be badly protected convoys, selected by the intelligence service. It was thought that success in this new area of operations would be far more damaging to the enemy than the sporadic one-off sinkings achieved so far.

Admiral Scheer (Kpt.z.S. Theodor Krancke) was the first purpose-built raider to sail during the autumn of 1940 and the first to adopt the new policy. The Royal Navy was unaware of *Scheer*'s movements until she attacked a convoy guarded by the AMC *Jervis Bay*. The heavy cruiser *Admiral Hipper* (Kpt.z.S. Wilhelm Meisel) followed *Scheer* into the North Atlantic during December, but her thirsty turbines, with their limited range, prevented the heavy cruiser from pursuing the pocket battleship into the southern oceans. Instead *Hipper* ran out from the North Sea and then became the first large German ship to enter a French Atlantic port. *Hipper* was further handicapped by persistent engine trouble, which recurred

at critical periods and had a major bearing on the outcome of several battles.

The year 1941 started well for Germany, with *Admiral Scheer* and five auxiliary cruisers in southern waters, and *Kormoran* (Fregkpt. Theodor Detmers) ready to start her offensive. *Scharnhorst* (Kpt.z.S. Kurt Caesar Hoffmann) and *Gneisenau* (Kpt.z.S. Otto Fein) appeared briefly on the scene, only to be forced back into the dockyard by storm damage. The two battleships and *Hipper* subsequently had successful cruises in the southern reaches of the North Atlantic, despite the heavy cruiser's unreliable engines proving a far greater handicap than the Royal Navy.

The end of March 1941 saw another lull in raider activity in northern waters with all regular warships back in port. The Kriegsmarine had good reason to be satisfied with its efforts, especially when one considers that the successes were at the expense of the world's most powerful navy. *Hipper* had proved that the limited range of the heavy cruiser did not prevent it from being an effective weapon against merchant shipping, while *Thor* had shown that auxiliary cruisers could successfully combat their Royal Navy counterparts. But raider activity had reached its peak and the long-term situation looked bleak. German shipyards were working to capacity and there was no hope of additional auxiliary cruisers being converted for the remainder of 1941 because U-boat production had priority. The tell-tale signs of defeat were hidden amid the still flourishing campaign, and it was hoped that 1942 would bring further successes.

BACKSTAGE DURING THE PEAK

The Raider Section of the Admiralty's Operational Intelligence Centre compiled a detailed dossier on each German ghost cruiser, and by the end of May 1941 their reports were being supplemented by regular newsletters. To get over stubborn ship-masters or those who could not digest so much new information, the Admiralty changed tack and made the information available to all the crew. Whence there came a growing awareness of the threats which men had to face on the high seas.

At first the Royal Navy was hampered in its efforts to check the identities of merchantmen because too many failed to follow the official guidelines and did not respond correctly when requested to do so. The time-consuming process of boarding each ship to check credentials was replaced by the introduction of a secret identification system for all merchant ships under British control. The new process was supported by a facility known as the 'Checkmate System' which could speedily provide warships with up-to-date information on the whereabouts of any Allied ship, making it almost impossible for an enemy masquerading under a false identity to maintain its pretence for long once it had been challenged.

Initially many masters of merchant ships were loath to broadcast distress calls when they were approached by a suspicious ship in case the transmission was detected by German radio monitors. The Admiralty continually pressed upon them the fact that the enemy did not possess such facilities, and that the Royal Navy desperately needed all information which might help in pinpointing the positions of raiders. A system was introduced whereby a sighting report was transmitted as soon as a dubious-looking ship came into sight, but no action was taken if this was later cancelled because it turned out to be a false alarm. The Germans captured documents containing details of this procedure and on occasions were able to use the victim's own transmitter to cancel such distress calls themselves.

Radar also started making a significant contribution to raider warfare. The first effective equipment was fitted in British operational ships early in 1941, at a time when

The bridge of the submarine escort ship *Otto Wünsche* with the usual spider's web of radio aerials in the background.

German development in this field was beginning to lose its advantages and lag behind as a consequence of Hitler's decision to halt research. German radar aerials were huge, bedstead-like frames mounted on a high part of the ship and, to maintain secrecy, they were dismantled once the ship approached coastal waters. *Hipper* used radar to track convoy SLS64, which she subsequently attacked on 12 February 1941. The convoy had first been detected by the radar the previous night, but the heavy cruiser did not close-in until after the strength of the escorts had been ascertained. Then, at first light, seven ships were quickly sunk and two more damaged. Both *Gneisenau* and *Scharnhorst* had used radar a month earlier to avoid the British fleet during the break-out for Operation 'Berlin'. The pocket battleship *Admiral Scheer* was also equipped with such apparatus for her cruise into the Indian Ocean. She used it in the North Atlantic to avoid lone merchant ships while waiting for her designated target, the convoy escorted by *Jervis Bay*.

BRITAIN HITS BACK

The sinking of the battleship *Bismarck* (Kpt.z.S. Ernst Lindemann with the entire Fleet Command under Admiral Günther Lütjens on board) marked the turning point in the Royal Navy's battle against raiders, and was the first occasion on which a large German ship was caught while attempting to break out into the Atlantic. What is more, radar played an important part in the hunt. In May 1941, *Bismarck* set out in company with the heavy cruiser *Prinz Eugen* (Kpt.z.S. Helmuth Brinkmann) for her first and only raiding operation. Around this time the Royal Navy capitalised on its success by severing the vital link without which raiders could not operate at all – the supply system. Raiders took food and provisions from their victims, but ammunition could not be acquired in this

way. An efficient supply network was therefore essential, especially as it was becoming more difficult to capture ships in conditions favourable to the attacking raider. Many merchant ships were now more alert to possible danger and no longer carried full bunkers of useful fuel, being issued with only sufficient to reach the next port of call.

For many years after the war, it was thought that the supply ships were caught fortuitously in the net drawn for *Bismarck*, but this was not the case. Later released 'Enigma' documents have revealed that the operation against the supply network was a well-planned, independent exercise. May and June 1941 were indeed black months for the Kriegsmarine, which lost a blockade breaker (*Elbe*, sunk off the Azores by aircraft from the carrier *Eagle*) and nine supply ships, all as a result of a well-executed hunt. These losses had a catastrophic effect on the raiders in the southern waters, especially *Orion* (Fregkpt. Kurt Weyher) whose engines were also giving trouble, and whose bunkers were almost empty and ammunition too low for further prolonged action. In the end *Orion* had to be refuelled by the auxiliary cruiser *Atlantis* (Kpt.z.S. Bernhard Rogge), which could ill-afford to sacrifice the precious oil, though it was essential for *Orion's* desperate dash to the French Atlantic coast. Incidentally, *Prinz Eugen's* refuelling positions were also known and the heavy cruiser would have been another sitting target had engine trouble not forced *Prinz* to make for port.

The Following Supply Ships were Sunk during June 1941
Alstertor, scuttled on 23 June in 41°12'N 13°10'W during an attack by Royal Navy forces.
Babitonga, scuttled on 21 June in 01°05'N 27°42'W when HMS *London* approached.
Egerland, sunk on 5 June in 07°N 31°W by HMS *London* and HMS *Brilliant*.
Esso Hamburg, supply tanker for *Bismarck*, *Prinz Eugen* and U-boats, scuttled 4 June in 7°35'N 31°25'W when HMS *London* approached.

Boat drill aboard the blockade breaker and supply ship *Anneliese Essberger*. Although a nuisance, this was a vital part of the survival routine. Not only was it necessary in case the ship had to be abandoned, but it was also vitally important to fool a British warship. To keep up their disguise when a warship approached, part of the crew might have to imitate a panic to get off.

Friedrich Breme, supply tanker for *Bismarck* and *Prinz Eugen*, sunk on 12 June in 44°48' 24°00'W by HMS *Sheffield*.

Gedania, supply tanker for *Bismarck*, *Prinz Eugen* and U-boats, captured by HMS *Marsdale* on 4 June in 43°38'N 28°15'W.

Gonzenheim, supply ship for *Bismarck* and *Prinz Eugen*, scuttled on 4 June in 43°29'N 24°04'W when several British warships appeared.

Lothringen, supply tanker for *Bismarck*, *Prinz Eugen* and U-boats, intercepted by HMS *Dunedin* and aircraft from the carrier *Eagle* on 15 June in 19°49'N 38°30W.

Spichern (ex-*Krossfonn*) was the only supply ship at sea to slip through the net and return to her home base at St Nazaire.

THE END OF THE CRUISER WAR

During the summer of 1941 the general progress of the war at sea may have looked relatively promising for the Germans, especially when one considers in retrospect the terrific successes still to come in American waters during the first months of 1942. The underlying trend though was grim. After the loss of *Bismarck*, only two pocket battleships and two heavy cruisers remained operational. *Lützow* (ex-*Deutschland* under Fregkpt. Bodo Heinrich Knoke) was almost ready for action after lengthy repairs when raiding plans were frustrated by a single torpedo dropped from a British aircraft in Oslo Fjord. *Admiral Scheer* was undergoing a routine refit in readiness for a foray into the Arctic in early autumn. Engine trouble still kept *Hipper* out of action; and *Prinz Eugen*, *Gneisenau* and *Scharnhorst* were undergoing repairs in France. This damage was the result of bombing by the Royal Air Force and there was no prospect of these vessels becoming operational until the following year. Auxiliary cruisers fared a little better; only one (*Pinguin* under Kpt.z.S. Ernst-Felix Krüder) had been sunk by enemy action. The others

had either returned to port or were still at large, but their successes had dwindled considerably in the face of anti-raider measures introduced by their opposition.

After the destruction of the original supply network in June 1941, the Kriegsmarine failed to re-establish another European-based provisioning system. Instead Germany looked to the Far East to obtain supplies from Japan. Sailings from Europe did not come to a complete halt, as has often been imagined, but only a few ships managed to run in and out of France.

By the end of 1941, Britain could already decode a substantial proportion of German radio traffic, and by the end of the following year this intelligence had been considerably increased. *Atlantis*, the first auxiliary cruiser to have sailed, was sunk in November 1941 as a direct result of the code breakers at Bletchley Park having read her radio instructions to *U126* (Kptlt. Ernst Bauer), with details of their meeting place. The Z-ship (supply ship for U-boats) *Python* suffered a similar fate a short time after she had picked up survivors from *Atlantis*. She had been ordered to the scene after the Germans had intercepted the raider's English language distress call in correct British code. Incidentally, the auxiliary cruiser code was never broken and Bletchley Park obtained the raider's positions through U-boat ciphers.

In February 1942, *Prinz Eugen* (Kpt.z.S. Helmuth Brinkmann), *Scharnhorst* (Kpt.z.S. Kurt Caesar Hoffmann) and *Gneisenau* (Kpt.z.S. Otto Fein) scored a psychological victory over the Royal Navy by passing through the English Channel from Brest. The so-called 'Channel Dash' came about as a direct result of Hitler's hunch that Britain would invade Norway; consequently he ordered Grand Admiral Erich Raeder to send these three major units into northern waters. Raeder was opposed to the move, but Hitler argued that the ships would be better employed in Norway and suggested a

Prinz Eugen during the Channel Dash (11–13 February 1942) when a squadron of heavy ships ran into northern waters from Brest (above and below). The entire operation so close to the English coast made the men tense. Every position on board fully occupied them and all guns were constantly ready for action. Many men hadn't expected to live through the reckless venture and seeing the sun rise over the Elbe estuary was a great relief.

An escorting destroyer seen from the heavy cruiser *Prinz Eugen* during the Channel Dash.

quick dash through the Channel. Raeder protested about the choice of route, but was overruled and the three ships left under command of Admiral Otto Ciliax (Commander-in-Chief for Battleships). This daring venture was executed without too much difficulty, but it spurred the British into making a strong effort to prevent similar feats from being performed in the future. British vigilance increased, making the Channel route a dangerous proposition for the second wave of raiders leaving Germany. *Thor* (Kpt.z.S. Günther Gumprich) managed to pass through without too much trouble during November 1941, but *Michel's* (Kpt.z.S. Hellmuth von Ruckteschell) attempt almost came to grief. *Stier* (Kpt.z.S. Horst Gerlach) was the last to get through, in May 1942. *Komet* (Kpt.z.S. Ulrich Brocksien) was sunk in the Channel during October and *Coronel* (Kpt.z.S. Ernst Thienemann) was recalled to prevent her certain destruction. The few ships which did break out into the southern waters were reasonably successful, although none of them achieved the high sinking figures of their predecessors. However, they created a great deal of commotion, delayed sailing schedules, forced merchant ships to make lengthy detours, kept the Royal Navy from other duties and, on the whole, produced favourable results.

The last plans to employ large regular warships in the Atlantic were formulated on 26 August 1942 when, at a meeting with Hitler, Raeder and Vizeadmiral Theodor Krancke (Permanent Representative of the Navy's Supreme Commander-in-Chief at Hitler's Headquarters and earlier captain of *Admiral Scheer*) and Kpt.z.S. Karl-Jesko von Puttkammer (Hitler's Naval Adjutant) discussed the possibilities of sending the pocket battleship *Admiral Scheer* to the South Atlantic. Raeder was convinced that *Scheer* had a good chance of slipping through the Allied net, and that the political and psychological rewards of such a voyage were

potentially great. However, Hitler refused on the grounds that he anticipated an Allied invasion of Europe and he thought that air support was not strong enough to give *Scheer* the help she needed for such a venture.

After this meeting, the general situation regarding the war at sea declined rapidly and the prospects of sending auxiliary cruisers out of Europe receded exceedingly quickly. In December 1942 Raeder announced the cancellation of conversion work on the last raider (*Schiff 49*, previously known as *Amerskerk*). This 7,900 grt (gross registered ton) vessel had been commandeered in

Prinz Eugen's signal nest during the Channel Dash. Flags were still favoured for close-range communications when it was prudent to maintain radio silence.

41

Prinz Eugen during the Channel Dash.

The German war flag flying aboard auxiliary cruiser *Widder*, with the rear gun uncovered for action. When not in use this was made to look like a deck cabin, hence a bullseye has been painted on the side.

Holland in April 1940 and handed over to North German Lloyd. She would have been called *Coburg*, had the commissioning taken place. Ship *14, Coronel*, was almost ready to sail and an attempt was made to get her out during early January, 1943. However, by this time British ships operated freely along the French coast without fear of hindrance from the Kriegsmarine, even during daylight. *Coronel*'s chances of making it were slim. Yet the sailing orders were issued and progress carefully monitored until it became clear that the Royal Navy was too powerful, at which time the ship was recalled. Auxiliary cruiser *Michel* was still at sea, off Japan, but without a single supply ship to support her. Consequently her operations were restricted, but this hardly mattered since raiders had ceased to be an effective force and success could now be measured only in terms of the length of time ships succeeded in staying afloat. The surface war on far distant seas had ground to a halt.

INCIDENTS AND OPERATIONS

THE GERMAN ATTACK ON POLAND

The war at sea was opened at 0445 hrs on 1 September 1939 by the old, and obsolete, battleship *Schleswig-Holstein*, under Kpt.z.S. Gustav Kleikamp, with a bombardment of the Polish-held Westerplatte, a spit of land in the estuary outside Danzig (East Prussia). The four 280-mm and six 105-mm guns were ideally suited for such a close-range attack which would weaken the defences before landings by several naval assault groups. However, the concrete bunkers did not succumb and it was a shortage of ammunition and food that eventually forced the Polish garrison there to surrender four days later.

This event, and indeed the entire German invasion of Poland, is today often regarded as the unwarranted attack of a powerful force against a small nation but in those days many Germans saw this in a different light. Modern

Autumn manoeuvres, 1937. The laying of smoke screens is being practised.

44

history books frequently fail to explain that the Polish people had maintained their language, culture and nationality for several centuries without a government because a variety of nations had laid claim to the territory in which they lived. In 1919, after the First World War, the victorious Allies used this Polish determination as a tool for further weakening Germany, Austria and Russia. Large areas of their countries were hived off for the founding of a new nation, the Polish Republic. Twenty years later, when the Second World War started, many men who marched into Poland had already been born when their homeland had been taken away and they had grown up during a time when the education system had further ingrained this resentment.

One cannot condone the military attack on Poland or even hope to understand the barbarism with which the Poles were treated. Even regular soldiers of the German Army were appalled by the brutality activated by the Nazis. Yet it is also important to remember that the majority of soldiers who marched into Poland did not look upon their move as an invasion of a foreign country, but rather as a reoccupation of their homeland. A good number of them had been forced out of their homes and the little compensation which they had received was lost as a result of the devaluation of the German Mark during the dramatic inflation of the 1920s. Their ancestors had settled in the sparsely inhabited regions of the east 150 years earlier, long before the area had come under the military rule of a French army of occupation under Napoleon. Therefore some of these German soldiers had long-established roots in the fertile plains which are now Poland.

ALTMARK INCIDENT

After having run the blockade from the South Atlantic, *Admiral Graf Spee*'s supply ship *Altmark* under Kpt. Heinrich Dau was intercepted by neutral Norwegian warships. The subsequent radio traffic gave away the position to the Royal Navy and when the destroyer HMS *Cossack* (Cdr P.L. Vian) appeared, *Dau* sought shelter in Norwegian territorial waters. There he was attacked by a boarding party on 16 February 1940 who shot a number of unarmed German sailors and released the prisoners aboard *Altmark*. The fact that nearby Norwegian warships did not make an effort to prevent this armed intrusion of their waters made the Germans realise that the country was supporting the Allied side rather than remaining neutral. This action, together with a similar incident involving the United States freighter *City of Flint*, contributed towards Germany making plans for the invasion of Norway.

ATHENIA INCIDENT

On the first day of the war Kptlt. Fritz-Julius Lemp in *U30* disobeyed standing orders and torpedoed the 13,581 grt passenger liner *Athenia* without warning. Since he also failed to report the incident, the German propaganda system accused the British Secret Service and the Prime Minister, Winston Churchill, of deliberate sabotage for the purpose of casting Germany in a bad light. Some weeks later, when *U30* returned home and the truth came out, Hitler ordered the relevant pages of the boat's log to be removed and to obliterate all reference to the sinking. At the same time, the crew was sworn to secrecy and the prohibition of attacks against passenger ships, even those sailing in convoys under military escort, was further emphasised. This order remained in force until the summer of the following year. This rather unfortunate incident led Britain to conclude that Germany had issued orders for unrestricted sea warfare, although the exact opposite was true.

CITY OF BENARES INCIDENT

The passenger liner *City Of Benares* was torpedoed during the first minutes of 18 September 1940, just a few weeks after the Naval High Command had allowed this category of ship to be a legitimate target. Although she was sailing in an escorted convoy without lights, the passengers on board had hardly practised lifeboat drill and a large number of children were killed by the sinking. After the war, the U-boat commander, Kptlt. Heinrich Bleichrodt of *U48*, was accused of knowing that the ship carried children and a concerted attempt was made to force him into making a confession that he deliberately singled them out to be killed. This accusation was absurd inasmuch as Bleichrodt neither knew which ship he was attacking nor what it was carrying. In the darkness of night, it was a legitimate target. Despite considerable pressure brought by the British authorities, levelling the accusation for the rest of his life, Bleichrodt had the strength of character to resist making such a confession and the case collapsed due to a lack of evidence. It is interesting to add that a number of sea-going Royal Navy officers also regarded this unwarranted attack on Bleichrodt to have been unjust and helped by warning him that the authorities were making a concerted attempt to get him hanged.

CITY OF FLINT INCIDENT

A United States merchant ship captured on 9 October 1939 by the pocket battleship *Deutschland* at the beginning of the war which became the centre of a diplomatic row and indicated that Norway was not going to maintain its neutrality. Thinking that she would side with the Allies against Germany resulted in plans being made to invade the country before it became a British base. See also the section on *Deutschland*.

'DEADLIGHT', OPERATION

The code-name for the Allied operation to scuttle U-boats after the war. Boats still at sea when the war ended were ordered to surface, hoist a black flag and await instructions to make for a specified Allied port. Boats in German-held ports were disarmed and later taken to isolated assembly points mainly at Loch Eriboll (on the west side of Scotland's north coast), Loch Ryan (west of Dumfries, Scotland) and to Lisahally (often also called Lisnahilly) in Loch Foyle (near Londonderry, Northern Ireland). From there they were moved in small groups to be sunk in deep water. A few didn't make it and went down where they could be reached by divers. The first wave left towards the end of November 1945 and the last waves were sunk in January of the following year. A survey conducted during the 1980s of known U-boats in shallow waters revealed that every one had been raided by relic hunters.

GIBRALTAR (OPERATION 'FELIX')

Pre-war plans for capturing Gibraltar were further evaluated during August 1940 under the code name of Operation 'Felix'. The main objectives were to cut off British dominance in the western Mediterranean and to make it more difficult for the Allies to run convoys along the African coasts. At the same time, German possession of Gibraltar would have provided an ideal base for U-boat operations in the Atlantic. However, the plan would have involved considerable assistance from Spain and General Franco felt his country had been too decimated by its civil war, and therefore resisted all efforts to become involved in a conflict against Britain. Consequently the German plans for attacking Gibraltar were abandoned.

U123. The large Type IX U-boats were also fitted with a 37-mm quick-firing gun on the upper deck, aft of the conning tower. The ship in the background appears to have several artillery hits in the side, but it looks as if this gun has not been used on this occasion. The gun had to be loaded by inserting each cartridge singly into the breech. The watertight tampon for sealing the barrel can clearly be seen. The later 37-mm anti-aircraft gun varied by firing smaller cartridges from a semi-automatic hopper.

GREER INCIDENT

On 7 September 1941, before the United States joined in the war, the position of *U652* (Oblt.z.S. Georg Werner Fraatz) was passed from a British aircraft to the United States destroyer *Greer* (Lt Cdr Frost). The boat dived but was still hunted with Asdic by the neutral ship and aircraft were directed to the spot for a depth charge assault. Thinking he was under attack from the destroyer, Fraatz fired two torpedoes but missed and *U652* was lucky to have escaped the subsequent depth charges from the destroyer. The United States president took this to have been an open display of aggression by a German U-boat and ordered naval forces to attack Axis ships on sight. Hitler, wishing to keep America out of the war, agreed that Fraatz's action had been correct, but he gave strict instructions to avoid conflict with American ships, saying that even when attacked, U-boats must not defend themselves by taking offensive action.

KEARNY INCIDENT

The United States destroyer *Kearny* participated in the defence of convoy SC48 in October 1941 at a time when the United States was still supposed to have been a neutral country. Following her identification as a British destroyer, *U568* (Kptlt. Georg Preuss) attacked with torpedoes, killing about a dozen of her crew. As a result Germany imposed still tighter restrictions on U-boats in the western Atlantic, while America used this as another example of murderous U-boat aggression.

LACONIA INCIDENT

Following the sinking of the troop transport *Laconia* on 12 September 1942, Kptlt. Werner Hartenstein (*U156*) discovered that there were some 1,500–2,000 Italian prisoners among the survivors. His immediate rescue operation was supported by the U-boat Command, who ordered other U-boats in the area to assist. At the same time Hartenstein broadcast a plain language appeal for help and covered his guns with Red Cross flags. Diplomatic negotiations with French authorities in West Africa resulted in warships being dispatched to pick up survivors. However a Liberator from the United States Army Air Force made five attacks on the lifeboats. As a result Admiral Karl Dönitz, the U-boat Chief, told his commanders to avoid such rescue operations in the future. After the war, this so-called 'Laconia Order' featured strongly at the International Military Tribunal in Nuremberg where it was claimed that Dönitz's decision amounted to an order for killing survivors. Although the court knew about the aircraft attack, it was assumed that this had been a spur-of-the-moment decision by the pilot who had been unaware of the rescue operation. The court was not told that this attack on survivors had been planned and ordered by Allied authorities.

PEARL HARBOR

An American naval base and anchorage in Hawaii, attacked by Japanese forces on 7 December 1941. In the attack 19 warships including 4 battleships were sunk, almost 200 aircraft destroyed, over 150 damaged and almost 2,500 men lost their lives, while Japan lost only 29 aircraft, 1 submarine and 5 midget submarines. The raid came about as a result of secret papers captured by auxiliary cruiser *Atlantis* being passed over to the Japanese, telling them about British military dispositions in the Far East. As a result of this attack, Germany declared war on the United States.

PELEUS INCIDENT

After the sinking of the 4,695 grt Greek freighter *Peleus* by *U852* in the South Atlantic off Africa, Kptlt. Heinz-Wilhelm Eck ordered floating debris to be sunk by gunfire to prevent it giving away his position to passing aircraft. A number of survivors were killed during this somewhat reckless action. Almost two months later an air induction pipe was damaged by aircraft and consequently *U852* was beached on the Somali coast, some 80 km south of Cape Guardafui. The crew managed to get ashore before blowing up their boat, but the wreck was found by HMS *Falmouth* and a boarding party examined the remains. At the same time the Germans were rounded up and taken prisoner. The 29-year-old Eck, Lt.z.S. August Hoffmann (IIWO) and the boat's medical officer, Walter Weisspfennig, were later forced into making confessions about the shooting of survivors and sentenced to death, despite the last two claiming that they were obeying orders. All three were executed by firing squad to the south of Hamburg on 30 November 1945. These were the only U-boat men to be sentenced to death for war crimes, although the Allies also tried forcing false confessions out of other men. This case is still a bone of contention among some submariners because they consider it not to have been a fair trial. There was hardly a case made for the defence and Allied officers who murdered U-boat men in life-rafts have never faced court martial.

'REGENBOGEN', OPERATION

German code-word ordering the scuttling of U-boats at the end of the war before they could be reached by Allied forces. As a term of surrender, Grand Admiral Karl Dönitz agreed to hand over all naval forces intact and even appointed two liaison officers, Fregkpt. Heinrich Liebe and Oblt.z.S. Martin Duppel, to ensure that the code word 'Regenbogen' should not be issued. However, neither of them believed this and called on Dönitz's Headquarters for verification, but his adjutant (Korvkpt. Walter Lüdde-Neurath) told them that as naval officers they should know their duty. Consequently the order 'Regenbogen' was transmitted by word of mouth because the use of radio codes had already been prohibited by the Allies. The distance to the North Sea base at Wilhelmshaven was too far, but the senior officer there (Korvkpt. Heinrich Bleichrodt) ordered boats to be sunk. Later, when he was reprimanded by the Royal Navy, he told the admirals that as a naval officer he did not need orders to scuttle. The fact that you don't surrender your ship had already been learned at school.

ST NAZAIRE (RAID ON)

A French port used as a German submarine base. Attacked by British forces in March

St Nazaire, showing the large lock that could also serve as dry dock for huge battleships and which became the main target for a daring commando raid on the port.

1942 with a view to destroying the locks leading to the inner port basin. The reason being that this was large enough to serve as dry dock for the battleship *Tirpitz*. Although the lock was put out of action by ramming the destroyer *Cambelltown* into the gates and detonating explosives inside her, tidal access to the U-boat pens remained. However this attack emphasised the vulnerability of the nearby U-boat Headquarters and shortly afterwards the staff was moved to Paris.

'SEALION', OPERATION

The code name for planned landings in England. Much of this operation progressed with a definite half-hearted atmosphere, giving the impression that it was a means of applying pressure to the British government for agreeing to cease-fire negotiations rather than a serious attempt to invade. Local commanders were given orders to mobilise considerable resources, but much of the support they needed from home remained lacking. The plan began during the early summer of 1940 and was abandoned in October. During this period, naval support units as well as barges for carrying troops were assembled in the following places: Flushing, Hook of Holland and Rotterdam, Zeebrugge, Antwerp, Ostend, Dunkirk, Calais, Boulogne, Le Havre and Cherbourg.

Landings were planned as follows:
Coast between Folkestone and Dungeness (Vizeadmiral Hermann von Fischel) with units from Rotterdam, Ostend and Dunkirk.
Coast between Dungeness and Winchelsea (Kpt.z.S. Gustav Kleikamp) with units from Calais and Antwerp.
Coast between Eastbourne Head and Bexhill (Kpt.z.S. Werner Lindenau or Eugen Lindau) with units from Boulogne.
Coast between Brighton and Selsey Bill (Kpt.z.S. Ernst Scheurlen) with units from Le Havre.

THE FLEET

L = Launched; C = Commissioned; S = Sunk; OoA = Out of Action

BATTLESHIPS

Bismarck
L: 14 February 1939 at Blohm und Voss in Hamburg; C: 24 August 1940; S: 27 May 1941.

Tirpitz
L: 1 April 1939 at the Naval Dock Yard in Wilhelmshaven; C: 25 January 1941; OoA after X-craft attack on 22 September 1943; S: 12 November 1944.

Gneisenau
L: 8 December 1936 at Deutsche Werke in Kiel; C: 21 May 1938; OoA during the night of 26–7 February 1942 as a result of an air raid on Kiel. The ship remained non-operational until 4 April when it was moved to Gotenhafen for decommissioning. Finally scuttled there towards the end of the war and scrapped between 1946 and 1952.

Scharnhorst
L: 3 October 1936 at the Naval Dock Yard in Wilhelmshaven; C: 7 January 1939; S: in the Arctic seas on 26 December 1943.

Schlesien
L: 28 May 1906 at F. Schichau in Danzig; C: 5 May 1908; S: by a mine on 3 May 1945 and beached.

Schleswig-Holstein
L: 7 December 1906 at Germania Werft in Kiel; C: 7 July 1908; OoA: 20 December 1944.

Bismarck
The Admiralty in London watched the building, launching, commissioning and subsequent work-up of the world's most powerful battleship with great anxiety until the giant moved to Gotenhafen for fitting out, where it was well out of range of even the longest ranging reconnaissance aircraft. When Hitler inspected the battleship there, he voiced his concern about the forthcoming foray into the Atlantic, but was assured by Admiral Günther Lütjens (Fleet Commander) that Bismarck had nothing to fear. Such an optimistic view was not shared by the entire Naval Command. Kpt.z.S. Karl Topp, captain of battleship Tirpitz, had conducted a lengthy wargame with his officers to determine the odds of reaching foreign waters. Their grim conclusion was that once the Royal Navy knew that the ship was underway, its chance of survival was nil. There was no way that Britain could afford to allow such a powerful ship to wreak havoc in the vastness of the Atlantic, and the best way to prevent such potential disaster was to stop it getting there in the first place.

Shortly afterwards, on 18 May 1941, Bismarck (Kpt.z.S. Ernst Lindemann) and her consort, the heavy cruiser Prinz Eugen (Kpt.z.S. Helmuth Brinkmann), slipped out of the Baltic to embark on Bismarck's one and only war cruise. Although luck played a role in early reconnaissance reaching London, the Royal Navy was prepared to throw everything against the two giants. This, in itself was not as easy as might be imagined. A knowledge of the exact sailing time was vital, otherwise British ships might be sent to sea

A model of battleship *Bismarck* in the Naval Memorial at Laboe (Kiel). The magnificent collection of models makes a significant contribution to the value of the memorial because they help to explain the very reason for its existence. It is a pity that not more silent and cold stone memorials make such an effort and provide an informative display. To the right of the crane are two 150-mm turrets of the ship's secondary armament. The turrets of the smaller 105-mm guns can also be seen. The dome, perched on the top of a circular tower just forward of the two launches and a little below the bridge, contained a gyroscopically stabilised platform housing rangefinders and gunnery control for the secondary and anti-aircraft armament. To the left of the crane, just below the top of the funnel, is a similar-looking structure. This is the folded-down cover of a searchlight and has a ribbed appearance.

too early and run out of fuel just at the crucial time of coming to battle.

Using the cover of bad weather, Admiral Günther Lütjens (Fleet Commander aboard *Bismarck*) slipped out of his anchorage in Norway when low clouds and appalling weather prevented the usual enemy reconnaissance flights. But despite the poor visibility and the experience gained earlier with *Scharnhorst* and *Gneisenau*, he was now

out of luck. London knew that the ships were on the move and the skilful pluck of a lone pilot, Michael Suckling, confirmed that they were on their way. The German Intelligence Service (B-Dienst) failed to extract any relevant news from the ether, and at one critical period of time informed Lütjens that the Royal Navy was still at Scapa Flow when in fact HMS *Hood* and HMS *Prince of Wales* were just over his horizon and *Bismarck* was already on a collision course with these two powerful opponents.

The knot was first tied when the cruiser HMS *Suffolk* sighted the German squadron steaming on a south-westerly course north of Iceland. This made it clear where they were going and *Suffolk* conveniently found a mist bank for covering her presence. Using radar, she kept contact, reporting details of position and course. The B-Dienst aboard the German ships intercepted these signals and fog patches were used to shake off the pursuer. However, each time the visibility improved, the Germans found the cruiser still on their tail. The other method of throwing off the follower didn't work either. Turning round in fog and then attacking the pursuer didn't have much effect because the cruiser ran away before the heavy guns could be brought to bear. Baron Burkhard von Mullheim-Rechberg, one of *Bismarck*'s surviving officers, has written: 'We concluded the British must have an efficient long-range radar system, which threw the whole concept of surface warfare into a disturbing new dimension.'

On the morning of 24 May 1941, the German squadron was engaged by the battlecruiser *Hood* and the battleship *Prince of Wales*. This brief exchange ended with *Hood* sinking as a result of a direct hit in one or more of her magazines and *Prince of Wales* being driven away to nurse damage. *Prinz Eugen* came through unscathed, but *Bismarck* had sustained three hits, two of them heavy, the effects of which would now play a major role in the course of battle. A direct hit in one of *Bismarck*'s tanks in her forecastle isolated about a thousand tons of fuel, preventing all access to it. In addition to this, a considerable leak left a noticeable trail of oil in her wake for any reconnaissance plane to see. *Bismarck* had also suffered damage to her machinery, and a hole in her bows had slightly reduced her top speed. The German staff had thought it unnecessary to refuel the battleship in Norway, where *Prinz Eugen* had been topped up, and this now gave the Germans no alternative other than to make for the safety of the French coast.

Running engines at fast speeds meant it was necessary to refuel *Prinz Eugen* once more. Therefore the heavy cruiser was dismissed to rendezvous with a supply tanker before raiding merchant shipping in the North Atlantic. *Bismarck* headed towards Brest, thinking she had thrown off the pursuers. However, during the morning of 26 May 1941 *Bismarck* was sighted by a Catalina flying-boat from Coastal Command. That evening a Swordfish aircraft was able to score a torpedo hit on *Bismarck*'s steering gear, rendering it inoperable. *Bismarck* held off a destroyer attack from the 4th Flotilla during the coming night, but the heavy guns of the battleship *King George V* and *Rodney* crippled the doomed ship during the following day. Eventually, unable to manoeuvre and almost out of ammunition, the pride of the German nation was scuttled. Both Lindemann and the Fleet Commander went down with the ship on 27 May, two days after Lütjens' 52nd birthday. In addition to the ships mentioned above, *Bismarck* was hunted by 2 aircraft carriers, 12 cruisers, 21 destroyers and about 50 aircraft from Coastal Command, and in the final one-and-a-half hour battle it took some 3,000 heavy shells and several torpedoes to cripple her.

Tirpitz

Tirpitz, the lonely Queen of the North, achieved more notoriety by doing nothing than many smaller units which sank considerably more ships. Her mere presence was such a threat to the Allies that at one stage convoys to northern Russia were halted just because she *might* emerge from her hiding place deep in the Norwegian fjords. Describing the British attacks against her would fill an entire volume in itself, yet the decision to conceal her in the maze of jagged

Tirpitz's smallest fixed armaments: a quadruple 20-mm anti-aircraft gun.

rocks was not made by the German Naval Command. The Naval War Staff had planned a raiding sortie into the North Atlantic together with the pocket battleship *Admiral Scheer*. It was Hitler who intervened personally. Having watched *Tirpitz*'s (Kpt.z.S. Karl Topp) trials in the Baltic while *Bismarck* was being hunted to death, he ordered the Naval Command to cancel their planned operation. Hitler decided she should be moved to Trondheim, where she remained for about six months before venturing out for her first war cruise. This was a quick hit and run mission against convoys PQ8 and QP12 ('PQ' – signified Britain to North Russia, while QP signified Russia to Britain) which achieved very little, although one of *Tirpitz*'s escorting destroyers managed to sink a small, empty Russian freighter.

The first significant attack against *Tirpitz* came to an abrupt end in October 1942 when, just a few miles from its goal, a couple of human torpedoes (*Chariots* – torpedo-like submarines that carried two operators sitting piggy-back style on top) broke away from the fishing boat carrying them across the North Sea. This boat had left the Shetlands on 26 October under Leif Larsen. Despite the disappointment, the target was too powerful to be abandoned and the Royal Navy tried again with X-craft. In September 1943, these midget submarines succeeded in dropping specially designed mines under *Tirpitz*'s hull. The detonation caused all three propeller shafts to be bent, the rudder to be damaged, and cracks below the water-line which allowed significant quantities of water into the ship. Several turbines were also unseated and even one of the heavy 380-mm turrets was lifted out of its foundations. Almost half a year was required for repairs and trials were still under way when Britain mounted another massive

The warrant officers' mess aboard battleship *Tirpitz*.

attack on 5 April 1944. This time the aircraft carriers *Furious* and *Victorious*, the escort carriers *Emperor, Fencer, Pursuer* and *Searcher*, together with an escort of battleship, cruisers and destroyers brought 41 Barracuda carrier bombers, protected by 41 fighters, to the target. Their 14 hits resulted in 122 aboard *Tirpitz* being killed and a further 316 being wounded, while the attackers suffered the loss of only 4 aircraft. Consequently the Queen of the North was put out of action for another three months. This action makes one wonder about the efficiency of German anti-aircraft defences. If a stable battleship with powerful guns couldn't cope against an attack by relatively flimsy and small aircraft, then U-boats, with considerably less fire-power and a rocking gun-base, stood very little chance against the much larger and better armoured aircraft from the Royal Air Force's Coastal Command.

A most astonishing attack came a fortnight later, when a bomb penetrated the armoured deck, but failed to explode. Germany's masquerading was effective enough to keep drawing attacks onto the *Tirpitz*, although she was hardly fit for action. Finally, in mid-August 1944, another air attack put her totally out of action, but again Germany kept up the pretence and moved her out of her northern hideout by disguising the tugs as escorts. The trick worked, Britain mounted further attacks and *Tirpitz* was finally sunk by Lancaster bombers in November 1944. An action which also killed over 900 of her crew, leaving just 880 battered survivors.

Off-duty sailors taking advantage of *Tirpitz*'s band rehearsing on the open deck. The two 150-mm gun turrets can be seen in the background. Both *Tirpitz* and *Bismarck* had a pair of these turrets on each side of the hull pointing forwards and a single set pointing aft.

Gneisenau and *Scharnhorst*

These two ships were classed as battlecruisers by foreign navies, although the German administration system tended to refer to them as battleships.

Towards the middle of August 1939, when emergency war plans came into effect, *Gneisenau* (Kpt.z.S. Erich Förste) continued in her role as fleet training ship, meaning she was not fully operational until later in the autumn. Her first war cruise took her into the North Sea with the light cruiser *Köln* (Kpt.z.S. Theodor Burchardi) and several destroyers. Both *Gneisenau* and her sister ship *Scharnhorst* were back in port towards the end of October to be kitted out for a strike against British blockading cruisers. The idea was to test the

opposition's vigilance and to make life easier for German merchant ships running the blockade through the North Atlantic. In the end the venture had to be written off as a magnificent shakedown cruise because the Royal Navy was unaware of the German presence and, of course, the anticipated cruiser blockade didn't exist. In fact, Britain's knowledge of German ship movements was so sketchy that when *Scharnhorst* (Kpt.z.S. Kurt Caesar Hoffmann) was sighted by the auxiliary cruiser *Rawalpindi*, she was identified as pocket battleship *Deutschland*, whose presence had been reported earlier. The sinking of *Rawalpindi* (Capt R.C. Kennedy) on 23 November 1939 was the only noteworthy brush with the Royal Navy and *Gneisenau*

The bridge and command tower of the battleship *Gneisenau*, photographed in Brest in 1941. The basic features were similar to those seen on the model of *Bismarck*, only there was just one 150-mm gun turret pointing forwards. The main mast, attached to the rear of the funnel is a valuable identification feature. The sister ship *Scharnhorst* had her main mast further aft, between the aircraft catapult and the rear rangefinder.

Pocket battleship *Admiral Graf Spee* on the left and battleship *Gneisenau* on the right. Both *Gneisenau* and *Scharnhorst* had two triple gun turrets pointing forwards and one triple turret on the stern, while *Bismarck* and *Tirpitz* had two double turrets fore and aft. The main artillery control position was located on the top of the command tower, just below the 10-metre-long optical rangefinder. A further artillery control centre with 10-metre-long rangefinder can be seen forward of the bridge.

suffered far more from storm damage than from bruising inflicted by Britain.

Following this, both the elusive sisters were deployed on a variety of short sorties before participating in the invasion of Norway. Plans to send them raiding into the North Atlantic in mid-June 1940 were frustrated by Lt Cdr David Ingram in HM Submarine *Clyde*, who scored several good torpedo hits against *Gneisenau*. Ironically, *Scharnhorst* was also limping back to Germany, having been torpedoed by the destroyer *Acasta* (Cdr Glasford).

Following repairs, the ships' natural enemy, the weather, prevented progress. Facilities in Stavanger did not allow the storm damage aboard *Gneisenau* to be repaired, so the giant was forced to return to Gotenhafen in the far eastern Baltic and it was the end of January 1941 before the two warships ventured out for

the second time. It was thought that had the B-Dienst not been aware of an increase in radio traffic, both ships might have ended their days at the mercy of a powerful hunting force sent out to sink them. Admiral Günther Lütjens, aboard *Gneisenau*, was warned, and routed his ships away from the danger. In retrospect it seems likely that both ships would have reached the open Atlantic without interference, but at the time it was thought to be better to have the ships doing nothing than risking a tiff with British warships. Eventually, when they did break out, an encounter with the Royal Navy was still on the cards and supply ships were positioned both to the north and south of Iceland. The Germans refuelled north-east of Jan Mayen Island from the tanker *Adria*, after which the weather played into German hands. A gale

Battleship *Gneisenau*.

force 7–9 raged with temperatures of 18°C below zero. In addition to this, the Royal Navy was forced back to port by a shortage of fuel. However, the Admiralty in London was not going to send ships out too soon and make the same mistake again. The next ship to torment the Royal Navy was *Bismarck*.

To return to the cold storm in March 1941; when the weather abated *Gneisenau* and *Scharnhorst* encountered six unescorted ships. Three ships were sunk but the other three, all fully laden tankers, were captured and rerouted to France. One of them (*Polycarp* commanded by Lt.z.S. Klemp) reached the Gironde Estuary. The other two (*San Casimiro* under Lt.z.S. Alfons Grenz and *Bianca* under

Lt.z.S. Westip) had to be scuttled when they were approached by the Royal Navy. Success continued for the Germans. The day after the capture, twelve further ships were sunk, but an abundance of smoke also attracted the battleship HMS *Rodney*, surprising *Gneisenau* while picking up survivors from the blazing freighter *Chilean Reefer*. The Germans answered the signal 'What ship?' with 'HMS *Emerald*' before making off at fast speed.

Once again the British fleet erupted into activity, with a desperate effort to cut the Germans off before they reached home waters, but there was no need for Admiral Lütjens to run the gauntlet. Instead, the squadron was refuelled at sea and their luck

The man is carrying a billycan usually used for collecting food from the galley, but on this occasion there is a race to see who can get it the fastest around the ship. There is a fair amount of water in it to make sure the carrier cannot go too fast. The Navy had a vast number of such challenges and often they were taken far more seriously than official competitions. Another one of these games involved rolling an egg around the deck with one's nose.

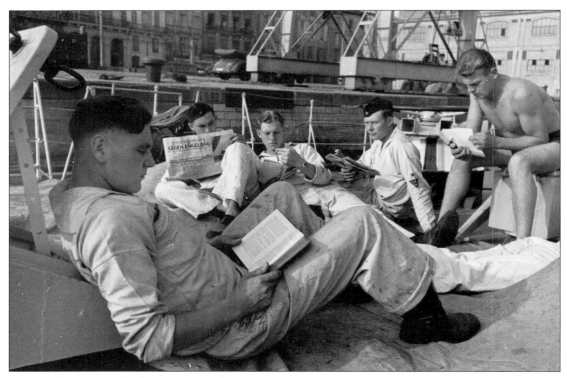

Taking a breather on deck. The man at the back is reading *Gegen Engeland*, a German newspaper produced in France.

held. A faulty radio prevented an approaching aircraft from *Ark Royal* from transmitting a sighting, and by the time it had returned to the carrier, the weather had intervened, keeping further flights firmly under deck. Consequently *Gneisenau* and *Scharnhorst* put into Brest on 22 March, bringing Operation Berlin to a most successful conclusion.

British air reconnaissance had improved considerably since *Admiral Hipper* paid her first visit to France on 27 December 1940 and Brest was uncomfortably close to British bases. It was not long before bombers arrived to plaster the two elusive sisters. British bomb aiming had also improved since the first attacks on *Hipper*. *Gneisenau* was hit by several bombs and by at least one aerial torpedo, launched by Flying Officer Kenneth Campbell, who lost his life in

the attempt. *Scharnhorst* was also damaged, meaning both ships could look forward to an enforced stay in port. Neither of them were used for raiding again. Instead they participated in the famous Channel Dash during February 1942, following which *Gneisenau* was used as training ship for most of the remaining war years. *Scharnhorst* participated in several more operations, mainly in the Arctic, where she was sunk during the Battle of North Cape on 26 December 1943.

Schlesien and *Schleswig-Holstein*

Both these old battleships were classed as training ships. Having been launched in 1906, they lacked underwater protection. Heavy losses sustained with this type of ship during the Battle of Jutland in the First World War relegated them to instant retirement until after the defeat, when the Allies dictated that they should form the backbone of the postwar fleet. Despite their shortcomings, both of them were designed at a time before the Versailles Diktat placed limitations on the calibre of guns, and in consequence *Schleswig-Holstein*'s artillery was used to open the Second World War by bombarding the Westerplatte in Danzig. Strangely enough both the old ladies saw limited operational service throughout the war. *Schleswig-Holstein* was sunk on 18 December 1944 and *Schlesien* was not put out of action until just a couple of days before the ceasefire in 1945.

POCKET BATTLESHIPS

Pocket Battleships were reclassed as heavy cruisers in February 1940.

Deutschland Renamed *Lützow* in November 1939

L: 19 May 1931 at Deutsche Werke in Kiel; C: 1 April 1933; S: in shallow water while lying at anchor near Swinemünde on 16 April 1945. Guns remained in action against land forces until 28 April 1945. The wreck was demolished by German forces after a heavy fire had destroyed much on board.

Admiral Graf Spee

L: 30 June 1934 at the Naval Dock Yard in Wilhelmshaven; C: 6 January 1936; S: scuttled during the early evening of 17 December 1939 in the estuary of La Plata.

Admiral Scheer

L: 1 April 1933 at the Naval Dock Yard in Wilhelmshaven; C: 12 November 1934; S: capsized on 10 April 1945 during an air raid on Kiel while lying at anchor at Deutsche Werke. Part of the wreck was buried under

Accommodation deck for the 2nd Division aboard the old battleship *Schlesien*.

rubble when the basin was filled in after the war.

Deutschland

Deutschland saw her first mortal action during the Spanish Civil War, on 29 May 1937, when she was attacked by aircraft in the Roads of Ibiza. At least two bombs exploded, killing more than thirty of her crew. *Deutschland*'s third target of the Second World War became a political football of considerable proportions. The United States freighter *City of Flint* (Cpt Joseph H. Gainard) was found to be carrying contraband, meaning she could be sunk, but Kpt.z.S. Paul Wenneker knew it was also necessary not to

Admiral Paul Wennecker who was commander of the pocket battleship *Deutschland* at the beginning of the war and then became Naval Attaché in Tokyo.

offend the Americans. He transferred prisoners captured earlier to the freighter and then sent her to Germany with a prize crew commanded by Lt.z.S. Hans Pussbach. Pursuing a northerly route to avoid the Royal Navy, *City of Flint* first made for the friendly port of Murmansk (in Northern Russia) for refuelling. Then Pussbach sailed southwards through coastal waters, but diplomatic relations with Norway were not as good as the German High Command had anticipated when *Deutschland*'s officers had been briefed during mid-August. The Norwegians considered the presence of an American ship with a German commander to be a violation of their neutrality and a warship was sent to intercept. As a result the Germans were interned, the prisoners released, the ship eventually handed back to US authorities and Germany lost the propaganda war.

Following this first war voyage, *Deutschland* went into dock for an overhaul which had already been scheduled for the previous August. She was renamed *Lützow* and then made ready for another raiding mission. At the same time there was a change in commander because Kpt.z.S. Paul Wenneker had previously served successfully as Naval Attaché in Japan and it was thought best that he should return to this challenging post. August Thiele was waiting to take command of an auxiliary cruiser when he was posted to *Lützow*. Nothing major developed from this point because the general raiding plans were interrupted by the invasion of Norway, and the world's first pocket battleship accompanied the newly commissioned heavy cruiser *Blücher* and the light cruiser *Emden* to Oslo. Again the German High Command took too much for granted; *Blücher* was sunk and *Lützow* damaged. Air reconnaissance had shown the Baltic to be clear of enemy forces and, having failed to detect the presence of British submarines, the Naval High Command ordered Thiele to proceed to

Pocket battleship *Deutschland* under way. The three main rangefinders can clearly be seen as large 'T'-shaped structures aft of the funnel, on top of the main control tower and on top of the bridge. There were also numerous smaller rangefinders on board.

Deutschland after her return to Germany from the Spanish Civil War, where a number of the crew were killed during an air raid on the ship. This shows the coffins being ceremonially brought ashore.

Guards of Honour aboard the pocket battleship *Deutschland* after her return from the Spanish Civil War where several of the crew had been killed.

Although many men serving in larger ships had bunks, there was still a considerable proportion who slept in hammocks and lived in incredibly cramped quarters. Some authors have claimed that alcohol was always prohibited on board ships, which is not quite supported by the bottles seen on this table. This photograph was taken long before the war and the man at the front might be Otto Schuhart, the famous U-boat commander who sunk the aircraft carrier HMS *Courageous* in the Western Approaches.

Germany without escort. Lt Cdr John Forbes in HM Submarine *Spearfish* took full advantage by scoring a direct hit on *Lützow*'s stern, putting her out of action. Boats from the 17th Submarine Chaser Flotilla, composed of converted trawlers, towed the pride of the nation back to Kiel, where she made fast on 13 April 1941.

Never again was the pocket battleship used for the purpose for which she had been designed – that of raiding merchant ships on far distant seas. In June 1941, she was on her way back to Norway for another break-out into the Atlantic when a single aircraft fooled the duty watch into believing it was German.

The subsequent torpedo hit was not too much of a problem, but shortly after the confusion *Lützow* scraped the rocky Norwegian bottom and a large tear forced her return to Kiel. The pocket battleship was back in Norway for the autumn and participated in several sorties into the Arctic seas, but very little was achieved and eventually, in autumn 1943, she returned to the eastern Baltic where she was used for training cadets. On 16 April 1945 *Lützow* was sunk in shallow water, which allowed her decks to remain above the surface and her heavy guns to be used against the advancing Russian armies.

A side view of *Admiral Graf Spee* after the Battle of the River Plate, but before the ship was scuttled. It looks as if people are still busy clearing up in the hope of attempting a run to Germany. An anti-aircraft control centre with rangefinder is visible on the left, looking like a circular tank. Below it and slightly to the right are the main controls for the crane. The aircraft has obviously seen better days. It could well have been that there was fuel in the tanks when the battle started, which would explain why so much has burned away. Aviation fuel was stored in a safe place, deep inside the hull and was brought up by pumping an inert gas like nitrogen or carbon dioxide into the tank, thus forcing fuel out of the filling pipe. This way there would never have been inflammable gas near the highly volatile liquid.

Admiral Graf Spee

Admiral Graf Spee, under Kpt.z.S. Hans Langsdorff, sailed from Wilhelmshaven on 21 August 1939 to take up a waiting position in the south Atlantic, some 1,500 km east of the Brazilian city of Salvador. On receiving permission to start offensive action, during the night of 25/26 September, some three weeks after the start of the war, *Graf Spee* immediately moved into the busy shipping lanes between Cape Town and Freetown on the African side of the Atlantic. Her first victim, the 5,000 ton freighter *Clement* was bagged on the 30th. When the rescued crew came on board they noticed the name 'Admiral Scheer' shimmering through a thin coat of paint on the side of the ship. Some of these prisoners were later handed over to a neutral ship, ensuring that the news of *Scheer*'s presence spread very quickly. At first glance it might be difficult to see the reason for such masquerading because even experts had problems distinguishing between the two ships, while performance as well as fire power was more or less identical. However, the object of the exercise was to give the impression that there were two raiders in southern waters.

Following this, *Graf Spee* was disguised as a British warship by covering the large optical rangefinder, forward of the bridge, with a wooden gun and adding large patches of dark-grey paint over the ship's light-grey peacetime colour. Bow waves were painted on the hull to complete the picture. Under this guise, *Graf Spee* headed for the Indian Ocean, where Langsdorff intended to sink a number of ships so as to make his presence known before crossing over to the other side of the Atlantic. He was thinking of returning home and thought the deviation would give the impression that he was going around Cape Horn. The sinking of a number of ships on the way made it fairly easy for the Royal Navy to estimate *Graf Spee*'s heading, and Commodore Henry Harwood guessed correctly that she would put in an appearance in the shipping lanes of the La Plata Estuary. On 13 December 1939 *Graf Spee* ran into Harwood's three cruisers to start the famous Battle of the River Plate, which ended with *Graf Spee* being scuttled off Montevideo and Langsdorff committing suicide in Buenos Aires. *Graf Spee* had sunk nine ships totalling just over 50,000 grt during her one and only war cruise, without the loss of a single life on either side. Kpt.z.S. Langsdorff was considered to have been a most humane officer by his British prisoners, who even sent a representative to his funeral (Cpt Pottinger of SS *Ashlea*) with a wreath, paid for by subscriptions from themselves.

THE BATTLE OF THE RIVER PLATE

So much has been written about *Graf Spee* and this famous seventy-five-minute battle that it would be superfluous to describe the details here. However, one important question must be answered: Why did it happen at all? Pocket battleships were supposed to have been able to outrun any battleship, and to have been able to blast any cruiser out of the water without going within range of the enemy's guns. So what went wrong at La Plata?

When the three British cruisers, *Exeter*, *Ajax* and *Achilles* were first spotted at 0600 hrs on 13 December 1939 at a range of about 18 km, they were identified as one light cruiser with two destroyers. *Graf Spee*'s officers took them to be convoy escorts and Langsdorff ordered full speed, action stations and headed towards them, expecting merchantmen to appear any minute. *Exeter*, instantly identifying *Graf Spee* as a pocket battleship, turned to challenge her while *Ajax* and *Achilles* moved over to the other flank for a well-rehearsed pocket battleship manoeuvre. *Exeter* and *Graf Spee* were approaching each other at a combined speed of about 50 kts. Although *Exeter* took the full brunt of *Graf Spee*'s first salvoes, she closed in so quickly that her guns could be brought to bear on the German ship, thus eliminating the pocket battleship's supreme advantage. *Ajax* and *Achilles* advanced to about 8 km for torpedo attacks. Frequently changing course, they avoided *Graf Spee*'s salvoes and in doing so got too close for the 280-mm guns to be accurately brought to bear on them. It is also important to remember that pocket battleships had only two large turrets, each with three barrels, making the division of fire-power into different directions quite a problem.

Graf Spee received fifteen hits, putting the middle gun of the forward turret out of action and damaging other vital equipment, including the central fire control position. Thirty-six of the crew were killed, more than fifty injured and, more importantly, insufficient ammunition was left for another lengthy action. At this stage it is necessary to take Langsdorff's character into account. He has been described as a humane man of great reputation, who had a deep concern for the well-being of other people, especially

He doesn't seem terribly happy. Action was usually very brief compared with the long periods of inactivity when men were just standing around, waiting for things to happen.

the men under him. Until this battle, he had not lost a single life, and now suddenly he was faced with the bloody, harsh reality of war. Langsdorff certainly considered his men during the decision-making of the next few days more than many other commanders might have done.

His decision to run into Montevideo for repairs has been criticised as having been wrong, but he radioed his intention to the Supreme Naval Command at 1937 hrs on the day of action and Berlin quickly sent a signal of approval. The events subsequent to the battle are also well known and hardly require elaboration. Thinking himself cut off by superior forces, Langsdorff decided to scuttle his ship rather than risk further loss of life. Again he communicated with the admirals of the Supreme Naval Command, who gave their permission. The men aboard *Graf Spee* had plenty of time to think about the destruction and rigged some unusual delayed-action devices. Torpedoes, for example, were hung from deck heads 'nose down' to blow the interior to pieces once the supporting ropes burned through. Nevertheless, despite these efforts, many important pieces of equipment remained in good order and British agents succeeded in removing *Graf Spee*'s secret radar, giving the Royal Navy a valuable insight into its performance.

Admiral Scheer

Admiral Scheer's big guns were used for the first time in earnest during the Spanish Civil War to bombard the town of Almeria in retaliation for an attack on *Deutschland*, but they were out of action at the beginning of the Second World War. When the emergency war programme was ordered, *Scheer* (Kpt.z.S. Hans-Heinrich Wurmbach) was lying in the Schillig Roads outside Wilhelmshaven with a great deal of machinery already dismantled for a major refit. The work went ahead as scheduled and consequently the ship was out of action for the next twelve months. However, keeping the anti-aircraft armament operational paid dividends when a Vickers Wellington bomber was shot down during the first British air raid on the city. After the refit, *Admiral Scheer* (Kpt.z.S. Theodor Krancke) was not released for raiding operations until the projected invasion of the United Kingdom had finally been cancelled. Then, in October 1940, Krancke received instructions to continue with *Graf Spee*'s role in southern oceans. His confinement in German waters while the first raiders were enjoying their initial successes had enabled him to glean useful information from them and to plan improved techniques of attack.

Admiral Scheer left Gotenhafen on 23 October 1940, passed through the gigantic locks of the Kiel Canal at Brunsbüttel four days later and then nosed cautiously out of the Elbe Estuary behind *Sperrbrecher XII* (ex-*Petropolis*) to dash north into the Atlantic, hoping for

good (i.e., foul) weather. She cleared the narrow Denmark Strait between Iceland and Greenland on 31 October, during a severe storm which washed two men overboard, despite extra precautions having been taken to prevent such an occurrence.

Following this, several promising lone targets were avoided. Krancke had learned from his predecessors that attacking a ship resulted in the ocean being swept clear of all other targets. So once mast heads came into sight, radar was used to determine whether they were a lone ship or convoy. This equipment had initially been developed as a radio rangefinder, to be used after a target had been visually sighted. It did not sweep through a complete circle nor was it continuously rated. Instead a comparatively narrow beam was directed towards the target for short periods to determine the range, or, as in this case, to keep the enemy under surveillance while remaining out of view.

Krancke did not have to wait long for his first convoy. The B-Dienst had already informed him that it was on its way, so it was only a case of finding the ships. This was done by using the ship's reconnaissance plane, whose pilot (Oblt.z.S. Ulrich Pietsch) had instructions not to use his radio and to return unseen. Krancke was fairly certain that the Royal Navy did not know of his whereabouts and he wanted to exploit the element of surprise to its fullest. However, fate decided otherwise. It was beginning to get dark by the time the aircraft was back on the ship, and Krancke had the ship ready for an attack because he did not want to risk losing the targets during the coming night.

At about the same time as Pietsch was being fished out of the water, on that fateful 5 November 1940, the fast banana boat *Mopan* overtook the much slower Convoy HX84 and soon afterwards ran into the guns of the pocket battleship. Thinking the lone ship was an auxiliary cruiser running ahead of the

Admiral Scheer flying the old ensign made up of red, white and black stripes behind an iron cross. The flag in the foreground is the Merchant Marine flag.

Pocket battleship *Admiral Scheer* after the conversion in which the large, triangular command tower was replaced by the slimmer, tubular structure seen in this photograph.

convoy, Krancke chose to sink her instead of concentrating on the mass of ships a short distance behind. After having lost more daylight by picking up survivors, fate intervened once more. The thirty-seven ships were indeed being escorted by an auxiliary cruiser, HMS *Jervis Bay*, under command of Cpt E.S.F. 'Fogarty' Fegen, who at first did not expect the warship on the horizon to be German. When he did identify it as an adversary, Fegen ordered the merchant ships to disperse while he faced certain death by challenging the giant. He was posthumously awarded Britain's highest reward for bravery, the Victoria Cross, for this action. Fegen's half hour battle did more than just give the ships in his charge a few precious minutes to scatter, it also forced *Scheer* to consume half of the ammunition for its main artillery and a third of the shells for the smaller guns. Many more

merchant ships would have been sunk had it not been for the fast banana boat *Mopan* and for the bravery of the men in HMS *Jervis Bay*.

Admiral Scheer's action had far-reaching consequences. Other convoys under way were immediately recalled and kept in port until battleship escort could be provided and, at the same time, heavy warship squadrons were sent to sea with the objective of blocking *Scheer*'s retreat to northern Germany or to the French coast. None of this affected Krancke because he set a course of 190° bound for the South Atlantic to be refuelled from the supply ship *Eurofeld* (Kpt. Blessin) on 12 November 1940.

Krancke now used every opportunity to exploit the advantages of cruiser war, by using provisions from his victims to keep *Admiral Scheer* as well as auxiliary cruisers and submarines supplied with food. Once his

A stunning close-up of *Admiral Scheer*. Both the aft and central fire control rangefinders are clearly visible. The other main features are: the single-barrelled 150-mm guns of the secondary armament. Just aft of the bridge but forward of the boat hanging over the side is a twin 105-mm anti-aircraft gun. There is also a twin 37-mm anti-aircraft gun in front of the rear optical rangefinder, but this blends rather well into the background. Just in front of the funnel and also visible on the far side are the anti-aircraft control centres with smaller optical rangefinders. In later years these were partly covered with dome-

shaped roofs. The man standing by the side of the searchlights near the funnel's rim gives some indication of size. The reflectors had a diameter of about 1.2 m. The captain's or main navigation bridge with chartroom has wings on both sides and is situated just forward of the 105-mm gun and below the hook of the crane. The windows above it, but below the searchlight, belong to the so-called admiral's bridge. This searchlight was situated on the signal platform from where flags could be hoisted or messages sent by a huge Morse lamp.

position in one area became known, he moved off to create havoc somewhere else. This process took the pocket battleship far into the Indian Ocean. Meetings with other German ships, especially auxiliary cruisers, played an important role in the initiative. Invitations for 'Kaffeetrinken' (afternoon coffee) were more than a desire to see new faces; they were intended as an aid to exchange news, experiences, library books, cinema films, magazines and anything else which could be swapped to make life more endurable.

By January 1941 Krancke had learned enough about the behaviour of enemy warships for *Admiral Scheer* to impersonate a British cruiser, thus making it possible to get close to unsuspecting merchant ships without them sending distress calls. Although the majority of ships were sunk, some were kept as supply ships and others were sent back to Europe with prize crews. The Norwegian tanker *Sandefjord*, for example, captured on 17 January 1941, became a prison ship for 241 people and successfully arrived in the Gironde Estuary on 27 February under command of Lt.s.S.(S) Erwin Goetsch.

A week earlier, *Admiral Scheer*'s luck had almost run out. A reconnaissance plane from the cruiser HMS *Glasgow* caught a glimpse of the raider, giving an accurate fix for the aircraft carrier *Hermes* and the cruisers *Canberra, Capetown, Enterprise, Hawkins* and *Shropshire*. On the British command chart it certainly looked as if the days of the marauding *Scheer* were numbered. Yet luck was once more on the German side. The crucial factor was a deterioration in the weather, causing *Glasgow*'s aircraft to lose contact and *Scheer* to slip out of the noose. Another, almost deadly situation occurred a few days later when the pocket battleship was steaming towards two enemy ships. A British merchantman stumbling upon them first sent an 'RRR' distress call. *Scheer* intercepted it and turned away before the ships came into sight.

At this point in time the Naval Command in Germany was also getting nervous, thinking the *Scheer* in mortal danger. Consequently Krancke was ordered to set a course of 370°. (Home!) However, before heading north there was another major meeting with a number of ships and with the tiny *U124* (Kptlt. Wilhelm Schultze), one of the first long-range U-boats to operate in southern waters. *Scheer* eventually crossed the equator on 15 March, passed through the Denmark Strait and arrived in Bergen on the 30th. Bringing his ship safely home must have been Krancke's best birthday present; he was forty-eight years old on that day. The tension of 161 days at sea began to ease once the ship made fast in Kiel during the late hours of the following day. Some 85,000 km had been covered, 15 ships sunk and 2 more captured bringing the complete bag to 113,000 grt, making this the most successful cruise of any German purpose-built surface warship.

Admiral Scheer went into dock for a well-earned overhaul and then saw some action in Baltic under the command of Kpt.z.S. Wilhelm Meendsen-Bohlken. Very little has been written about *Scheer*'s next major voyage, probably because hardly anything was sunk and there were no brushes with the Royal Navy. Yet Operation 'Wunderland' must rank as one of the most dramatic voyages of the Second World War. This started during the late spring of 1942 when Japanese intelligence notified the Germans of a Russian convoy leaving Vladivostok to make passage through the Siberian Sea. This involved a treacherous, ice-bound voyage of almost 12,000 km without any significant ports *en route*. The German Supreme Naval Command was only able to draw on the experiences of auxiliary cruiser *Komet* (Adm. Robert Eyssen) and therefore reacted by ordering Group Command North to prepare a memorandum about

Sailors in small boats lived in considerable discomfort but larger ships offered almost luxurious accommodation, in some cases better than what men would have had at home. This shows a warrant officer on the right with his gas mask container by his hand. Another bunk could have been folded down on top of his and he seems to have had the comforts of a small cooker and a fan.

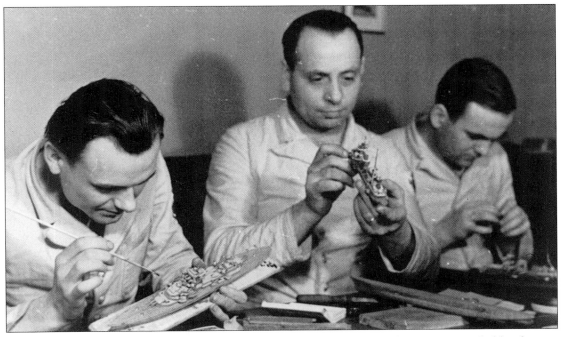

Although often busy, sailors still found time for hobbies and clubs. These pictures were probably taken aboard the heavy cruiser *Prinz Eugen*.

sending warships into the Siberian Sea. The results were quick in coming and mostly negative: too little was known about the ice; there had been no regular weather patterns during the past ten years; there was no hope of sending reconnaissance planes; and the Intelligence Service had not included the region in its studies. These deliberations were still under discussion when Japan provided details of yet another convoy having sailed. The German High Command bit the bullet and ordered *Admiral Scheer* (Kpt.z.S. Wilhelm Meendsen-Bohlken) to intercept them in the Kara Sea.

There was a meeting with *U601* (Kptlt. Peter Ottmar Grau) on 18 August 1942 to collect reports of a detailed reconnaissance of the pack ice and another meeting with *U252* (Kptlt. Heinrich Timm). The information provided by the two U-boats was supplemented with reconnaissance from *Scheer*'s plane, which eventually even sighted nine ships battling their way westwards. However the natural elements played against the pocket battleship and none of them came within range of the guns. Later the aircraft found ten more ships in the Wilkitzki Strait, but this time the raider did not have accurate enough charts to penetrate into those dangerous waters.

Two astonishing incidents came a few days later, during a skirmish with the 1,384GRT icebreaker *Sibirikow* which was sunk on 25 August 1942. Surprisingly this little ship, in the lonely vastness of an icy wilderness had been fully prepared for war and fought back with unexpected determination. Afterwards the Germans found a similar reaction while attacking the isolated outpost at Port Dixon. Plans to land a demolition squad had to be abandoned because two coastal batteries were so well hidden that German observers had not noticed them until they initiated their own vigorous retaliation.

HEAVY CRUISERS

Admiral Hipper
L: 6 February 1937 at Blohm und Voss in Hamburg; C: 29 April 1939; S: scuttled on 3 May 1945 while lying in Kiel. The wreck was later moved to the Heikendorfer Bay and scrapped.

Blücher
L: 8 June 1937 at Deutsche Werke in Kiel; C: 20 September 1939; S: 9 April 1940 in Oslo Fjord.

Prinz Eugen
L: 22 August 1938 at Germania Werft in Kiel; C: 1 August 1940. S: 13 January 1946 as target for American atom bomb tests at Kwajalein Atoll.

Although pocket battleships were reclassed as heavy cruisers, there were some significant operational differences between these two classes. Technical data suggests that heavy cruisers had only a slightly shorter range than the other class but their incredibly thirsty turbines could not be shut off at sea. This meant that their time at sea was always limited to just over a fortnight, unless tanker support could be provided. Diesel engines in pocket battleships, on the other hand, could be slowed down to consume very little fuel or even turned off to use none at all.

Admiral Hipper
Sea trials during the summer of 1939 suggested it would be wise to carry out a number of modifications rather than send *Admiral Hipper* (Kpt.z.S. Hellmuth Heye) to battle. Although she had been commissioned only four months before the beginning of the war, some parts of the ship had to be completely redesigned. Probably the most obvious of these alterations was the adding of so-called 'clipper bows' to prevent the forepart from being submerged during

Heavy cruiser *Prinz Eugen*. Carrying ammunition to the 105-mm guns and feeding it manually into the breeches was hard work and often had to be carried out in appalling weather on slippery decks.

An escort coming alongside the heavy cruiser *Prinz Eugen*.

The bell from *Admiral Hipper* on display at the Naval Memorial at Laboe (Kiel). The approaches to the solemn Hall of Commemoration have been tastefully decorated with a number of relics which create a stimulating maritime atmosphere in this austere building.

rough weather. This was rather important because water washing over the deck flooded the foremost gun turret. Consequently *Hipper* was not released until the Norwegian campaign of April 1940. The famous ramming by the British destroyer *Glowworm* on 8 April resulted in a fairly large hole being torn in the heavy cruiser's side, meaning it was June before *Hipper* could reappear. The following months were filled with more ill fortune. *Scharnhorst* and *Gneisenau* were damaged in separate incidents by torpedoes, leaving *Hipper* alone in the Polar seas. Only one small steamer, the 1,940 grt *Ester Thorsen*, was sunk before Kpt.z.S. Hellmuth Heye received orders to

bring his ship back to port, where the cruiser then lay idle, but in constant readiness, until after the postponement of the planned invasion of the United Kingdom.

Meanwhile a drastic change in the scenario had made it possible to send the fuel-thirsty ship south into the Atlantic and then to France for refuelling. By this time, October 1940, Hellmuth Heye had been promoted to Chief of Staff of the Security Forces for the Baltic. He was replaced by Kpt.z.S. Wilhelm Meisel, who also received more than his share of bad luck. First, the supply ship *Uckermark* (Korvkpt. Josef Amfaldern) was mined and the Supreme Naval Command could not organise another tanker, meaning that *Hipper* had to be recalled. Then, when the supply ship *Friedrich Breme* was ready, and Group Command West put their tanker *Thorn* at *Hipper*'s disposal, the heavy cruiser suffered a breakdown of vital pumping gear. After this had been repaired, another section of the pumping system failed. Following further repairs, Hipper had just left Kristiansand in Norway when a large pipe burst, squirting a jet of oil onto a hot boiler. The resulting fire dictated another return to the dockyard in Kiel.

The only consolation for this chain of disasters was that the delay made it possible to fit out another fast substitute for *Uckermark*. The supply ship *Dithmarschen* (Korvkpt. Walter von Zatorski) followed *Hipper* into the Atlantic to act first as mobile filling station and then as independent raider in her own right. Earlier suggestions to use these purpose-built supply ships as raiders were rejected on the grounds that the typical tanker silhouette could not be disguised. However, by this time the Supreme Naval Command realised that the opposition was not as sharp as had been anticipated and it was well worth taking the risk. After all, with three 150-mm guns, the tanker was well equipped to deal with the majority of merchant ships. Once again, well-made plans were laid to rest. *Dithmarschen*'s engines played up, forcing her back to port and this necessitated sending out the tanker *Adria* to refuel *Hipper* north-east of Iceland.

In mid-December 1940 *Hipper* proceeded north without great incident, was refuelled in Bergen by the tanker *Wollin*, and passed through the Denmark Strait to be refuelled by *Friedrich Breme* before bad luck played its trump card again. This time the entire set of starboard engines broke down. They were just about repaired when a convoy approached with powerful escorts, meaning it was best avoided. On 22 December, *Hipper*'s

aircraft disappeared, never to be heard of again. More bad luck followed on Christmas Eve when convoy WS5A was located by radar, but also found to be escorted by too powerful a force. This time *Hipper* got close enough to the heavy cruiser HMS *Berwick* for an exchange of gunfire. When *Hipper*'s torpedo officer was given permission to shoot, his orders were answered by a loud hiss of compressed air but without the torpedoes being ejected. Although some artillery hits were observed on *Berwick*, no serious damage was done to either side and *Hipper* made fast in Brest during the late afternoon of 27 December 1940 with many people aboard more frustrated than elated.

It took just seven days for the Royal Air Force to find the cruiser and to aim ninety tons of high explosives at her. Luckily for the Germans, the bomb aiming was not up to much and no serious damage resulted, although the surrounding town received quite a battering. British propaganda of the time has recorded how pleased the French were with these attacks. It appears that those who lost their property or were injured rushed out into the streets in joy to encouragingly wave British flags at the passing aircraft.

On 1 February *Hipper* was ready again. A considerable proportion of the crew had been replaced, and this made itself felt a few days later when the filling of the bunkers from tanker *Spichern* took an exceptionally long time, but the new hands also brought a change of luck. While making for a convoy being shadowed by *U37* (Kptlt. Nicolai Clausen) *Hipper* ran into a different group of ships heading north from Freetown in West Africa. Seven of them were sunk and two more damaged with radar ranged guns, but once again *Hipper*'s built-in handicap took control. Being at sea for twelve days meant the bunkers were running dry, making it impossible to pursue the other targets.

Fritz Kiemle as Obermaschinist by his desk aboard the light cruiser *Köln*. The cylinder on the table is a gas mask container and a torch is lying by its base. The hat was known as '*Schiffchen*' (Small Ship) and was favoured because it could be folded flat.

This time British air reconnaissance was a little quicker off the mark and the first wave of aircraft arrived the day after *Hipper* had put in to Brest, but bomb aiming had not improved. Although more houses were devastated, *Hipper* did not sustain any significant damage. It was the temperamental engine syndrome, not the bombing which kept the cruiser in port. Following a selection of words not usually found in dictionaries, the Naval Command ordered the ship back to Germany for repairs. The subsequent voyage was uneventful because the opposition did not notice the sailing until it was too late. After twice refuelling, first from tanker *Thorn* before the Denmark Strait and

from *Wollin* in Bergen, *Hipper* arrived back in Kiel at 1430 hrs on 28 March 1941. Following this the heavy cruiser was laid up and never again used for raiding in the Atlantic. Britain was probably aware of this because the ship remained untroubled from military opposition for much of the war and was finally blown up by German forces just a few days before the instrument of surrender was signed on 5 May 1945.

Blücher

Blücher's (Kpt.z.S. Heinrich Woldag) one and only war cruise ended rather abruptly shortly after first light on 9 April 1940. Sailing up Oslo Fjord with a view to landing troops in

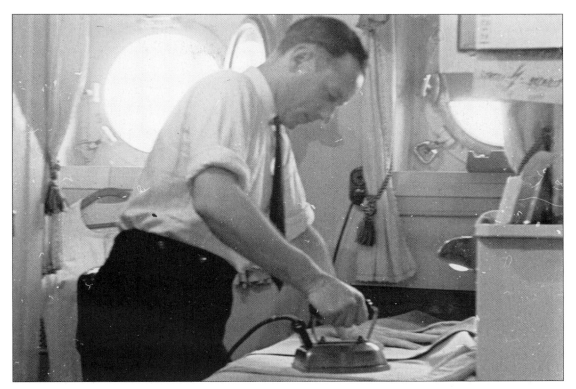

Fritz Kiemle demonstrating the versatility of the Obermaschinist's desk. Such space was not provided as a perk for higher ranks. The paper war had become so important that a great deal of time had to be spent dealing with administrative matters.

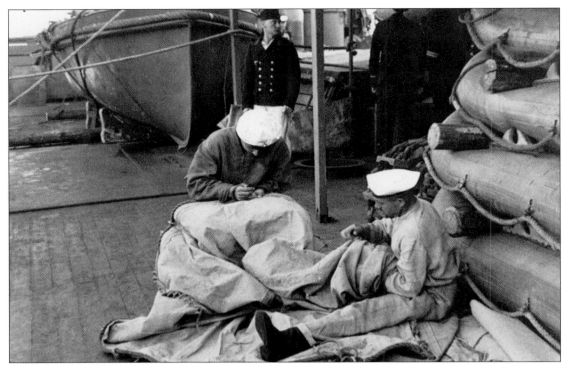

Old crafts, such as sail-making, were still in demand, even aboard the modern warships of the Second World War.

the capital for the invasion of Norway, the heavy cruiser was hit by two torpedoes fired from a land battery at the Dröbak Narrows and sank. The wreck is still lying there in exceptionally deep water.

Prinz Eugen

Prinz Eugen's maiden voyage under Kpt.z.S. Helmuth Brinkmann was delayed by several bomb hits received during an air raid on Kiel in April 1941 and then, shortly after this damage had been repaired, the *Prinz* ran on to a mine. Damage was again slight and a few weeks later the ship accompanied battleship *Bismarck* into the North Atlantic. There the heavy cruiser missed being sunk by the vast numbers dispatched from Britain because the ship had slipped away for a solo raiding

mission at a time when the opposition had lost contact. It was the heavy cruiser syndrome – engine trouble – which eventually forced Brinkmann to make for France. Repairs were well in hand when the ship became a target for the Royal Air Force. The First Officer, Fregkpt. Otto Stooss, and sixty men were killed, and the ship had to be laid up until the end of the year. In February 1942, *Prinz Eugen* participated in the famous Channel Dash to finish up in Norwegian waters, where HM Submarine *Trident* (Lt Cdr George Gregory) scored at least one well-placed torpedo hit on 23 February 1942. Blowing off part of the stern meant there was no prospect of engaging the ship in the near future. Instead a temporary rudder was rigged for a slow crawl to Trondheim where

The heavy cruiser *Prinz Eugen*.

Prinz Eugen – clearing up after exercises. The men are handling shells from the main 203-mm guns.

emergency repairs were carried out before continuing with the dangerous passage to the dockyard in Kiel.

Prinz Eugen was laid up there until the end of the year, but plans for further raiding never materialised. The *Prinz* ended its days as a target at Bikini Atoll for American atom bomb tests. One of the propellers has since found its way back to Germany and rests as a monument at the Naval Memorial in Laboe (Kiel).

AUXILIARY CRUISERS

The use of merchant ships as men-of-war, or privateers as they were called in olden days, helped in alleviating the expensive and lengthy problem of building warships. This system of waging war went out of business during the middle of the nineteenth century when the operating authority, the so-called 'Letter of Marque', was abolished at the Paris Congress of 1856. Prussia planned to engage armed merchant ships against France during the Franco-Prussian conflict of 1870–1, but both Britain and the United States were so much against the practice that it was abandoned. It

was not until the autumn manoeuvres of 1895 that the German High Command tried an experiment of converting the merchant ship *Normania* into a cruiser. Ten years later, during a war against Russia, Japan's accidental attack on a British merchant ship resulted in a conference being called at The Hague (in Holland) to consider some basic regulations for warfare with merchant ships.

This conference agreed on the following main points. A converted merchant ship or auxiliary cruiser must fly a flag identifying it as a warship and it must belong to the nation represented by that flag. The commander must be a bona fide officer of that nation's navy and must obey military law. The aim of this was to prevent civilian ships from fighting under merchant ship masters. Disguises were allowed, as long as this was cast off and the true identity made known before an engagement started. So, since the beginning of this century auxiliary cruisers were regarded as bona fide men-of-war and were subject to different laws which regulated the conduct of merchant ships with defensive armament. Merchant ships could be armed and the guns used in

Auxiliary Cruisers, left, *Kulmerland*, centre, *Triona* and, right, *Komet*.

The breech end of what looks like a twin 37-mm quick-firing gun. Shells were fed singly into each barrel. This common calibre has been deduced from the man's hand.

self-defence, but merchant seamen would have put themselves outside the law and made themselves pirates, had they used their weapons to start a fight with another ship.

Auxiliary warships presented an attractive proposition for the German High Command and such projects were eagerly discussed with private shipping firms while the trials with *Normania* were still fresh in the Navy's memory. Generous subsidies and a little arm-twisting provided some agreement on the basic facilities which needed to be incorporated in ship designs, but these details had hardly been circulated when the First World War broke out. Grabbing the initiative, Germany set about arming a number of ships and sending them out to raid merchant shipping on far distant

oceans. A number of them had highly successful careers, taking enormous pressure off European waters by keeping warships tied up in foreign parts. Later, the introduction of reliable oil-fired engines made the proposition of converting auxiliary cruisers even more attractive at the outset of the Second World War. The handful of these 'ghost' cruisers in far-off waters had highly successful operations and achieved more than the majority of purpose-built warships.

Auxiliary cruisers were originally called '*Handelsschutzkreuzer*' (Trade Protection Cruiser) and later became known as '*Handelsstörkreuzer*', but their abbreviation of HSK remained the same. These ships were first identified by an administration number from 1–8 and prefixed with the letters 'HSK'. Later, for operational purposes, they received another administration number which was always prefixed with the name 'Schiff' (Ship). Commanders had the privilege of also giving their ships a traditional name, while the Admiralty in London identified them with a letter in sequence order in which the raiders were discovered. Whence *Pinguin, HSK5, Schiff 33* and *Raider F* all refer to the same ship.

Atlantis

Originally *Goldenfels* from DDG Hansa Line of Bremen; *Schiff 16*; *HSK2, Raider C.* Left Kiel on 11 March 1940 under command of

Konteradmiral Bernhard Rogge wearing the uniform of the Federal German Navy. He himself used to joke that his career ranged from pirate to admiral, although his arduous time as commander of the raider *Atlantis* gained him deep respect from his colleagues, opponents and historians.

Kpt.z.S. Bernhard Rogge and remained at sea for a period of 622 days without putting into a port. S: 22 November 1941 by the cruiser HMS *Devonshire*.

Although many authors have added spice to their adventure stories by claiming that some small action resulted in a dramatic change in world history, the vast majority of such assertions must be treated with a large pinch of salt. However, *Atlantis*'s capture of the 7,528 grt freighter *Automedon* resulted in the Japanese attack on Pearl Harbor and America officially joining in the war, so this one single action did indeed make a major contribution to world history. *Automedon* was carrying a number of highly secret documents from Britain to Far Eastern military commanders when she was intercepted by auxiliary cruiser *Atlantis*. The papers were so sensitive that they were not locked in the ship's safe with the usual valuables. Instead, the heavily weighted bundles were kept on the bridge so that they could be thrown overboard in the unlikely event of the ship falling into enemy hands. Rogge's shot across the bows on the morning of 11 November 1940 resulted in *Automedon* increasing speed and sending distress calls. Consequently the auxiliary cruiser opened fire and the next salvo hit both the bridge and radio room, instantly killing all the officers who knew about the sensitive mail in their care.

Rogge and his adjutant (Dr Ulrich Mohr) recognised the importance of the papers, but thought they were of such value to the Japanese that they would probably be taken to be fakes. The information gave details of troop strengths in the Far East as well as outlines of Britain's policies in the event of an outbreak of hostilities there. Less than a week later, the captured tanker *Ole Jacob*, already under command of Kptlt.(S) Kamenz (the pre-war master of *Atlantis*) was dispatched with a couple of crates of captured documents for Admiral Paul Wenneker, the German Naval Attaché in Tokyo. This top secret information provided the Japanese with the necessary intelligence and confidence to bring them into the war.

Bletchley Park, the secret decrypting centre in Britain, intercepted a radio signal from Tokyo to Berlin on 12 December, but couldn't do anything to prevent the consequent chain of events leading to Japan's dramatic entry into the war by attacking the United States fleet at anchor in Pearl Harbor. Rogge became one of only three Germans to be awarded the high honour of being presented with the Sword of the Samurai. Although perhaps insignificant to the outcome of the war, it might be interesting to add that Kamenz made his way back to Berlin along the Siberian Railway. From there he travelled to France and then a submarine took him to a supply ship in the South Atlantic and from there he eventually returned to join his old ship, *Atlantis*.

Coburg

Originally the Dutch *Amerskerk*, allocated the number *Schiff 49*, but not converted into an auxiliary cruiser.

Coronel

Originally *Togo* belonging to Woermann Line AG in Hamburg; *Schiff 14*; HSK number not allocated; *Raider K*. Shortly after setting out in January 1943 under Kpt.z.S. Ernst Thienemann, opposition turned out to be too strong and the raider was recalled to prevent her annihilation. She reverted to the name *Togo* and later became the Norwegian *Svalbard*.

Hansa

The name *Hansa* was not adopted until plans to employ the ship as an auxiliary cruiser had been scrapped. Originally the *Glengarry* belonging to the Glen Line in London; then *Meersburg* belonging to the Hamburg–America Line; *Schiff 5*; HSK number not allocated. After the war she became *Empire* *Humber* and then *Glengarry* again, both under British flag.

Iller

Belonged to North German Lloyd and was considered for conversion, but work never went ahead.

Komet

Originally *Ems* belonging to North German Lloyd in Bremen; *Schiff 45*; *HSK7*; *Raider B*. Left Germany in July 1940 under Kpt.z.S. (later Admiral) Robert Eyssen, travelled along the Siberian Sea Passage and entered the Pacific through the Bering Strait. Returned to France in October 1941 and then sailed through the English Channel back to Germany, arriving in Hamburg on 31 November 1941.

Komet II, although sometimes written in such a way that it could be a different ship, the name refers to the second voyage, which started in October 1942, this time under Kpt.z.S. Ulrich Brocksien. S: in the English Channel by the British MTB 236 while breaking out into the Atlantic. There were no survivors.

Kormoran

Originally *Steiermark* belonging to the Hamburg–America Line in Hamburg; *Schiff 41*; *HSK8*; *Raider G*. Left Gotenhafen on 3 December 1940 under Fregkpt. Theodor Detmers. S: after combat with the Australian cruiser HMAS *Sydney* 29 November 1941.

Detmer's earlier experience with temperamental high pressure steam turbines in the destroyer *Hermann Schoemann* stood him in good stead when it came to dealing with *Kormoran*'s chain of disastrous engine breakdowns. By the time she was sunk, the engineering officer (Kptlt.(Ing.) Stehr) had supervised 350 bearing replacements! The end came quickly, but brought with it a mass of intrigue which has lasted to the present day and is rekindled every time a historian is

Germany's smallest raider *Komet*, under Kpt.z.S. Robert Eyssen, while meeting with *Anneliese Essberger*. *Komet* reached the Pacific Ocean by travelling eastwards along the Siberian Sea Passage. She was probably the first non-Russian ship to have attempted the venture and, what is more, there had only been a few ships before her that had proved the feat was possible during one summer's season. Her accompanying Russian icebreaker did not make it! It got stuck in the ice and was forced to spend a winter frozen in before it reached the Bering Strait.

searching for mysterious drama. *Kormoran* was sunk as a result of a duel with the far superior Australian cruiser *Sydney*, which went down with all hands. The unbalanced nature of the duel, fuelled by a mass of erroneous information, gave rise to all manner of stories involving everything from Japanese submarines to German flying saucers having been responsible for sinking the *Sydney*. As a result the straightforward account by men from *Kormoran*, who reached Australia, has often been discounted.

Being in home waters, the Australian cruiser was lured into a false sense of security by the German disguise. Consequently it approached too close and positioned itself sideways-on, making it an ideal target for the auxiliary cruiser's inferior, hidden armament. *Kormoran* fired several effective broadsides from incredible short range before the Australians realised what was happening, and they were hardly able to recover from the onslaught. However, one retaliatory shell detonated inside the ghost cruiser's engine room, giving Kpt.z.S. Detmers no alternative other than to scuttle on his 350th day at sea. Eighty men were killed during the brief action on that hot

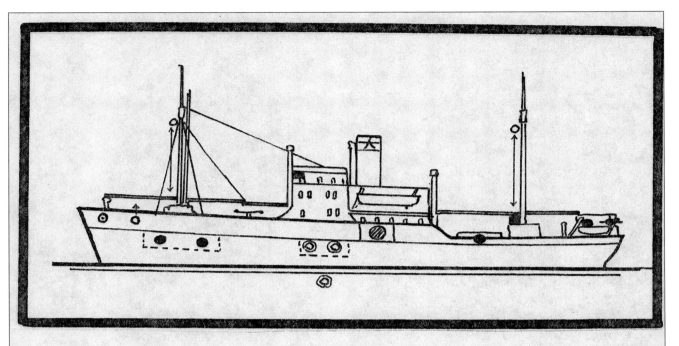

○ = 4 - 2 cm (o.79 inch) A.A.guns, during action hoisted up on both masts and on foxle deck

✦ = 1 - 3.7 cm (1.46 inch) double A.A.gun aft

☉ = 1 - 6 cm (2.36 inch) gun for warning ships on the foxle deck

● = 6 - 15 cm (5.91 inch) guns, of which 4 guns could fire to either side simultaneously

◎ = 4 surface and 2 underwater torpedo tubes

◼ = 2 fire control positions

⊤ = 1 range finder, during action raised

Not shown, 1 Arado-seaplane and 1 light speed-boat, especially constructed for mine laying purposes.

I FOUND THIS IN MY LOG. SOMEHOW, I HAD BEEN ABLE TO JOT IT DOWN, BASED ON MY OWN OBSERVATIONS AND DISCUSSIONS. HOWEVER, I CANNOT GUARANTEE, THAT IT IS ABSOLUTELY CORRECT. PERSONALLY, I BELIEVE YES IT IS. IN EYSSENS BOOK "KOMET", I DO NOT SEE ANY SUCH SKETCH.

Auxiliary cruiser *Komet* drawn by Otto Giese.

afternoon of 29 November 1941, but a good number of survivors later reached the Australian mainland to become prisoners of war. It is difficult to explain why there were no survivors from the *Sydney*, but it must be remembered that her decks were heavily raked with gunfire and the action took place in shark-infested waters.

The subsequent argument about this engagement also illustrates how history can easily be distorted. While learning English as a prisoner of war, one of *Kormoran*'s engineers translated a newspaper article of what a reporter had imagined might have happened. This translation exercise was then seized by authorities and taken to be an eye-witness account, although the author had been in the engine room all the time and had not witnessed what was going on outside. In addition to this, several historians have made up their own versions of the sinking, saying *Kormoran*'s records are inaccurate because no one can even agree on the time when *Sydney* was first sighted. Even auxiliary cruisers, with their somewhat primitive facilities, did not relay messages by shouting them across the deck! Instead telephones were used. The first person to have spotted the Australian cruiser would have been the lookout in the crow's nest and none of the other lookouts would have been aware of his sighting report. Therefore the next person, located half way up the mast, would have made his own report a few minutes later and deck lookouts would have been the last to relay their news. Consequently, if the reports are accurate, there must be a time lapse when different people sighted the same object.

Michel

Originally *Bielsko* belonging to the Gdynia–America Line in Gdingen (in Poland); then *Bonn* under the German flag; *Schiff 28*; *HSK9*; *Raider H*. Left Kiel on 9 March 1942 under Kpt.z.S. Hellmuth von Ruckteschell and

passed through the English Channel to Far Eastern waters. A return voyage to Europe was thought to involve too much risk and *Michel* ran into Kobe (Japan) on 2 March 1943. For her second voyage she left Japan on 21 May 1943 under the command of Kpt.z.S. Günther Gumprich. S: by US Submarine *Tarpon* on 17 October 1943.

Michel's cruise did not get off to a good start! During the night, while the majority of the crew were enjoying a last run ashore in Cuxhaven, the ship tore free from her moorings. The most senior officer on board, Kptlt. Konrad Hoppe (the ship's aircraft pilot) took the sensible option of allowing the ship to drift out into the Elbe Estuary and await daylight before redocking. A few days later, near Ostend, the opposite happened, *Michel* ran aground. The voyage ended a year later in Kobe (in Japan) because the return run into Europe had been considered too dangerous. Ill-health forced the commander, Kpt.z.S. Hellmuth von Ruckteschell, to seek medical attention and he was replaced by Kpt.z.S. Günther Gumprich for a second cruise. Sailing from Yokohama in May 1943, *Michel* accidentally ran into an Allied convoy and sailed with it for some time until a spell of bad visibility allowed Gumprich to turn away. After the war, von Ruckteschell was accused of war crimes and sentenced to ten years in jail for having allowed *Michel* to attack too aggressively. This seems rather strange, especially since many Allied forces attacked with considerably more severity than *Michel*, but Ruckteschell had already singed Britain's beard as a U-boat commander during the First World War and it seems highly likely that his prison sentence was revenge for this earlier defacing of British pride.

Orion

Originally *Kurmark* belonging to the Hamburg–America Line; *Schiff 36*, *HSK1*;

Auxiliary cruiser *Michel* seen from *Stier* during one of their rare meetings on southern oceans.

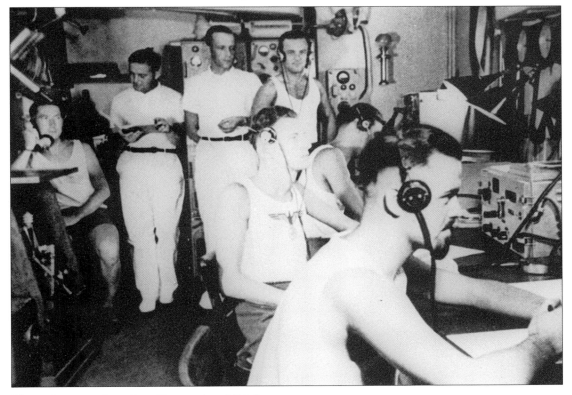

The radio room aboard auxiliary cruiser *Michel*.

Raider A; later renamed *Hektor*. Left Kiel on 30 March 1940 under Fregkpt. Kurt Weyher and returned to the Gironde Estuary on 23 August 1941. Following this the ship was used for training purposes.

Being fitted with high-pressure steam turbines meant the engines could not be switched off to conserve fuel. Consequently *Orion* covered the longest distance of all the ghost cruisers, a staggering 235,600 km. She dropped anchor off Royan (in France) in August 1941 after having been at sea for 511 days. Following this she was renamed *Hektor* and used as a gunnery training ship.

Pinguin

Originally *Kandelfels* belonging to DDG Hansa of Bremen; *Schiff 33*; *HSK5*; *Raider F.* Left

Germany in June 1940 under Kpt.z.S. Ernst-Felix Krüder to become the most successful surface raider in terms of tonnage sunk. S: by the British cruiser HMS *Cornwall* on 8 May 1941.

Stier

Originally *Cairo* belonging to the Atlas–Levante Line of Bremen; *Schiff 23*; *HSK6*; *Raider E.* Left Kiel on 9 May 1942 under Kpt.z.S. Horst Gerlach and sunk on 27 September 1942 as a result of combat with the United States auxiliary cruiser *Stephen Hopkins*. Survivors arrived in Royan on 2 November 1942 aboard the supply ship *Tannenfels*.

Thor

Originally *Santa Cruz* belonging to the Olderburg–Portugiesische Dampfschiffahrts

The officers of the raider *Pinguin* with Kpt.z.S. Ernst-Felix Krüder in the middle and the youngest officer aboard auxiliary cruisers, Hans Karl Hemmer, on the extreme right. It is a tradition that the most important member of the ship's company always sits on the floor.

Reederei; *Schiff 10*; *HSK4*; *Raider E*. Left Kiel on 6 July 1940 under Kpt.z.S. Otto Kähler and returned to Hamburg on 30 April 1941. Following a refit the ship, under command of Kpt.z.S. Günther Gumprich, left Kiel on 30 November 1941 for Bordeaux in France. Several problems frustrated the first two departures from there and it was 14 January 1942 before the *Thor* sailed from the Gironde Estuary with plans to operate in the Antarctic seas. Destroyed on 30 November 1942 in Yokohama (in Japan) while moored next to the supply ship *Uckermark*. A fire, which started in the tanker, gutted both ships. During the first voyage, *Thor* fought three duels with British auxiliary cruisers: *Alcantara*, *Carnarvon Castle* and *Voltaire*.

Widder

Originally *Neumark* of the Hamburg–America Line; *Schiff 21*; *HSK3*; *Raider D*. After the war

One of auxiliary cruiser *Thor*'s lookouts half way up the mast. A canvas screen has been put up to give some protection from the weather.

The rear guns of auxiliary cruiser *Widder* in action.

became *Ulysses* (British) and then *Fechenheim* (German). Left the Elbe Estuary on 5 May 1940 under Kpt.z.S. Hellmuth von Ruckteschell and returned to Brest (in France) on 31 October 1940. The ship was constantly plagued with unreliable engines which made a second voyage impractical. *Widder* was converted into a floating workshop and employed in Norwegian waters.

LIGHT CRUISERS

Emden
L: 7 January 1925 at the Naval Dock Yard in Wilhelmshaven; C: 15 November 1925; OoA: during an air raid on Kiel in April 1945, beached at Heikendorfer Bay and later scrapped.

Karlsruhe
L: 20 August 1927 at Deutsche Werke in Kiel; C: 6 November 1929; S: 9 April 1940 after having been hit by torpedoes from HM Submarine *Truant.*

Köln
L: 23 May 1928 at the Naval Dock Yard in Wilhelmshaven; C: 15 January 1940; S: 31 March 1945 as a result of an air raid on Wilhelmshaven.

Königsberg
L: 26 March 1927 at the Naval Dock Yard in Wilhelmshaven; C: 17 April 1929; S: in Bergen (in Norway) as a result of an air attack on 10 April 1940.

Leipzig
L: 18 October 1929 at the Naval Dock Yard in Wilhelmshaven; C: 8 October 1931; OoA: on 15 October 1944 as a result of having been rammed by *Prinz Eugen.* S: by the Allies in the North Sea on 16 December 1946 after having loaded the ship with canisters containing poisonous gases.

Nürnberg
L: 8 December 1934 at Deutsche Werke in Kiel; C: 2 November 1935; after the war became *Admiral Makarow* under the Soviet flag.

Although the appearance of some light cruisers was modified as time went on, at least the designers were helpful to historians seeking to identify this class by fitting each one with a set of torpedo tubes in a shallow well by the side or slightly ahead of the foremost funnel. Having been conceived at a time before radar, and when effective radio still had some way to go, light cruisers were thought of as the eyes and ears of battleships. The idea was that they should be powerful enough to cope with light opposition and fast enough to run away from superior fire-power.

By the early 1920s technology had advanced sufficiently to add considerable versatility to this concept, and cruisers found themselves becoming the wonder ships of the future. Turbines for high speeds were supplemented with diesel engines to provide exceptionally long ranges, and the improvement in armament made their artillery effective enough to suggest that they might also serve as lone surface raiders and minelayers. The possibilities seemed vast; and it was not only the Germans who were thinking about this. The people who imposed the limitations of the Versailles Diktat did not pick a maximum of 6,000 tons for light cruisers out of thin air. They knew full well that the modern role for such a ship could never be squeezed into such a tiny size. So, when the Reichsmarine started building its new generation of cruisers, something had to give, and it is not difficult to see where the designers saved weight. A quick glance at the armament of the first new cruiser (*Emden*) reveals the main target for the economies. Sea-going officers, who might one day have to take the ship to war, were not terribly impressed at the lack of firepower, but at the

Karlsruhe entering New York harbour with the crew assembled on deck for a traditional welcome.

Karlsruhe's main artillery control centre with 10-metre-long optical rangefinder situated at the top of a high tower which also supported a spider's web of radio aerials.

time there was nothing to shoot at anyway, so it was not deemed important.

The next type, based on the design of *Königsberg*, was far more impressive. The armament looked good, the performance was almost exciting and the sea-keeping qualities excellent. In all the ship performed well, but – and this was rather a big but – it achieved compliance with the limitations imposed by the Versailles Diktat by being rather thin on the sides. New techniques of welding steel made it possible to use thinner plates than those necessary when bolting them together with rivets and the navy quickly discovered that the stress from heavy seas was too much for some parts. Storm damage became an embarrassing feature at times, especially in *Karlsruhe*, where

cracks appeared in the hull while battling up America's west coast during a pre-war training and flag-showing cruise. The damage was sufficient for water to leak in, forcing the cruiser into dry dock at San Diego, California.

Leipzig, *Köln* and *Nürnberg* participated in the Spanish Civil War, where they proved to be admirable ships. When the Second World War began none of the light cruisers were actually put to the ultimate test of having to defend themselves in tricky sea battles. *Königsberg* was put out of action by coastal batteries near Bergen and sunk the following day in port by naval dive bombers. *Karlsruhe* was torpedoed by HM Submarine *Truant* (Lt Cdr C.H. Hutchinson) and the wreck later sunk by two torpedoes fired from the German torpedo

A good view of the rear turrets of what is probably the light cruiser *Köln*. Although the majority of men are wearing the white summer or tropical uniform, this was by no means compulsory for everybody because there is one man on the left with a different combination.

Light cruiser *Nürnberg*. German designers have helped historians by including a well for torpedo tubes somewhere near the forward funnel. In this case the black box-like feature can be seen between funnel and bridge.

The light cruiser *Karlsruhe* before the war at the Kiel Naval Week. It was not just a case of hanging such decorations anywhere. The Navy supplied quite a substantial book with regulations about the correct order in which the flags should be displayed.

The light cruiser *Karlsruhe*.

The K-Class cruisers were slightly thin on the sides to comply with the limitations imposed by the Versailles Diktat and *Karlsruhe* suffered some serious storm damage while battling along America's west coast. Consequently she had to go into dry dock in San Diego. The quantity of washing hanging up suggests the men inside her have had rather a rough time.

Karlsruhe kitted out for an official reception. This time identification can be quite positive because a nameplate has been attached to the outside of the ship.

Karlsruhe. In their traditional role, cruisers would have to spend more time drawing superior forces towards battleships rather than attacking smaller ships, therefore two turrets of the main armament pointed backwards. These were staggered to give them a greater arc of forward fire, as can clearly be seen here.

boat *Greif*. The initial attack inflicted only one mortal casualty and the rest of the crew were taken off. *Köln* was also bombed just before the end of the war and sank on even keel in shallow water with her decks still clear of the water. *Emden* also almost saw the end of the war, being bombed in 1945 and then beached near Kiel. After the war *Leipzig* served as an accommodation ship in Wilhelmshaven before being sunk in the North Sea during 1946 as a dustbin containing unwanted gas bombs. (Gosh, the military do think of some productive uses for good quality steel and unwanted poisons.) *Nürnberg* was in Copenhagen when the war ended and then sailed under the Soviet flag until she was scrapped between 1959 and 1960.

DESTROYERS AND TORPEDO BOATS

1st Destroyer Flotilla
Founded during the autumn of 1938 by amalgamating the 1st and 3rd Destroyer Division and disbanded in April 1940 after heavy losses during the Norwegian campaign. Surviving vessels then joined the 5th Flotilla. Units: *Richard Beitzen, Friedrich Eckholdt, Friedrich Ihn, Erich Steinbrinck, Max Schultz* and *Georg Thiele*. Flotilla Chief: Kpt.z.S. Wilhelm Meisel until October 1939, then Fregkpt. Fritz Berger.

2nd Destroyer Flotilla
Founded during the autumn of 1938 from the 2nd Destroyer Division and disbanded in April 1940 after the Norwegian campaign. Remaining ships joined the 6th Flotilla. Units: *Bruno Heinemann, Paul Jacobi, Leberecht Maass, Theodor Riedel* and *Hermann Schoemann*. Flotilla Chief: Kpt.z.S. Friedrich Bonte until October 1939 then Fregkpt. Rudolf von Pufendorf.

3rd Destroyer Flotilla
Founded during December 1939 from the 5th Destroyer Division and disbanded in April 1940 after the Norwegian campaign. Units: *Karl Galster, Hermann Künne, Hans Lüdemann, Diether von Roeder* and *Anton Schmidt*. Flotilla Chief: Fregkpt. Hans-Joachim Gadow.

4th Destroyer Flotilla
Founded during April 1939 and disbanded in April 1940. The one surviving destroyer was taken over by the 6th Flotilla. In 1942 the 4th Flotilla was re-founded with new boats. Units: *Bernd von Arnim, Erich Giese, Hans Lody, Erich Koellner* and *Wolfgang Zenker*. After 1942: *Z31, Z32, Z33, Z34, Z37, Z38* and *Z39*. Flotilla Chief: Fregkpt. Erich Bey until 1940. Korvkpt. Georg Langheld until April 1943, then Kpt.z.S. Rolf Johannesson until December 1944 and Kpt.z.S. Freiherr Hubert von Wangenheim until the end of the war.

5th Destroyer Flotilla
Founded during May 1940 with survivors from the 1st Flotilla. Units: *Richard Beitzen, Friedrich Eckholdt, Friedrich Ihn, Erich Steinbrinck* and *ZH1*. Flotilla Chief: Fregkpt. Alfred Schemmel until August 1940, then Kpt.z.S. Fritz Berger until July 1942, Kpt.z.S. Schemmel again until December 1942, Kpt.z.S. Max-Eckhart Wolff until February 1944 and then Kpt.z.S. Georg Langheld until the end of the war.

6th Destroyer Flotilla
Founded in May 1940 with survivors from the Norwegian campaign. Units: *Karl Galster, Bruno Heinemann, Paul Jacobi, Hans Lody, Theodor Riedel, Hermann Schoemann, Z35, Z36* and *Z43*. Flotilla Chief: Kpt.z.S. Erich Bey (at the same time Flag Officer for Destroyers) until November 1940, Kpt.z.S. Schulte-Hinrichs until April 1943, then Kpt.z.S. Friedrich Kothe until December 1944 and Kpt.z.S. Heinz Peters for the rest of the war.

7th Destroyer Flotilla
Not operational.

The destroyer *Z10* (*Hans Lody*) in a Norwegian fjord near Skjeberg. This remarkable radio-controlled model was built at a scale of 1:32 by Ivar Berntsen.

Another view of Ivar Bernsten's magnificent model photographed in a Norwegian fjord, where so many destroyers saw heavy action.

A destroyer in the Kiel Canal.

Ivar Bernsten's model of *Hans Lody*.

8th Destroyer Flotilla (The Narvik Flotilla)
Founded in December 1940 and disbanded in August 1944 after heavy losses. Re-founded in November 1944.
Units: *Z23, Z24, Z25, Z26, Z27, Z28, Z29, Z30.*
Flotilla Chief: Kpt.z.S. Gottfried Pönitz until March 1943, Kpt.z.S. Hans Erdmenger until December 1943, Fregkpt. Georg Langheld until April 1944, Freiherr Theodor von Mauchenheim until June 1944 and Fregkpt. Georg Ritter und Edler Herr von Berger until August 1944. Following the re-founding Kpt.z.S. Heinrich Gerlach until the end of the war.

List of Destroyers (Z = Zerstörer)
Z1, Leberecht Maass
Z2, Georg Thiele
Z3, Max Schultz

Z4, Richard Beitzen
Z5, Paul Jacobi
Z6, Theodor Riedel
Z7, Hermann Schoemann
Z8, Bruno Heinemann
Z9, Wolfgang Zenker
Z10, Hans Lody
Z11, Bernd von Arnim
Z12, Erich Giese
Z13, Erich Koellner
Z14, Friedrich Ihn
Z15, Erich Steinbrinck
Z16, Freidrich Eckoldt
Z17, Diether von Roeder
Z18, Hans Lüdemann
Z19, Hermann Künne
Z20, Karl Galster
Z21, Wilhelm Heidkamp

The torpedo boat *T18*. Once again a remarkable model by the Norwegian Ivar Berntsen. The paravane, lying on the deck just forward of the bridge, was part of the bow protection gear for clearing mines from the boat's path.

A close up of *T18*'s bridge. One really has to look exceptionally hard to realise that this is not the real vessel but a model made by Ivar Berntsen.

Berntsen's model of *T18*, showing the positions of the torpedo tubes and a quadruple 20-mm anti-aircraft gun.

Z22, Anton Schmidt
Z23 – Z39, names not allocated
Z43, name not allocated
ZG3, Hermes
ZH1, name not allocated

TORPEDO BOATS

1st Torpedo Boat Flotilla
Employed in the North Sea for laying offensive and defensive mine barrages until spring 1941. Moved to the Baltic and then disbanded.

2nd Torpedo Boat Flotilla
Active in the North Sea on a variety of operations including minelaying until the spring of 1941, then moved into the Baltic. Used in northern areas for convoy escorts during the summer of 1942 and then with the Torpedo School for training. Employed in the Baltic until the end of the war.

3rd Torpedo Boat Flotilla
Engaged in the North Sea and western areas from early 1942 until the spring of 1943, at the same time other boats from the flotilla were moved into northern areas. Employed in Danish waters during the summer of 1943 and then for training. Operated in the Baltic and its North Sea approaches until the end of the war.

4th Torpedo Boat Flotilla
Established during the autumn of 1943 in French waters for escort duties and the laying of defensive mine barrages.

5th Torpedo Boat Flotilla
Employed in the North Sea and later in Dutch and French waters until the entire flotilla was annihilated. Towards the end of the war the flotilla was re-established in the Baltic with new boats.

6th Torpedo Boat Flotilla
Operational in the North Sea, participated in the invasion of Norway and disbanded in February 1941.

7th Torpedo Boat Flotilla
Engaged for a variety of duties, but mainly as escorts in both North Sea and Baltic. Used for training from June 1940 and disbanded in December 1940.

8th Torpedo Boat Flotilla
Not operational.

9th Torpedo Boat Flotilla
Founded in September 1943 in the Aegean Sea and disbanded in October 1944. Then re-established shortly before the end of the war and employed in the Adriatic.

10th Torpedo Boat Flotilla
Founded in January 1944 for employment in the Mediterranean to the north of Corsica.

The engine room of a torpedo boat. If the men's hat bands are to be believed then this could be *Seeadler*, one of the early boats launched in 1926.

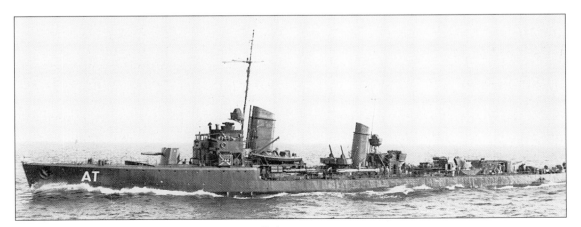

Torpedo boat *Albatross*, which looked like a small destroyer.

The development of German destroyers can easily be compared with the introduction of the Ferguson agricultural tractor. When these first appeared, the majority of people preferred to stick with older proven workhorses, but later, when a variety of useful accessories were added, the vehicles became an indispensable tool. After the First World War, destroyer development followed slightly different lines of thinking in Britain, in the United States and in Germany because each country had different uses for them. Britain needed convoy escorts, capable of dealing with submarines, while Germany was still shrouded in Grand Admiral Alfred von Tirpitz's vision of a torpedo carrier. Hence the first destroyer-type vessels were called 'Torpedo Boats'. Germany's lack of interest in destroyers was illustrated by the fact that the first post-First World War destroyer was not commissioned until 1937, and then this class came under the jurisdiction of the Flag Officer for Torpedo Boats. It was not until the outbreak of the Second World War that people realised that these larger vessels of about 1,500 tons offered incredible diversity. Their torpedoes made them capable of attacking large warships; depth charges made them ideal as submarine chasers; their artillery could cope with aircraft and the majority of fast moving boats; and the ability to lay mines gave them a fourth vital role. It was not long before destroyers became the most important workhorse for the fleet and saw action in every theatre of war where the Navy operated.

The office of Flag Officer for Torpedo Boats, established in Swinemünde on the Baltic coast in September 1933, was renamed Flag Officer for Destroyers in November

A minesweeper or M-boat at sea.

T157 during the early days of the Reichsmarine.

This is an example of a First World War torpedo boat which was not scrapped by the Diktat of Versailles and formed part of the backbone for the new fleet.

1939. At the same time a new administrative network for torpedo and motor torpedo boats was created. Both the FdZ (*Führer der Zerstörer* – Flag Officer for Destroyers) and FdT (*Führer der Torpedoboote* – Flag Officer for Torpedo Boats) came under the direct jurisdiction of the Commander-in-Chief of Reconnaissance Forces. For much of the time these had only administrative responsibility because the boats came under the operational command of other local officers. Some of the vessels were never even attached to a flotilla because they were always serving with other units. The position of Flag Officer for Torpedo Boats was eventually abolished in April 1942 and the remaining units passed over to the Flag Officer for Destroyers. However, as before, for much of the time operational control remained with other local commanders.

Shortly after the beginning of the war, the majority of torpedo boats and destroyers operated in the Baltic and only a few in the North Sea. Many of them were employed for the laying of defensive mine barrages until the coming of long winter nights and seasonal bad weather gave them the opportunity of approaching Britain's east coast for offensive mining operations. In spring 1940 destroyers and torpedo boats were employed during the invasion of Norway and Denmark, where they functioned as autonomous flotillas assisting task force commanders. The FdZ (Kpt.z.S. and Kommodore Friedrich Bonte) was killed while leading the assault on *Narvik* aboard *Wilhelm Heidkamp* while the FdT (Kpt.z.S. Hans Bütow) led the attack on Kristiansand in torpedo boat *Luchs*. Following heavy losses

The aftermath of Operation *'Weserübung'*, the invasion of Norway and Denmark. This shows the area near Narvik.

in Norway, the entire torpedo boat and destroyer arm was reorganised, although much of this was only for administrative purposes and the boats continued operating under local commanders.

Following the invasion of the Low Countries, destroyers and torpedo boats followed the Army westwards, using places in Holland such as Den Helder, Scheveningen and Rotterdam as bases; and continuing the chain of re-fuelling stations through Ostend in Belgium to Boulogne, Cherbourg and on as far as the Biscay ports of France. By this time destroyers had become such indispensable workhorses that the Navy looked around for supplementing its meagre fleet with foreign acquisitions. The first additional boats were commandeered from the Royal Norwegian Navy. Some of these new names fitted so well into the existing German naming pattern that one could easily mistake them for the home-produced articles. For example *Löwe* (ex-*Gyller*), *Leopard* (ex-*Balder*), *Panther* (ex-*Odin*) and *Tiger* (ex-*Tor*) could well be mistaken for vessels of the *Raubtier* (Beasts of Prey) Class. The origin of other boats is more easily determined because the letter 'A' (meaning *Ausland* – Foreign) was added to their number, for instance, as TA9 was the ex-Italian *FR2*, which had earlier been the French *Bombarde*. A similar identification was used for foreign destroyers, but instead of the 'A', a letter of the country of origin was added, such as *ZG3* (Destroyer from Greece) and *ZH1* (Destroyer from Holland). The first German purpose-built destroyers were also known by a name in addition to the official 'Z' number (Z meaning *Zerstörer*). These were not just pet names given to the boat by the crew, but officially recognised means of identification.

MOTOR TORPEDO BOATS

The MTB or Motor Torpedo Boat was called E-boat (Enemy boat) in England and *S-boot* or *Schnellboot* (Fast Boat) in German. They differed from torpedo boats by having a much smaller displacement and a very high speed. All of them definitely looked like MTBs rather than small destroyers.

1st S-boat Flotilla
Operational in the Baltic, then in the North Sea for the invasion of Norway, and along the Dutch and French coasts. Returned to the Baltic in 1941 and moved to the Black Sea during the spring of 1942 where it remained until October 1944.

2nd S-boat Flotilla
Operational in the North Sea, participated in the invasion of Norway and then returned to the North Sea before being moved into the English Channel. In 1941, for period of five months, the flotilla was operational in the Baltic, but for most of the time it remained in French waters.

3rd S-boat Flotilla
Founded in May 1940 and operated along the Dutch coast and in the English Channel. For a time based in Boulogne and Ostend. Then moved into the Baltic before being transported overland to Italy and from there to Tunisia. Remained in the Mediterranean until the end of the war.

4th S-boat Flotilla
Operational in the English Channel and the area between Britain and Belgium from 1940 until 1944.

5th S-boat Flotilla
Founded during the summer of 1941 in the far eastern Baltic and then engaged in the English Channel until June 1944, by which time the majority of boats had been sunk. Reformed with new boats and employed in the Baltic.

6th S-boat Flotilla
Founded 1941 and operated mainly in the North Sea and English Channel, although at one stage the flotilla was moved into the Baltic for a brief period.

7th S-boat Flotilla
Founded in October 1941 in the Baltic and then moved to the Mediterranean.

8th S-boat Flotilla
Founded in November 1941 for employment in Norwegian and northern waters. Disbanded in July 1942.

9th S-boat Flotilla
Founded in April 1943 for employment in the English Channel.

10th S-boat Flotilla
Founded in March 1944 for employment in the English Channel.

11th S-boat Flotilla
Operational for nine months from February 1943 in the Baltic and possibly in French waters.

21st S-boat Flotilla
Founded in the Baltic and then moved into the Mediterranean.

22nd S-boat Flotilla
Founded in December 1943 in the Baltic and disbanded in October 1944.

24th S-boat Flotilla
Operational in the Mediterranean, mainly from Greek waters.

After the First World War the majority of maritime nations neglected MTB development. Britain seemed to continue building them only for export, and the limitations imposed by the Versailles Diktat made it impractical for Germany to contemplate this type of craft. It

S9 (left) and *S11*, both examples of the early types of motor torpedo boats with a flotilla of small U-boats in the background.

seems that only France and Italy saw a future for such small fast torpedo carriers; probably because the Mediterranean offered ideal areas for their employment. Germany was also fascinated by the possibilities of engaging fast craft and a saga of amazing clandestine development can be uncovered before this type of boat reappeared from under the Versailles cloak. The Reichsmarine's first S-boats were powered by petrol engines, which made them somewhat undesirable for combat because the majority of people did not fancy the idea of sitting on top of such volatile fuel while being shot at. However, these designs proved to be better than expected and modifications soon gave rise to five more petrol-engine S-boats.

Several engine manufacturers attempted to find a solution by squeezing more power out of the diesel principle, and such engines were incorporated in the next sets of boats. The results were so promising that Germany soon reached a stage where the basic diesel design was improved with superchargers. They then had to find ways of preventing boats from drowning in their own bow waves. Consequently, the general shape of the hull was improved to provide better sea-keeping qualities. *S38* became the basis for this new fast, supercharged type, which saw effective service towards the end of the war.

The basic anti-aircraft armament was improved as soon as aircraft became a significant threat during the war, but the problem was difficult to solve because a fast boat, bobbing about on top of waves, always provided an unstable gun platform. Furthermore, it was found that the majority of aircraft could turn tighter circles than the

Two flotilla commander pennants and a long, thin commander's pennant.

boats, although a number failed to regain height in the process and ended up going for a swim. However, the aircraft threat not only persisted, but worsened because aircraft were being fitted with more powerful guns and cannon. The protective steel cladding which was added to torpedo boats resulted in them becoming slightly more unstable, and losses to aircraft continued at an alarming rate. Eventually the entire bridge became an armoured box. Yet, despite the threat from the air, S-boats continued to be successfully employed until the end of the war and saw action in a vast diversity of areas.

At first S-boats came under the jurisdiction of the Flag Officer for Torpedo Boats and later under the Flag Officer for Destroyers. It was not until April of 1943 that they were given their own autonomous command and the first *Führer der Schnellboote* (FdS – Flag Officer for S-boats), Kpt.z.S. and Kommodore Rudolf Petersen, remained in office until the end of the war. Much of the FdS's work involved administrative duties because operational command was held by local commanders. Unlike torpedo boats and destroyers, S-boats tended to operate more often as autonomous flotillas without having to fit in directly with other forces. The main reason for this was that there were not that many other forces in the areas where they were fighting. S-boats also achieved incredible successes at times when the sinking figures of other forces, such as

A photograph of the 'man overboard' procedure on small vessels. It was customary for one man to balance over the water at the end of a long ladder to retrieve whatever needed picking up. Usually a lifebelt was thrown overboard for the purpose of practising the manoeuvre.

A wreath made from a simple cross, with a hat band from the 2nd Minesweeping Flotilla at the top. The boat was passing a spot where comrades had been killed during the First World War. The man is wearing standard working rig with official woollen hat, tight-knit jumper and denim trousers.

U-boats, had dwindled considerably. For example, a single operation in April 1944 killed more Allied soldiers than all the combined German forces on D-Day. This happened when a handful of boats from the 9th S-Flotilla under the leadership of Götz Freiherr von Mirbach penetrated into Lyme Bay on the south coast of Devon. Following an analysis of radio signals it was fairly obvious that there was considerable movement of Allied shipping in the area and when the 9th Flotilla struck, it hit a number of ships carrying soldiers practising landings for D-Day. The official figures state that about a thousand Allied servicemen were killed, although locals living along the coast have suspicions that the real number, hushed up at the time, was considerably larger.

LIGHT S-BOATS

The concept of LS-boats or *Leichte Schnellboote* (Light Speedboats) had been formulated before the turn of the century. As early as 1895 the experimental auxiliary cruiser *Normania* had been equipped with two steam-driven motor torpedo boats. The main stumbling block in the craft's development was the lack of reliable engines which could be started quickly and which would not be affected by the damp conditions they were likely to meet at sea. Even after the First World War, when diesel engines made the concept possible, it was found that the weight of normal torpedo tubes made the craft too unstable at speed and the idea was more or less abandoned. It was only because of the persistence of one visionary, Heinz Docter, who experimented in his spare time, that small motor torpedo boats became operational during the Second World War.

A few LS-boats saw service in the Aegean Sea, and a number were carried by auxiliary cruisers. The majority were troubled with a chain of embarrassing mechanical failures and their torpedoes were found to be hardly powerful enough to stop merchant ships, yet they fooled some people into stopping because it was thought that the attack had come from a submarine. Kpt.z.S. Hellmuth von Ruckteschell (Commander of the auxiliary cruisers *Michel* and *Widder*) told the High Command that every raider should be equipped with two such craft, but with reliable engines. The torpedoes carried by LS-boats were small aerial torpedoes, not the standard type carried by S-boats and U-boats.

SUPPLY SHIPS

The following supply ships and tankers have been included because they operated in areas where they came into contact with enemy forces and they frequently feature in histories of the war.

Adria
Motor tanker used as supply ship. Taken over by Britain after the war and renamed *Empire Tageos*. Later she became the Russian *Kazbek* and then the Polish *Karpaty*.

Alstertor
V-ship, scuttled on 23 June 1941 when HMS *Marsdale* appeared.

Alsterufer
V-ship and blockade breaker. S: by aircraft on 27 December 1943.

Altmark
Purpose-built naval supply ship. Renamed *Uckermark* shortly after the beginning of the war.

Anneliese Essberger
Blockade breaker and later V-ship, scuttled on 21 November 1942 when USS *Milwaukee* appeared.

Babitonga

Scuttled on 21 June 1941 when HMS *London* approached.

Belchen

Supply tanker for U-boats, *Bismarck* and *Prinz Eugen*. S: 3 June 1941 by HMS *Aurora* and HMS *Kenya*.

Burgenland

Blockade breaker and designated supply ship for *Michel*.

Charlotte Schliemann

Blockade breaker and designated supply ship for *Stier* and *Michel*.

Coburg

V-ship. Commandeered in Holland in May 1940. It was first planned to engage the vessel as a raider, but she was later used as a supply ship. Scuttled on 4 March 1941 when the cruisers *Leander* and *Canberra* approached.

Otto Giese, *Anneliese Essberger*'s second officer, on the open bridge. Otto Giese joined the Merchant Navy as an officer candidate long before the beginning of the war. One of the first things he purchased with his accumulated salary was a Leica camera, which then accompanied him until he surrendered in the Far East in 1945. Consequently he has the most exciting collection of photographs documenting Germany's turbulent past.

Anneliese Essberger supplying provisions and about 700 tons of fuel through fire hoses to the smallest auxiliary cruiser (*Komet* under Kpt.z.S. Robert Eyssen). At this stage, sometime between 15 and 22 July 1941, *Anneliese Essberger* was still disguised as a Japanese ship.

The bridge of *Anneliese Essberger* while supplying *Komet* with fuel through fire hoses. Sitting high up is a signalman from the auxiliary cruiser.

Anneliese Essberger's Chief Mate Koch and the signalman from *Komet*. One problem with such meetings was that the crews from merchant ships often did not have trained men for the vast variety of skills required by a warship.

Dithmarschen
Purpose-built fleet supply ship which became British-flagged *Southmark* after the war and later *Conecuh* (USA).

Doggerbank
Captured on 31 January 1941 by auxiliary cruiser *Atlantis* as *Speybank* and dispatched to Europe as prize. Later used as an auxiliary minelayer, blockade breaker and V-ship.

Dresden
Supply ship for *Atlantis*. Scuttled in the Gironde Estuary on 25 August 1944. Raised by the French and renamed *Doba*. Stranded at Ras Hafonn in Somalia on 21 July 1950. Also known as *Schiff 171*.

Duquesa
Refrigerated ship carrying food which was captured by *Admiral Scheer* on 18 December 1940 and later scuttled on 20 February 1941, because there was no more fuel to keep refrigerators or engines running. Used as supply ship and unofficially known as Supply Depot Wilhelmshaven – South.

Elsa Essberger
Designated supply ship for *Orion*. Scuttled in the Gironde Estuary during August 1944.

Emmy Friederich
Supply ship for *Admiral Graf Spee*. Scuttled in the Caribbean on 23 October 1939 when HMS *Caradoc* appeared.

Ermland
Blockade breaker. The ship was in the Philippine capital Manila when the war started and from there put into neutral Formosa. She left there on 28 July 1940 to be fitted out in Japan for running the blockade back to Europe. Sailing on 29 December 1940, she picked up prisoners from *Orion* and *Komet* before arriving in the Gironde Estuary on 4 April 1941. Following this she was engaged as a supply ship.

Esso Hamburg
Supply tanker for *Gneisenau*, *Admiral Scheer* and *Prinz Eugen*. Scuttled on 4 June 1941 when HMS *London* and HMS *Brilliant* approached.

Friedrich Breme
Supply ship for *Admiral Hipper*, *Scharnhorst* and *Gneisenau*. Scuttled on 12 June 1941 when HMS *Sheffield* approached.

Gonzenheim
Supply ship and reconnaissance vessel for *Bismarck* and *Prinz Eugen*. Sunk on 4 June 1941 by HMS *Nelson* and HMS *Esperance Bay*. Earlier known as *Kongsfjord* and also as *Sperrbrecher 15*.

Ill
Motor tanker which was used as supply ship for raiders. Known as *Turicum* before the war and became *Funta Aspra* (Italian) afterwards.

Kertosono
Captured by *Thor* and sent to France as prize.

Ketty Brovig
Captured by *Atlantis* on 2 February 1941 and scuttled on 4 March 1941 when the cruisers *Canberra* and *Leander* approached.

Königsberg
Supply ship for *Widder*. Scuttled on 16 June 1940 when French warships approached.

Kota Nopan
Captured by *Komet* and sent to France. Later used as blockade breaker. For her last cruise she left Singapore on 4 February 1943 and was scuttled off Cape Finisterre after having been stopped by the mine-cruiser *Adventure*.

Krossfonn
Captured by *Widder*, renamed *Spichern* and used as supply ship.

Kulmerland
Supply ship for several raiders. Damaged beyond repair on 23 September 1943 during an air raid on Nantes.

Lothringen
Supply tanker for *Bismarck* and *Prinz Eugen*. Surrendered to aircraft carrier *Eagle* on 15 June 1941. Earlier known as *Papendrecht*. Became *Empire Salvage*, then *Dunedin* and later *Papendrecht* again.

Monsun
Captured on 18 January 1941 by *Admiral Scheer* as *Sandefjord* and scuttled in Nantes on 11 August 1944.

Münsterland
Supply ship for auxiliary cruisers. Sunk near Calais on 20 January 1944.

Nordmark
Purpose-built supply ship. Earlier known as *Westerwald* and after the war commissioned in the Royal Navy as *Northmark* and after that as *Bulawayo*.

The engine room of the *Ermland*. Although oil-fired engines were more convenient and made a good deal less mess, working in the engine room was still a hot and dirty job.

Blockade breaker *Rio Grande* arriving in Bordeaux, France, April 1942.

Nordstern

Captured by *Admiral Scheer* on 20 February 1941 when the ship was known as *British Advocate*. Sunk in French waters on 24 July 1944.

Nordvard

Captured by *Pinguin* on 15 September 1940 and sunk in Oslo Fjord on 29 December 1944.

Ole Jacob

Captured by *Atlantis* on 10 November 1940 and used as supply tanker and blockade breaker. Sunk off Spain on 24 December 1941.

Osorno

Designated supply ship for *Michel* and also used as blockade breaker.

Portland

Supply ship for *Admiral Scheer*. Scuttled on 13 April 1943 when the French cruiser *Georges Leyques* approached.

Prairie

The ship with this name seen in photos of several books is the German purpose-built supply ship *Nordmark* disguised as an American tanker.

Python

Z-ship, supply ship for U-boats. Sent to rescue survivors from *Atlantis*. Scuttled on 1 December 1941 while under attack from the British cruiser *Dorsetshire*.

Regensburg

Supply ship for auxiliary cruisers. Scuttled on 30 March 1943 when the British cruiser *Glasgow* approached.

Rekum

Supply tanker sunk near Boulogne on 21 March 1944.

Rhakotis

Left Japan as blockade breaker to supply *Michel*. Scuttled on 1 January 1943 after being challenged by the light cruiser *Scylla*.

Rio Grande

Blockade breaker which served as supply ship for several auxiliary cruisers. Scuttled on 4 January 1944 near Ascension Island when USS *Omaha* approached.

Rudolf Albrecht

Supply ship for *Kormoran*. Taken over by Britain after the war and renamed *Empire Taginda*, then *Basing Steam*, then *Oil Steam* and finally *Vrissi* (under the Greek flag).

Schlettstadt

Earlier known as *Coryda*. Supply tanker for *Scharnhorst* and *Gneisenau*. Taken over by Britain after the war.

Spichern

Captured by *Widder* as *Krossfonn*. Supply ship for heavy cruisers and *Thor*. Scuttled in Brest during August 1944. Raised and then known as *Rigsfjell* and later as *Ringsacker*.

Tannenfels

Blockade breaker and supply ship. Scuttled in the Gironde Estuary during August 1944.

The supply ship *Tannenfels* in the Gironde Estuary.

Thorn

Supply ship for *Admiral Hipper*. Sunk on 2 April 1941 by HMS *Tigris*. Earlier known as *Ruth*.

Uckermark

Purpose-built supply ship which was earlier known as *Altmark*. Destroyed on 30 November 1942 in Yokohama during a fire, which also put auxiliary cruiser *Thor* out of action.

Weser

Captured as *Vancouver Island* on 25 September 1940 and later used as supply ship for *Orion*. Sunk accidentally on 15 October 1941 by *U558* (Kptlt. Günther Krech).

Westerwald

Purpose-built supply ship. Renamed *Nordmark* shortly after the start of the war.

Winnetou

Supply ship for *Orion*. Sunk on 12 August 1944 by US Submarine *Puffer*.

Wollin

Supply tanker used in European coastal waters to refuel raiders in Norway.

By the beginning of 1942 Germany had established seven categories of supply ship. These were: fleet supply ships (*Trosschiffe*); auxiliary fleet supply ships (*Hilfstrosschiffe*); escort tankers (*Begleittanker*); supply ships known as V-ships (*V-Schiffe* or *Versorgungsschiffe*); submarine supply ships known as Z-ships (*Uboots-Zufuhrschiffe* or *Ubootsversorger*); port supply ships (*Etappen V-Schiffe*); and port supply tankers (*Etappentanker*). Merchant ships with civilian crews, known as blockade breakers, were also used to supply raiders at sea and, of course, many raiders extracted provisions from their victims before sinking them.

Fleet supply ships, such as *Altmark* and *Nordmark*, were purpose built with trained military crews and a fairly impressive armament of at least three 150-mm guns. The original design concept allowed for them to be also employable as merchant raiders after their cargo had been off-loaded. Auxiliary fleet supply ships were basically similar, but these ships had neither been built as men-of-war nor had they been permanently employed by the Navy before the start of the conflict. However, after the outbreak of the war they were staffed by naval personnel and sailed under the same command as regular warships. In port, supply ships came under different administrative authorities for loading. Both categories carried the majority of items which warships might need, such as fuel, various types of oil, ammunition, food, general cargo and spare parts for machinery. Since they were often sent out to supply specific raiders, they also delivered mail and personal items.

Escort tankers were similarly employed, but their sole objective was to refuel other ships at sea. The majority of these were tankers running under charter from their private owners and they carried only a small military section in addition to a civilian crew. The naval contingent would have helped with manning the defensive armament, signalling and advising the master on military matters.

V-ships operated in a similar fashion to fleet supply ships, but usually carried only general supplies with little or no liquid fuel. The main objective of Z-ships was to take fuel and supplies to U-boats. Specially converted merchant ships were used for this purpose. Port supply ships and port tankers were originally conceived as a means of getting provisions from one port to another, but some of these ships were large ocean-going vessels which could also be used for provisioning vessels far offshore.

Although an ocean-going supply network had already been considered vital long before the beginning of the First World War, this was one of the last branches to be developed by

The Merchant Marine flag flying aboard *Anneliese Essberger* in 1941 after her arrival in Bordeaux.

The quartermaster's stores. The diary for 1942 on display helps to name and date this picture, but take away the uniforms and this could have been in any navy, any place on earth. Stores like this were such a vital necessity that ships could not have operated without them.

the Kriegsmarine. During the 1920s there was no need for such vessels and in any case no one knew how goods could be transferred on the high seas. The absence of fast fleet supply ships became quite a problem as early as 1928, when the light cruiser *Emden* (Kpt.z.S. Richard Foerster) embarked on a cadet training cruise which was also one of the first long-distance, oil-fired voyages. The voyage was made possible by chartering the tanker *Hansa* from Atlantik Tank Reederei. She had been specially built with a cruiser stern for refuelling experiments and later even became the property of the Reichsmarine. Such close cooperation was possible, without excessive incentives, because two directors of the shipping firm were ex-navy officers.

Trials with the 6,000 grt *Hansa* eventually led to the development of the next stage in the supply ship design process. Two ships of this modified type (*Adria* and *Rudolf Albrecht*) later saw service with raiders in the Atlantic. The first specially designed fleet supply ships were not laid down until 1937 and only two (*Westerwald* and *Altmark*) were operational at the start of the Second World War. *Dithmarschen* and *Ermland* were still undergoing trials, *Franken* was under construction and the sixth, *Havelland*, was launched in Kiel during 1940, but was never completed. A side view of these ships resembled modern tankers of the period. Only when flying directly overhead was it possible to see the slim, curved lines of a warship, rather than the rectangular box shape of a tanker. This streamlined shape was even more pronounced at the waterline and helped to make the ships economical in the consumption of fuel and gave them a top speed of 22 kt. The designs also incorporated other typical warship features such as having two sets of engines, two independently operating rudders and the internal layout compartmentalised so that a hit in one section would not easily put another out of action as well.

Crow's nest lookout, *Doggerbank.*

Once at sea, supply ships came under the jurisdiction of the same authority which controlled the warships, but the administrative work of acquiring stores was carried out by a special supply department within the Supreme Naval Command and loading became the headache of the Naval Ship Yards. In May 1940, the decision to pass the responsibility for loading the ships over to the two Naval Commands for the Baltic and North Sea, produced such wild groans from overworked officials that it was decided to create a special fleet supply arm. Known as the *Trosschiffverband* (TSV), this was founded in Wilhelmshaven under Fregkpt. Alfred Stiller.

Stiller started with the four purpose-built supply ships already in commission, but his authority was quickly enlarged with the 9,323 grt Norwegian tanker *Krossfonn*, which had been captured by auxiliary cruiser *Widder*. The men for the new ships were recruited from the merchant navy, where a considerable proportion of well-experienced personnel was lying idle due to the war. The volunteers underwent a period of eight to ten weeks of military training at a special supply ship school in Wilhelmshaven. Since a number of these ships kept their civilian crews, being technically under charter from their original owners, their commanding officers had the title of 'Kapitän' without the military 'zur See' suffix. Naval ranks with the letters 'Sdf' or 'S', meaning Sonderführer (Special Leader) often indicated that the man had been promoted from the merchant navy.

Fitting out supply ships in home waters was only part of the story. The majority of raiding operations took place in southern waters, where it was not necessary to sail ships from Europe. Quite a number of German freighters were scattered around the globe in neutral ports, unable to move because of the war. The basic difficulty in engaging them lay with neutrality regulations which prohibited the fitting out of warships in neutral ports, and supply ships counted as men-of-war. So everything had be done under a great cloak of secrecy. The general decline in world trade, as a result of the war, meant it was not too difficult to find suppliers in foreign waters, but accumulating and loading vast stocks was a major undertaking. The situation was not helped by a strong presence of British interests which kept watchful eyes on German ships in neutral ports.

Since the sheer effort of loading a single ship was well beyond the capabilities of an individual, the Navy established a special supply system, called the Special Naval Service (Marinesonderdienst). The foundations for this organisation had already been laid long before 1939, although the Service itself was not founded until after the start of the conflict. One could visualise this set-up as a normal shipping office, working under exceptionally difficult conditions. In Japan, where most of the activity took place, the Service came under the control of the 50-year-old Kpt.z.S. Werner Vermehren, who had been born in El Paso in Texas. His immediate superior was the German Naval Attaché in Tokyo, Admiral Paul Wenneker, who had earlier been captain of the pocket battleship Deutschland.

MINESWEEPERS

Although minesweepers were one of the last types of ship to be developed by the old Imperial Navy, their high seas design proved so successful that it continued in service with only minor modifications until well after the Second World War. Known as Type 35 or M35, the design formed the basis for new minesweepers built for the Reichsmarine, and in 1939 it was even simplified for war production to be known as Type 40 or M40. Later in the war it was further modified and enlarged to become Type 43 or M43. Boats belonging to these three types became the workhorses for the majority of minesweeping duties. However, they were too big for the vast stretches of the shallow coastal waters or tidal rivers, which required special shallow draught vessels known as Räumboot or R-boat (Motor Minesweepers). The R-boat types built by the old Imperial Navy had been rather disastrous inasmuch as they did not manoeuvre well and their poor sea-keeping qualities made them unsuitable for use in rough water. Consequently the Reichsmarine completely redesigned this type to produce a highly successful craft. The third major variety of mine clearance vessels, known as Sperrbrecher (Barrier Breakers), were old merchant ships filled with cork, sealed air-filled tins or other flotation aids, intended for sailing in front of other, more valuable vessels to detonate mines in their path.

By the end of the Second World War, European waters had been filled with some 600,000 mines plus probably another 50,000–100,000 types of other explosive barriers. Germany alone employed about 3,000 vessels and over 100,000 men to help clear them from areas where they were not wanted. Of this, some 500 minesweepers and 25,000 men were stationed in the Channel ports of occupied France. Such vast numbers make it obvious that all types of ships from

After the First World War the majority of minesweepers were converted to burn oil instead of coal, but shortages meant they were changed back again for the Second World War. This shows coal sacks being brought aboard a minesweeper.

The German Navy still follows in the old tradition of celebrating every possible event in history, and when there is nothing to celebrate, they simply celebrate the fact that there is nothing to celebrate. Having emptied a coal barge was as good a reason as any for letting your hair down.

Coaling was a filthy job, but it was no worse than the work done by thousands of people in factories. This shows men aboard *M133*.

The coal-burning furnaces aboard one of the minesweepers. This filthy work was essential because without it there was no power for anything else.

A minesweeper at sea. The flag flying on the stern suggests that this photo was taken before the autumn of 1935 when Hitler introduced the new ensign with swastika.

The so-called 'whisper bag' or megaphone, consisting of funnel-shaped trumpet, featured frequently throughout the war, and even today men still prefer to shout orders rather than use more sophisticated personal radios.

fishing boats and tugs to unwanted ferries were commandeered for minesweeping duties. They certainly formed an incredibly large proportion of the German fleet.

Before the beginning of the war, the position of Flag Officer for Minesweepers had already become somewhat impractical, and the control of port protection flotillas had passed to the Naval Commands for the Baltic and North Sea. The conflict later made coastal protection much more of a priority than it had been, and special coastal protection units were established in Germany and along the coasts of the occupied countries. As with other ships, operational control was often handed over to other naval commanders who were responsible for big ships in the particular area.

M-BOATS

As has already been mentioned, there were three basic types of minesweeper developed with very little modification from a successful First World War design. One of the main reasons for changing from Type 35 to Type 40

Minesweeper *M133*. Quite a number of other small boats with three digit numbers were in fact identified only by the last two digits, the first one sometimes being the number of the boat's flotilla.

was to simplify the specifications so that boats could be built in small shipyards, which had previously not been involved with such complicated craft. The third variation of the basic design, Type 43, came about as a desire to improve the general performance by increasing range and armaments. Minesweepers were identified by a number prefixed with the letter 'M'. As with other small ships, during pre-war years the first digit of many three-figure numbers indicated the boat's flotilla. The different types of minesweeper mentioned above were identified by the year when they first went into production. During the war many minesweepers were modified to burn coal instead of oil and they carried a wide variety of artillery. In fact the basic Type 35 design was equipped with such powerful guns that it was nicknamed 'The Channel Destroyer'. Before the war some of the boats were also used for training and even had torpedo tubes fitted for practice purposes.

By the end of the war minesweepers were equipped with more than twelve different types of mechanical apparatus for clearing standard moored mines. Although, of course, not all twelve types were found on the same ship at the same time. In addition to this, Germany had developed more than eight different sets of apparatus for dealing with acoustic mines and there were ten different sets of gear for coping with magnetic varieties. Mine clearing had indeed become an exacting art, although the danger of the boat being destroyed in the clearing process always remained high. In addition to the various types of sweeping apparatus, ships were also protected by so-called Bow Protection Gear which was supposed to push moored mines away from the ship's hull. This equipment was somewhat unsuitable for large ships and it could not be used for speeds over 16 kt, though it had been fitted to giants such as *Bismarck*. It consisted of a set of wires and paravanes and should not be confused with an armoured shield placed over

A close up of *M145*'s hull showing the multitude of rivets holding the iron plates together.

small craft, especially U-boats. Armoured shields were intended as temporary protection from ice while passing through coastal waters and along the Kiel Canal.

MOTOR MINESWEEPERS

The Reichsmarine developed small mine-sweepers under the guise of tugs. They were also called Fleet Escort Vessels or F-boats (*Fangboote* – Catching or Retrieving Boats) by some people because they were frequently engaged for catching torpedoes during exercises. However the 'F' seems to stem from *Flachgehendeboote*, meaning Shallow Draught

A small motor minesweeper flying an admiral's flag. In this case it is bringing Admiral Carls alongside *U408* for an inspection of the assembled crew. The photo was taken in Norway at about the time of the battle for the famous convoy PQ18. This could well be at Bergen with the submarine pens under construction in the background.

Boats. The vast majority of this type were called R-boats, short for *Räumboot* (Clearance Boat).

Many of the R-boats were fitted with Voith-Schneider or cycloidal propellers. These make rudders obsolete because they can drive the boat in any direction. What is more, it is possible to change directly from fast ahead to fast astern without stopping the engines and reversing them. This makes for super manoeuvrability, but has the disadvantage inasmuch as the system seems to lose about 10 per cent of power over similar hulls with conventional propellers. Incidentally, M1 and

M2 were also equipped with this type of propeller and although their commanding officers used the system to much effect, it was never universally adopted for larger vessels. The Reichsmarine's R-boats were such a success that after the war they were used for a variety of other purposes and many saw sterling service as cutters, pilot vessels or launches where small, fast and stable craft were required. They could be engaged with their clearing gear in winds up to Force 6–7.

R-boats, originally with a displacement of about 65 tons and later increased up to 175 tons, were still too big for use in the confined waters of Norwegian fjords, and Kptlt. Hans Bartels took it upon himself to build his own tiny minesweepers by adapting a Norwegian fishing boat design and buying the engines in Sweden. He invited the Supreme Commander-in-Chief of the Navy to the commissioning ceremony of his '*Dwarfs*' before sending him the bill for the project. But this form of independence was not appreciated and Bartels found himself being 'promoted' to become first officer aboard the destroyer *Z34*. Yet, the tiny *Dwarfs* provided an excellent service by 'de-lousing' the narrow confines of the fjords.

SPERRBRECHER (BARRIER BREAKERS OR AUXILIARY MINESWEEPERS)

Referring to these craft as minesweepers is a little misleading inasmuch as they were not employed in the role of fishing for mines. Instead they sailed in front of warships, escorting them in and out of ports and providing good anti-aircraft cover at the same time. They were fitted with powerful electro-magnets and a means of detonating acoustic mines. The idea was that unsavoury objects in their path would be disposed of. To cope with such explosions, crew accommodation was specially insulated to absorb shocks and excessive noise. Despite this, serving aboard

A motor minesweeper being used as escort for submarines and made fast next to *U48*, the most successful U-boat of the Second World War.

A *Sperrbrecher* or barrier breaker lying at anchor. These ships were filled with flotation aids so that they could sail in front of others to detonate mines. Life aboard them must have been somewhat uncomfortable, despite living quarters having been provided with extra insulation.

Sperrbrechers was somewhat nerve-racking because the force of exploding mines broke many ships in half. The only consolation was that often there were ships behind who could stop and pick up survivors. Since a vast variety of old and obsolete vessels were used for conversion to barrier breakers, there were no special designs for this type of ship.

MINELAYERS

Although Germany designed a number of purpose-built minelayers, these large ships were only suitable for laying defensive barriers. They would have attracted too much attention had they approached too close to foreign harbours. So offensive mines were laid by smaller ships such as destroyers, submarines or even minesweepers. M-boats could carry some thirty standard mines and the larger, Type 43, even managed to store forty-four. Since these boats were fast and reasonably well armed, they found themselves being employed for a variety of offensive mining operations. Cruisers also carried mines, although approaching close to shallow enemy shipping lanes was more than impractical. Several auxiliary cruisers laid mines in far distant ports where intrusions would not be anticipated while *Pinguin* went one better by converting a captured ship, *Storstad*, into a minelayer on the high seas and then sending it along its original route into Australian waters. *Pinguin* also used a captured whale hunter (renamed *Adjutant* by the Germans) for mining Lyttleton and Wellington in New Zealand, but *Pinguin* was herself sunk

Men aboard the minesweeper *M18* doing what comes naturally. Second from the right is the commander, Kptlt. Otto Köhler.

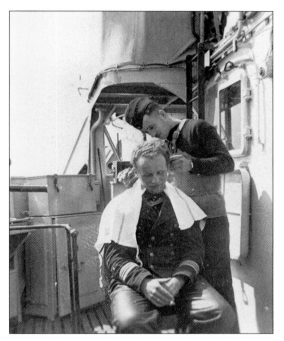

Kptlt. Otto Köhler having his hair cut aboard *M18*.

Kptlt. Otto Köhler writing in his personal 'Observations Book' while an Obermaat holding a box camera is enjoying a moment of peace. Both of them are wearing '*Schiffchen*' (Small Ship). The man on the left is wearing a white denim working jacket while Köhler is dressed in naval leathers.

before the operation could be put into practice.

Passat

A name given to the 8,998 grt Norwegian freighter *Storstad* after she had been captured by auxiliary cruiser *Pinguin* in October 1940 and converted into a minelayer under command of Kptlt.(S) Erich Warning. She was used for laying thirty mines in the Banks Strait between north-east Tasmania and Barren Island during the night of 29/30 October, each with four-day delayed action fuses. Another forty were deposited on the eastern side of the Bass Strait during the following night and then another forty in the approaches to Port Phillip Bay for catching traffic running in and out of Melbourne. Following this, *Passat* reverted to her original name and was used as a reconnaissance vessel under Oblt.z.S. Walter Lewit. Eventually the ship made a successful voyage to France. Following this, *Storstad* was used as a supply ship until she was damaged in Nantes during August 1944.

Adjutant

Whale hunter *Pol IX* was captured by auxiliary cruiser *Pinguin* in the Antarctic and commissioned on the high seas in February 1941 as an official unit of the *Kriegsmarine* under command of Oblt.z.S. Hans Karl Hemmer, the youngest officer aboard auxiliary cruisers. The removal of the harpoon and catwalk made her look like a fishing boat, suitable for reconnaissance and for laying mines. However, *Pinguin* was sunk before much of this plan could be put into

135

Adjutant, under Hans Karl Hemmer, being refuelled. This was captured as a whaler, but once the harpoon and catwalk had been removed it resembled a nondescript fishing boat, suitable for laying mines close to enemy harbours.

Adjutant coming alongside auxiliary cruiser *Pinguin*.

Hans Karl Hemmer, the youngest officer aboard auxiliary cruisers, as commander of the captured whale hunter *Adjutant*.

Mast-top lookout of the auxiliary minelayer and blockade breaker *Doggerbank*.

practice and Hemmer sailed dramatically across the Pacific. Being first refuelled from *Kormoran*, he eventually joined auxiliary cruiser *Komet* under Admiral Robert Eyssen. This cooperation was not a happy affair because Hemmer received a severe backlash from an earlier bitter disagreement between Eyssen and *Pinguin*'s commander. Hemmer was relieved of his command and replaced by Oblt.z.S. Wilfred Karsten, who mined Lyttleton and Wellington in New Zealand. The mines were probably defective because nothing was sunk with them and the Royal Navy did not discover their whereabouts until reading German log books after the war. The 350-ton *Adjutant* had been built in Middlesbrough (in England) during 1937 and was scuttled off Chatham Island in the Pacific.

Doggerbank

Originally *Speybank*, belonging to Andrew Weir and Company, captured by auxiliary cruiser *Atlantis* and brought to France as a prize under command of Kptlt. Paul Schneidewind. After refitting and renaming, she left France in December 1941 to lay mines off Cape Town (South Africa) and to act as a submarine supply ship. The mining operation was successful, but there were no U-boats in the area, so *Doggerbank* continued to Japan and returned to Europe as a blockade breaker. On 3 March 1943, she was sunk by *U43* (Kptlt. Hans-Joachim Schwantke), who had been told there were no German ships in the area. A small group of men, including the commander, remained alive in a lifeboat for twenty-five days. Being without food and water, Schneidewind then shot himself, and other survivors, except Fritz Kuert, followed suit. Kuert was finally picked up by a US ship, taken to America and returned to Germany during the prisoner swap.

SAIL TRAINING SHIPS

The Imperial Navy abandoned sail training four years before the beginning of the First World War because it was considered to be an outdated method of educating future officers. Instead of wind, the cadets were presented with the power of steam and gunpowder. A few years later, it became apparent that sailors' worst enemies would always remain the restless sea and the unpredictable weather. Consequently the Reichsmarine reintroduced sail training as an essential part of its officer education programme. The first new ship, the four masted gaff-sail schooner *Marten Jensen*, acquired from Denmark, received a thorough refit before being commissioned under the name of *Niobe* in 1923. A top-heavy tendency remained and, less than ten years later, she capsized during a sudden and fierce summer storm off the Island of Fehmarn in the Baltic. Sixty-nine men were killed, including almost the entire intake of officer cadets for 1932. Following this, a political storm brewed for some time with numerous influential people calling for an

end to what was considered to be an outdated extravaganza. However, the naval command won the argument and set about designing better and safer sailing ships. The fact that this generation of vessels not only survived the war, but that the designs are still in service today shows the high standards which were achieved.

Niobe
The regular crew consisted of 7 officers and about 27 men, who looked after a maximum of about 65 cadets. C: 19 December 1923; S: by capsizing during a sudden summer storm on 26 July 1932. Raised and later sunk as a target for testing torpedoes.

Gorch Fock
The regular crew was made up of 9 officers and about 58 men, plus a maximum of 198 cadets. C: 27 June 1933; survived the war to become *Towarischtsch* (Soviet).

Horst Wessel
C: 17 September 1936; survived the war to become *Eagle* (USA).

Albert Leo Schlageter
C: 12 February 1938; survived the war to become *Guanabara* (Brazilian) and in 1961 *Sagres* (Portuguese). Both the last two had a permanent crew of 9 officers and about 69 men plus room for 220 cadets.

WHAT THE NAMES MEAN

Bismarck

Otto, Count and later Prince von Bismarck (1815–98) took this name from his home town, which lies just over 100 km west of Berlin. He was a powerful force in the unification of the German Nation. As Chancellor and Minister President, his aim was to stabilise the Germanic states as one nation, to make them powerful enough to stand up against the French and other European nations. Differences with the new Emperor, Wilhelm II, forced his retirement from political life in 1890.

Blücher

Gebhard Leberecht von Blücher, Prince Blücher von Wahlstadt (1742–1819) became a famous field marshal in the Prussian Army, who fought on the British side against the French at Waterloo. One of the great achievements of this conflict was getting his forces across the Rhine during the hours of darkness and in deepest winter. A memorial still stands near Kaub (between St Goarshausen and Bingen in the Rhine Gorge) to mark the event. His army was the subject of a famous remark by the English Duke of Wellington during the Battle of Waterloo, 'I wish it were night and the Prussians were here.'

Prinz Eugen

Prince Eugen von Savoyen (1663–1736) was an Austrian field marshal who fought in the wars of liberation from domination by the French.

Gneisenau

August Neidhardt von Gneisenau, born in 1760, was made a count in 1814. He was a general on Blücher's staff and worked for some time with Gerhard von Scharnhorst. He died of cholera in 1831.

Graf Spee

Maximilian Reichsgraf von Spee, born 1861 in Copenhagen and killed during the Battle of the Falklands in 1914. As Chief of the East Asia Cruiser Squadron, he attempted a homeward run shortly after the outbreak of the First World War, but was cut off by British warships, which annihilated most of the Germans, including Admiral von Spee and both his sons.

Hipper

Franz, Ritter von Hipper, born in 1863 and joined the Navy in 1881. Devoted many of his younger years to the development of torpedoes. As Commander-in-Chief for Cruisers he led the German onslaught for the Battle of Jutland during the First World War and died in Hamburg-Altona in 1932.

Lützow

Adolf, Freiherr von Lützow (1782–1834) was a cavalry officer during the early wars of liberation when he was severely defeated by superior French forces, but succeeded in re-establishing the decimated units.

Scharnhorst

Gerhard von Scharnhorst (1755–1813) was a social reformer and Prussian general, responsible for the introduction of national conscription. Among other things, he abolished degrading and demoralising punishments, and brought about a system of promotion according to ability rather than social standing. He died from his wounds while serving on Blücher's staff during the campaign against the French.

Scheer

Admiral Reinhard Scheer (1863–1928) was a famous advocate for the use of cruisers and Chief of the High Seas Fleet. When he became Fleet Commander he made it plain that he wanted to engage the ships under his command to the limits of their capabilities.

Seydlitz (incompleted cruiser)

Friedrich Wilhelm von Seydlitz (1721–73) a general of cavalry.

Tirpitz

Alfred von Tirpitz (1849–1930) started his career as an ordinary naval officer of average ability, but his enthusiasm for torpedoes brought him early promotion to *Korvettenkapitän*. Later he became State Secretary for the Naval Office and Grand Admiral. He was the driving force behind the development of the Imperial Navy. He has often been described as an armaments fanatic. His clever and most balanced proposals never resulted in a parliamentary defeat until a difference about unrestricted submarine warfare forced his retirement on 8 March 1916. He died in Ebenhausen in 1930 and lies buried in a cemetery near Fürstenried to the south of Munich.

Graf Zeppelin (incompleted aircraft carrier)

Ferdinand, Graf von Zeppelin (1838–1917) inventor, designer and developer of Germany's large airships.

U-BOATS

The terms of the Versailles Diktat prohibited the Reichsmarine from building or owning U-boats, but today it is well known that Germany kept pace with submarine development by opening a construction bureau in Holland. Soon after coming to power in 1933, Hitler boosted this clandestine development by telling the Army and Navy chiefs to plan for expansion because the shackles of the impossible restrictions would be thrown off as soon as possible. Two years later the unexpected happened. The Reichsmarine was secretly collecting parts for assembling a small number of tiny coastal submarines when the government stumbled upon what must have been the political opportunity of the century. The National Socialists were still balancing on politically weak foundations, when someone struck upon the idea of consolidating their standing by repudiating the Versailles Diktat. The situation had arisen because although Hitler had the highest number of votes, he still did not have unanimous support and his government could easily have been toppled by turbulence within the country.

The reason this must have been such a great political opportunity was that whatever happened, the National Socialists could not lose. Whatever the outcome, Hitler would end up holding the winning hand. A few years before the NSDAP came to power, the French had sent an army of occupation into the industrial heartland of the Ruhr because German war reparations were slowing down. Quite probably the National Socialists were expecting something similar on this occasion. Such an invasion would have given Hitler the unique opportunity of uniting the masses behind him while he appeared to stand firm in face of obvious oppression. But such a stance was not necessary. Instead, the Allies allowed the Versailles Diktat to be thrown out by the very people who were supposed to be suppressed by it. In retrospect it seems absurd and one wonders why Germany had been forced into signing the humiliating document in the first place. Following Hitler's famous proclamation, the Germans found that not only were the Allies sitting idly by while the Diktat was discarded, but influential foreign politicians were actually congratulating Hitler for the position he had taken. The National Socialists had won a terrific battle and, at the same time, spineless Allied politicians had allowed Europe on to the first step down the slide into anarchy and unimaginable suffering.

The repudiation of the Versailles Diktat and the reintroduction of national conscription were followed by changing the name of the Navy from Reichsmarine to Kriegsmarine. A few weeks later Hitler was rewarded with the so-called Anglo-German Naval Agreement, although Germany gained the most and it should therefore really have been called the German-Anglo Agreement. Hitler's achievements with these negotiations went so far beyond the admirals' wildest dreams that they presented the Naval High Command with several unforeseen problems. Earlier, when the first U-boat parts started arriving secretly in Kiel, Admiral Raeder (Supreme Commander-in-Chief of the Navy) had visions of perhaps being allowed to

The semi-automatic 37-mm quick-firing anti-aircraft gun aboard *U181* under the command of Kpt.z.S. Kurt Freiwald. It appears that the weapon is being cleaned because there are no cartridges in the clip above the breech.

assemble a few small submarines. These would have been attached to some existing surface ship flotilla, but the unexpected boost from the Naval Agreement meant there would soon be too many submarines for such plans and an autonomous unit had to be established.

Creating a new submarine flotilla presented a few tricky problems because the majority of men who had served in submarines during the First World War were now too old, somewhat out of touch or dead, and Germany's new generation of submariners was still too inexperienced to lead a flotilla. Men were being secretly trained under the guise of the Anti-Submarine School in Kiel and a few of them,

mainly engineers, had also participated in trials with boats built by German businesses in foreign countries. So, there was a tiny core of men capable of coping with the three-dimensional thinking necessary for controlling submarines, but the Naval High Command didn't have anyone in the running for leading such a group of specialists.

At this stage fate played a hand. Just at this critical moment, when the Supreme Naval Command was looking for a likely candidate to push into what the majority considered to be a hideous position, the light cruiser *Emden* returned from a flag-showing tour around the world. Her commander, Karl Dönitz, had already been nick-named 'Star' as cadet; he had commissioned two brand-new units; he preferred to make up his own rules rather than follow those written by others; and, most important of all, he was one of the few likely officers who had actually commanded a submarine during the First World War.

Dönitz guessed that he would leave *Emden* for one of the bigger, more prestigious ships and after that probably become a cruiser squadron commander or an officer within the Naval High Command. The idea of returning to a small flotilla of stinking submarines didn't appeal at all, but he was assured that it was only a temporary measure for a couple of years while a new commander was being brought up for the role. Dönitz took command of the first U-Flotilla in 1935. However, the war started before such plans could be put into operation and Dönitz was promoted from Flotilla Commander to Flag Officer in January 1936 and later, in October 1939, to Commander-in-Chief for U-boats. Many historians have fallen into the trap of taking this to have been a process of planned progression and made Dönitz responsible for pre-war submarine development, which is a long way from the truth. His brief was severely limited to welding the U-boat flotilla into a fighting force. Training new personnel

U307 under Oblt.z.S. Friedrich-Georg Herrle showing how anti-aircraft guns dominated conning towers towards the end of the war. In this case there appears to be one double 20-mm on the upper platform, and a 37-mm quick-firing gun on the lower *wintergarten*. Many boats were fitted with a quadruple 20-mm weapon on the lower platform and two 20-mm twins on the upper.

was not part of his duty. In fact the school flotilla came under the jurisdiction of the Torpedo Inspectorate while other submarine matters were decided by the U-boat Office at the Supreme Naval Command with whom Dönitz had little or no contact.

Being without definite directives for the new submarine flotilla, Dönitz started creating the foundations of his future vision, which was based on the concept that one day there would be about 300 U-boats. The declaration of war, just four years after taking up his appointment, made these plans redundant and Dönitz's entire administrative system had to be modified to meet the new demands put upon it. At first no one was sure how the conflict would develop and it was not until the beginning of 1940 that the U-boat arm took on the shape it would keep throughout the ensuing years.

At first the admirals of the Naval High Command thought U-boats should be used for a variety of unproductive tasks such as acting as meteorological stations or escorting surface ships. Since the weather provided far better protection than tiny submarines, the majority of surface ships broke out of the dangerous European waters during storms, when U-boats had problems remaining on the surface and could never have engaged their weapons. Yet it was the summer of 1940 before Dönitz succeeded in bringing his superiors round to thinking that submarines would be better employed if they were pitched as an autonomous force against Allied convoys. In addition to this, U-boats were tied by Prize Ordinance Regulations prohibiting surprise attacks against merchant ships, unless they were sailing in convoy or were being escorted by warships. These rules were imposed so strongly

Top of the conning tower aboard *U510*.

Side view of a Type VII U-boat, *U756*, with an open hatch.

that the war was almost a year old before U-boats were free to attack all merchant shipping in the Western Approaches to British ports.

By that time, August 1940, control of the majority of submarines at sea had passed to what became known simply as the 'U-boat Command' under the leadership of Admiral Karl Dönitz and the head of its Operations Department, Kpt.z.S. Eberhard Godt. Everything else came under the control of Kpt.z.S. Hans-Georg von Friedeburg, who was in charge of the Organisation Department. U-boat flotillas, although plentiful in number, acted as a means of provisioning boats and looking after the welfare of the men in port. In most cases, as soon as boats were clear of coastal waters they came under the direct jurisdiction of the U-boat Command.

Radio communications were so good that Dönitz's small staff could broadcast to boats submerged off America's east coast. The entire equipment occupied a small van and accompanied the U-boat Command to wherever it was located. At times, of course, messages would be boosted by big stations such as Goliah near Magdeburg, where some twenty masts supported a spider's web of high voltage antennas some 150–200 m up in the air. Efficient wireless communications had already been established before the First World War because the only telephone lines to German colonies and bases in Africa and the Far East had to go through British-controlled cables.

OPERATION AREAS

U-boats found their way into the Atlantic, the Mediterranean, the Black Sea and into the Caribbean. They operated in Polar waters, in the Indian Ocean and in the far eastern Pacific. In fact, if one believes a printing error in Dr Jürgen Rohwer's *Axis Submarine Successes* then *U13* (KL Karl Daublebsky von Eichhain) penetrated up the Avon Canal to sink the freighter *Magdapur* on the

racecourse at Stratford-upon-Avon in the heart of England. (The position is given as 52°11'N 01°43'W, but the 'W' should be 'E'.)

THE BALTIC

Even before the first shots, marking the German reoccupation of her former territories, were fired, the lack of opposition made it clear that there would be no U-boat activity in the eastern Baltic. So, in September 1939 as Britain declared war, the majority of submarines were already on their way west, leaving the Baltic free for training. This was ideal because most of the Baltic was out of reach of the Royal Air Force, meaning the education process could go ahead without serious interference. There was a little U-boat activity in the 'Finnish Bathtub' of the far eastern Baltic, but generally the bitter war of vengeance didn't arrive until the Russian armies started advancing westwards. Then, late in 1944, Germany mounted a massive operation for helping refugees fleeing the horrors of bitter war. Every available ship and boat was engaged to help the steady stream of ragged humanity across the ice-bound water. The losses inflicted on German civilians, many of them children and old people, make the figures for the Battle of the Atlantic or the British evacuation at Dunkirk drop into insignificance. For example *Goya* went down with 6,500 refugees, *Wilhelm Gustloff* with over 5,000 and *General von Steuben* with almost 3,000. Yet despite such large numbers being killed, only about 2 per cent of the total lost their lives, indicating the vast volume of humanity which fled westwards in front of the Red Army. As comparison it might be interesting to add that the losses suffered by the Germans during the three brief naval actions, mentioned above, were more than a quarter of the total number of British civilians killed during the entire war.

A flotilla of training boats in the Baltic.

U121 in Pillau, eastern Baltic.

THE BLACK SEA

The sixty smallish ships sunk during a period of almost two years makes one wonder whether the effort of bringing U-boats into the Black Sea was worth it, and whether these successes might not have been achieved more easily by, perhaps, aircraft. The 30th U-boat Flotilla, known as the Black Sea Flotilla, was based at Constanta (Romania) and also had a provisioning port at Feodosia on the Crimean Peninsula. It was founded by Kptlt. Helmut Rosenbaum in October 1942 and disbanded in October 1944 while under command of Kptlt. Clemens Schöler. During the summer of 1944 the flotilla came under command of Kptlt. Klaus Petersen. The boats were all of the small coastal Type IIB and consisted of: *U9, U18, U19, U20, U23* and *U24*. *U9* was destroyed during an air raid on Constanta and the others were scuttled near Turkey when the German positions became untenable due to the pressure of the surrounding Russian forces. Originally the boats were brought into the Black Sea by being dismantled and then carried on pontoons along the River Elbe. From near

Clemens Schöler, Chief of the 30th (Black Sea) U-boat Flotilla being escorted to the railway station in Constanta (Romania) at the end of his tour of duty (above and below). It was common for officers to be given a 'high class' send off. Note that the convoy is flying the pennant of a flotilla commander.

Dresden they travelled by overland transporter to Regensburg on the Danube. There they were placed back on the same purpose-built pontoons and carried downstream to be reassembled near the Black Sea. To do this, the hulls were cut into sections and engines, propellers, batteries and other heavy gear carried separately.

THE MEDITERRANEAN

Before the beginning of the war, Dönitz had already discounted the Mediterranean as a suitable hunting-ground for U-boats. The sea is too calm, the water too clear and the weather generally too good for submarine activity. His dislike for the area was strengthened in 1939 by Korvkpt. Klaus Ewerth (*U26*), following a reconnaissance of the Gibraltar area. However, later the Supreme Naval Command ordered Dönitz to send boats into the Mediterranean, thus founding a new submarine division in Italy under a newly created Flag Officer, Korvkpt. Victor Oehrn. After a while this post became known as Flag Officer for the Mediterranean. For most of the time there were two flotillas: the 23rd based chiefly in Salamis (Greece) and the 29th first in

Although household and luxury goods continued to be made for a much longer period of the war than in Britain, there were considerable shortages in Germany. However, men based in France could continue to buy a vast quantity of goods no longer available at home, making window shopping most attractive. Although these two could be mistaken for soldiers from the Afrikakorps, they are U-boat men on leave in Bordeaux.

Going home on leave from France. The spare hand was required for carrying the parcels lying on the floor. There were virtually no restrictions on what men could take home and those leaving France took full advantage of the many luxury goods which could be purchased there. The circular cylinder is a gas mask container.

La Spezia (Italy), then Toulon and later also in Pola (Pula, former Yugoslavia) and Marseille. When the position of flag officer was abolished in September 1944 the three surviving boats were moved east, under the command of the Admiral for the Aegean.

THE CARIBBEAN

Once opposition along the eastern seaboard of the United States became too determined, Dönitz moved long-range boats southwards until eventually they roamed through the Caribbean and on as far south as the delta of the Amazon. Although the U-boats enjoyed some initial successes, the enemy was quick to bite and for many it became a case of nurturing badly damaged machinery for a long trek back to France. Being surrounded by American radio direction finders made it easy for the enemy to track U-boats that were sending out distress calls.

To this day the Caribbean still holds one of the big secrets of the war. This is the mysterious disappearance of the world's largest submarine, the 2,880/4,304 ton French *Surcouf*. Much has been written about its enigmatic end, but no one seems ever to have pursued the research by the American historian Edward R. Rumpf, who has suggested it could well have been a target for *U502* under Kptlt. Jürgen von Rosenstiel. After the war it was easy to identify the ships which Rosenstiel claims to have sunk, but one particular 2,500 ton tanker in the Caribbean has eluded Rumpf and other historians. Rosenstiel's log clearly describes the sinking in some detail, saying that *U502* aimed at a tanker showing dim navigation lights. When the torpedo struck amidships, the target burst into a dramatic ball of fire and went down immediately. This description appears to be too vivid for anyone's imagination and it is pretty certain that *U502* hit something, but what? So far the United States has failed to match this reported sinking with the name of

a lost merchant ship and it seems highly likely that the men aboard *U502* would not have identified such a uniquely huge boat as *Surcouf* to be a submarine, unless, of course, they were expecting her. After all *Surcouf* was three times larger than the usual submarines they were used to seeing. So it could well be that they left the area thinking they had hit a tanker. The position, in about 50 fathoms of water, is some 32 nautical miles south-west of Aruba (West Indies) and 5 nautical miles off the lighthouse on the Peninsula de Paraguana, so the matter could be clarified by a diver.

THE FAR EAST

During March 1944, Fregkpt. Wilhelm Dommes founded the first Far Eastern U-boat base in Penang (Malaya) and later expanded his activities by spreading refuelling and repair facilities to other ports. Known as Chief of the Southern Area, he was supported with provisions supplied through the Special Naval Service via the Naval Attaché in Tokyo, Admiral Paul Wenneker. This Service had originally been set up for the benefit of surface raiders and blockade breakers. The problems of working with Japanese culture and the immense distances made things most difficult, yet despite these problems a number of boats made highly successful voyages to the Far East. They remained under the operational control of the U-boat Command and usually fought their way out, refitted in the Far East and then returned as cargo carriers with vital raw materials. At times, while there were still surface raiders at sea, boats refuelled from them or from their supply ships, but the very long-range U-boats could reach the Far East without support, although they did not carry sufficient fuel for a return journey. Some quite ambitious refits were carried out under makeshift conditions and much of the labour was provided by the crews. A number of commanders went with a one-way ticket and then stayed in the Far East for other naval duties while a different man brought the boat home. In some cases this was planned and in others such decisions were made on the spur of the moment. Over the years many stories emerged about U-boats carrying vast volumes of mercury in their ballast tanks. Mercury is a highly expensive metal and during the war it was used sparingly for making bomb fuses. Small quantities were carried from the Far East, but it was usually stored inside earthenware bottles stacked in wooden crates inside the pressure hull. The idea of such a heavy and expensive commodity being poured into diving tanks appears to be a little far-fetched. The following bases were established in the Far East:

Shonan-Singapore (Malaya) (Korvkpt. Wolfgang Erhardt)
Penang (Malaya) (Kptlt. Waldemar Grützmacher)
Djakarta (Java) (Korvkpt. Dr Hermann Kandeler)
Soerabaja (Java) (Kptlt. Konrad Hoppe)
Kobe (Japan) (Korvkpt. Eitel-Friedrich Kentrat)

THE SOUTH ATLANTIC

The original plans for submarine activities in the South Atlantic were for a couple of boats to raid the shipping lanes while supported by a surface ship stationed in an out-of-the-way location. However, Britain could understand a fair proportion of the radio code by the time the German forces moved into deep

Officers and crewmen aboard *U178* after her first cruise into the South Atlantic and Indian Ocean. Left, Admiral Menche, centre, Korvkpt. Klaus Scholtz and, right, the commander, Kpt.z.S Hans Ibbeken.

southern waters and Allied cruisers smashed the operations or rendered them virtually impossible. There were great individual successes, acts of ingenuity, bravery and survival, but U-boat operations aimed specifically at the deep South Atlantic did not achieve worthwhile sinking figures.

THE POLAR SEAS

U-boats were sent into the Arctic Seas as floating weather stations, for reconnaissance, to establish land-based automatic weather stations, to help set up manned weather stations, to plant automatic weather buoys and to harass convoys running to and from North Russian ports. At first ordinary boats with hardly any modifications were sent north, later some additional heaters were provided. For many it was a case of fighting the elements in ordinary unmodified boats, rather than being engaged against military opposition. Stories about the weather stations could easily fill a most exciting adventure book on their own, yet so little has been published. In addition to U-boats, the Luftwaffe also operated a vast number of weather data collecting flights. A very much neglected field of history which will hopefully one day be written down. Even if the results were not terribly significant within the context of world history, these theatres of operation generated a number of highly ingenious characters, many of whom unfortunately were not given an opportunity of enriching postwar life.

This is not a case of U-boats being supported by aircraft, but the other way round. The Blohm und Voss flying boat was carrying out a reconnaissance of the Arctic and *U255* under Kptlt. Reinhart Reche was acting as a floating fuel station.

THE BATTLE OF THE ATLANTIC

The Battle of the Atlantic was fought largely by U-boats pitched against merchant ships to prevent supplies being brought to Britain. This bloody conflict started within hours of Britain and France declaring war on 3 September 1939 and continued for several days after the cease-fire came into force on 5 May 1945. At the beginning of the war U-boats were allocated patrol areas and there they were obliged to stop merchant ships, establish whether or not they were carrying contraband and, theoretically, they should have seen to the safety of the crew before sinking the ship. The impracticability of these orders, together with a series of catastrophic torpedo failures, a shortage of torpedoes and a plentiful supply of torpedo mines encouraged the U-boat Command to mount an intensive mining offensive of British harbours during the first winter of war. This gave the Germans the advantage of using the small coastal boats of Type II to much greater benefit. Although these boats had three loaded bow torpedo tubes, they could carry only two spare torpedoes, meaning their employment was somewhat limited. The total of five torpedoes, however, could be replaced with up to eighteen mines making them far more practical in this role.

The spring of 1940 saw U-boats employed in a variety of pointless tasks connected with the invasion of Denmark and Norway, which meant it was summer before the U-boat Command could re-employ them against merchant shipping in the North Atlantic. The following autumn saw the so-called 'Happy Time' when every one of the dozen or so U-boats at sea was sinking more than an average of 5.5 ships per month. This was achieved by boats attacking on the surface at night and using their radios to advertise convoy positions.

This incredible massacre ended abruptly in the early spring of 1941 at the time when

'Silent Otto', Otto Kretschmer of *U23* and *U99* wearing the Knights Cross of the Iron Cross with Oakleaves around the neck and the ribbon for the Iron Cross 2nd Class through the top button hole. The national eagle with swastika on the right breast was worn by all ranks. The golden scalloped edge of the hat indicated his rank group.

the three aces Joachim Schepke, Günter Prien and Otto Kretschmer were sunk. From then on, sinking figures of merchantmen dwindled and never again were U-boats in a position of strength in the battles in the Atlantic. The declaration of war against the United States brought a brief respite because the Americans made very little effort in hunting U-boats. Indeed many convoys carrying highly flammable petroleum continued sailing, often with coastal illuminations revealing their positions to waiting U-boats further out at sea.

In the summer of 1942 opposition in American waters had become too intense and U-boats returned to the so-called Air Gap of the mid-Atlantic, which could not be reached by land-based aircraft, in incredibly large numbers. Two years earlier, during the 'Happy Time' of 1940, the average number of U-boats at sea each day never exceeded a dozen or so. By September 1942 this average had reached 100 boats at sea for every day, but sinkings had fallen dramatically. Instead of each U-boat sinking almost six ships per month, statistically the success rate had dropped to more than two U-boats being required to sink a single merchant ship.

A fact, often overlooked by historians, is that this incredibly high average of over 100 U-boats at sea had been maintained for more than half a year before a major convoy battle took place. This happened in March 1943 when the fast convoy HX229 ran into the slow convoy SC122 and almost a hundred merchant ships met a massive 'wolf pack' – a group of U-boats. Anyone claiming that this was the peak of the U-boat offensive should also explain why such a vast number of U-boats had been at sea for so long without a large-scale convoy battle having taken place. After all, avoiding such vast numbers of U-boats had been a terrific achievement.

By March 1943, Germany had realised that the Allies were gaining the upper hand and started preparing for some desperate but firm countermeasures. First, the surface fleet was scaled down, though without making the move too obvious so as not to encourage the enemy to unleash its forces against more valuable targets. Secondly, existing U-boats were modified to meet the new threats, mainly from the air. Thirdly, plans were made for the production of a new generation of so-called electro-submarines of Types XXI and XXIII.

May 1943, when a large number of U-boats were sunk, has often been described as the turning point in the Battle of the Atlantic, although the German High Command never recognised this and claimed it was a temporary setback. Grand Admiral Dönitz did withdraw U-boats from the danger area, but almost immediately made plans to send them back. The return to the Atlantic convoy routes took place in September, when boats were due to attack with new improved weapons. For the first time they had strengthened anti-aircraft guns, new direction-finding anti-convoy torpedoes and acoustic torpedoes for use against fast-moving warships. The idea was that the boats would attack at night on the surface. At the time, U-boat Command thought that Leuthen's efforts were a great turning point in the war, but this euphoria was short lived. The weather was in the convoys' favour and the escort screen had not been destroyed as imagined. This was due to submerged U-boats believing that the detonations they heard had sunk their targets. Most of the escorts had escaped, however, and the next convoy attacks turned out worse for the U-boats.

The struggle in the Atlantic continued until the summer of 1944 when the majority of U-boats were employed against the D-Day invasion forces. The Allied Operation 'Cork' to block off the Western Approaches of the Channel though was highly successful. It would seem very likely that U-boat losses here would have been considerably worse, had Admiral Eberhard Godt (Chief of the U-boat Command) obeyed Dönitz's instructions to send every available boat into the English Channel. However, when the crucial order, 'SEND ALL BOATS TO SEA' came, he sent the boats without schnorkels (which were more at risk) into the Atlantic, where they were relatively safe because they were some way from the enemy.

As a footnote, it might be interesting to add that comparing German and Allied statistics for the Battle of the Atlantic is not straightforward because Germany tended to include figures from the western North Sea and British waters as being part of the Atlantic. In Britain, however, these areas were classed as 'Home Waters' and the Atlantic started a little way further west.

THE BOATS

At the beginning of the war, all boats were based on modified First World War designs, meaning they were propelled by diesel engines on the surface, and then powered by electric drive when the air supply was shut off for diving. Although the limited battery power made them extremely slow once under the water and the U-boat Arm concentrated on practising submerged attacks until the summer of 1940, only very few people appear to have been interested in producing vessels capable of higher underwater speeds. It was as late as 1943, when defeat was staring the Germans in the face, that they stumbled upon the idea of adding extra batteries and developed the so-called electro-submarine. About a dozen of these new boats saw brief operational service before the end of the war, but their main contribution came much later when the Allies elaborated the principle further to produce the silent 'patrol submarine' of the Cold War era.

The speeds of submarines can best be illustrated by the Type VIIC, which was the largest U-boat class ever to have been built and Germany's main weapon in the Battle of the Atlantic. The top surface speed of 17 kt is about 30 km/h or just over 20 mph and the most economical cruising speed was 10 kt or 18 km/h or 11 mph. The difference in range was quite considerable: 3,250 nm or 6,000 km at fast speed and 9,500 nm or 17,500 km at the economical speed. Once submerged, the top speed was reduced to 7.5 kt or almost 14 km/h or 9 mph. This is slower than an average cycling speed and could only be maintained for a couple of hours before the batteries were exhausted. Generally boats would proceed at 2–4 kt (4 km/h or almost 2.3 mph – 7 km/h or just over 4.6 mph). This is walking speed or, at best, a brisk marching pace. The large Type XXI electro-boats could reach 10 kt submerged and maintain this speed for over 100 nm. At half that speed they could cover three times the distance.

At the beginning of the war, Germany had three main sizes of submarine: small coastal boats (Type II) of most limited use, sea-going varieties (Type VII and I) and a long-range class (Type IX). Of these, Type VII offered a good performance, making it suitable for operations as far as the Canadian coast, and a little further if it could be refuelled at sea. The larger ocean-going version was later developed for long-distance work for voyages to the Far East. The vision of supplying 'wolf packs' at sea from submarines converted into supply tankers was a novel idea in the 1930s but hardly materialised because no one came up with a practical solution for transferring heavy goods on the high seas. The main problems were the weather, rough seas and finding ways of safely opening hatches in mid-ocean. Usually only the conning tower hatch was used, but transferring goods through this 'main door' was very difficult. By the time these replenishment experiments started, Britain could already understand a large proportion of the U-boats' secret radio traffic and consequently the vulnerable supply submarines had rather short lives.

One strange part of U-boat development was that the German Navy never developed them as an integrated fighting force, and aircraft which are so vital for finding targets, played only a minor role. On top of this, the Navy never had a really effective weapon for U-boats. The torpedoes of the Second World War were in many ways inferior to their First World War predecessors. There were three

Before the war the majority of U-boats had their numbers painted on conning towers, and usually there were also bronze number plates on the bows, which can be seen in this picture as a black rectangle below the net cutter. The wire running from the net cutter to the top of the conning tower was originally intended to prevent boats being caught in nets. Although nets hardly played a significant role during the Second World War, the wires remained because they were used to anchor safety harnesses when men were working on the upper deck, and they also served as radio aerials. This shows *U30*, one of the early Type VIIA boats.

The bows of *U49* with net cutter clearly visible.

Atlantic boats had four bow torpedo tubes. The outside doors of these fitted flush with the casing, making them difficult to spot in photographs, even when the hull is out of the water. Large, long-range boats also had two stern tubes while the smaller Type VII boats had only one tube at the back. However, there were about a dozen or so Type VIICs built without rear tubes while a few more had them welded shut because damage allowed water to seep in. This boat is lying on the stocks. Technically it still belongs to the shipyard and the merchant flag can be seen flying on the bows. The large ensign with swastika would be hoisted for the first time during the commissioning ceremony.

major faults with the torpedoes and the last one to occur, a defect in acoustic torpedoes, seems to have been recognised by Britain long before Germany became aware of it. After the war, it was calculated that only about one in ten acoustic torpedoes actually sank its target.

The general situation with artillery was even worse. Before the war, commanders came to the conclusion that the large (88 or 105 mm) deck guns served no useful function and officers were loath to use them, except in exceptionally calm seas which were hardly ever encountered in the Atlantic. Gunners and men bringing up ammunition were frequently washed off the decks or injured, making the use of the big gun somewhat impracticable. Even in calm weather, aiming the gun from a rocking deck was not terribly easy. Yet, despite this, some boats fought incredibly long duels, in one instance expending over a hundred shells in an attack.

At times one gets the impression that anti-aircraft guns were added to the rear of conning towers because no one could think of anything better to mount in the space. The resulting designs, based on a single 20-mm gun, weren't terribly effective against fast, armoured aircraft of the Second World War, and it was only when air attacks began to pose a serious threat that Germany responded by modifying the conning towers. A variety of different designs were tried out, but generally the combination of two 20-mm twins on an enlarged upper platform and a 20-mm quadruple or a single 37 mm on an additional lower platform came into widespread use. Yet even this improved fire-power was not terribly effective. Again, the main problem arose from shooting from an unstable base. The gunners also found the range of their weapons inadequate and the ammunition tended to be consumed faster

UA was originally built for Turkey, but the war started before it could be handed over and the boat was commissioned into the Kriegsmarine. Being a large, long-distance type, it was often used as a supply boat. This was the only German U-boat of the Second World War with that typically large projection at the front of the conning tower.

An Arado seaplane being made ready for flight. Wings were removed for storage below decks and the aircraft was hoisted on to the water for take off. This looks very much like a cargo hatch, which would suggest the photograph was taken aboard an auxiliary cruiser. A purpose-built warship would have launched the aircraft from a catapult.

than men could bring it up from below. Furthermore, the additional bulk on the upper deck further reduced the slow underwater speeds of the boats.

Germany quickly discovered that its U-boats did not have a weapon against the large, well-armoured long-range planes employed by the Royal Air Force and that all they could do was to escape by diving; but this also had its drawbacks. Aircraft were faster than U-boats and many boats received fatal damage at the moment of disappearing below the waves, thus making diving speeds critical. This part of the operations became known as the Battle of Seconds and probably contributed more to U-boat losses than has previously been assumed. Yet there were also

a number of incredibly narrow and dramatic escapes where the resilience of the crew helped in bringing seriously damaged boats back to port, illustrating the high quality of German ship building.

The majority of U-boat operations had to be conducted without much-needed air support. This aspect of history has hardly been examined and one wonders who had actually failed the U-boat men. After all, of the almost 1,200 U-boats commissioned, about 800 never got within shooting range of the enemy. This means that only one third of the fleet attacked and at least damaged ships. What is more, half of this small fraction attacked fewer than five and most of the damage was done by 131 U-boats. It therefore becomes apparent that Germany had its priorities in the wrong place and should have provided more support rather than concentrate on building such vast numbers of submarines.

Instead of attacking the threat from aircraft, Germany responded by making it easier for U-boats to avoid the danger. This was done by providing a schnorkel or breathing pipe so that boats could remain submerged for longer periods. However, this hardly helped in making them more effective because the underwater speed was limited to a maximum of about 5 kt.

The idea of the schnorkel was by no means new. Breathing masts had first been developed during the 1930s by Kptlt. J.J. Wichers of the Royal Netherlands Navy with a view to allowing submarines in the Far East to escape the gruelling tropical heat by remaining under the surface. Modified versions of this equipment, fitted to O21–O23 (the Dutch submarines), fell into German hands during 1940, but then it was

discarded because the Kriegsmarine could not see a use for it.

The first German schnorkels consisted of a hinged pipe bringing air into the submarine while exhaust gases were carried back out through a separate duct inside the larger tube. A variety of different head valves were fitted to prevent water running down when waves washed over the top. When not in use, hinged schnorkels were lowered into the casing between the pressure hull and upper deck. They could be raised from the inside of the submerged boat and, once in this position, clipped into a bracket at the top of the conning tower. The new electro-submarines, designed from 1943 onwards, were fitted with a different design which could be raised and lowered in a similar manner to the periscopes. In fact a number of them had all three heads, that is the schnorkel, navigation periscope and attack periscope attached to a special collar that kept them rigid. However, the periscopes could be raised independently of the schnorkel.

MIDGET WEAPONS

Today it is easy to see German midget weapons as a desperate last attempt to prolong the war, although at the time men were hoping that these drastic measures would help to bring about a negotiated peace rather than the horrendous alternative, the unconditional surrender demanded by the Allies. The germination of numerous but isolated ideas of employing small sea-going vessels as major weapons of war took place while the incredible results of two British X-craft inspired people's thinking. In September 1943, the mighty battleship *Tirpitz* had been put out of action by eight men, two London bus engines and the sort of technology which an enterprising enthusiast could knock up in a garden shed. The salvaged X-craft, probably *X-6* (Lt Cameron) and *X-7* (Lt Plaice), were taken to a stretch of protected water at Heiligenhafen (East of Kiel, near the island of Fehmarn), to be restored and put through a series of trials. At the same time, Italian midget submarine activities came under scrutiny. From these foundations, a few dozen men, recruited from the Navy, Air Force, Army and SS, started training for what could be called sabotage operations.

Grand Admiral Dönitz (the U-boat Chief, who had been promoted to Supreme Commander-in-Chief of the Navy in January 1943) was more than sceptical when he chaired one of the first meetings to discuss midget weapons. A short presentation by Richard Mohr, a civilian designer from the Torpedo Trials Centre at Eckernförde (*Torpedo Versuchsanstalt* – TVA), sounded too simplistic and too impossible to be of any use. Mohr's answer to the Italian human torpedoes was to

sit a man inside one! He thought that in colder waters this would be preferable to the Italian model where men rode piggyback on top. The idea was to replace the warhead with a cabin and to attach another torpedo, complete with explosives, underneath the operator. Realising that the Torpedo Trials Centre had already built such a craft, Dönitz turned to Oblt.z.S. 'Hanno' Krieg and told him to go up there and try it out.

The 25-year-old Oblt.z.S., Johann Otto Krieg, had joined the Navy in 1937 to become First Watch Officer of *U81*, which had sunk the aircraft carrier *Ark Royal* in the Mediterranean while under command of Kptlt. Friedrich Guggenberger. Following this, Krieg commanded *U142* and then went back to his old *U81* for an incredibly difficult period during the turbulent year of 1943. The boat only just survived those twelve months. It was destroyed during an air raid on Pola (in the Adriatic) in January 1944, leaving Krieg without a command. Returning to Germany, Krieg expected to eventually continue his journey as far as the Baltic where he would be given a brand new U-boat. Instead, he ended up on his own, sitting inside a torpedo. The only compensation was that the controls were simple. There was the steering mechanism and a lever for turning the electric motor on and off. The craft was not even fitted with a way of varying the speed or a means for making it dive. Pressing the handle, while the craft pointed out to sea, made it dash off at about 50 kmh (30 mph). Astonishingly, it didn't sink! Krieg brought it back, and the batteries were rewired, but even at half speed it still went far too fast. In the end, the men

A midget weapon of Type *Neger* at the Deutsches Museum in Munich (above and below). Although a long way from the coast, the museum has an interesting naval section which includes the *U1* boat from before the First World War, a *Seehund* and a number of surface craft. The tubular window is a postwar addition. Originally it would have been fitted with a Plexiglas dome.

reduced the speed to less than 4 kt by merely wiring batteries in parallel rather than in series. This had the advantage of giving them a very slow speed and an incredibly long running time of ten or more hours.

Thus, with very little effort, a new weapon, named *Neger* ('Negro'), was born. What was more, the Navy already had a use for the curiosity. By this time Allied forces had established a firm foothold in Italy's deep south. Dönitz realised that such simple one-man torpedoes would have been handy for striking at the support ships bringing in supplies. Recognising that small, special weapons might have a significant role for the future, the Naval High Command appointed Vizeadmiral Eberhard Weichold to look into the possibilities and to coordinate development. However, he was not given any special organisational support or many additional resources for tackling the problems ahead. Despite this lack of investment, it quickly became obvious that traditional chains of command would have to be abandoned because future success was going to depend on the abilities of unconventional men creating unorthodox concepts. As a result, early in the summer of 1944, when Konteradmiral Hellmuth Heye took over command of Weichold's groups, they were amalgamated into an autonomous force, known as the Midget Weapons Unit (*Kleinkampfverband* or *K-Verband*).

Heye started by looking around for characters too strong for moulding into the conventional Kriegsmarine form. One of the first people to spring to mind was Korvkpt. Hans Bartels, who had already built his own minesweepers in Norway during 1940 and was consequently promoted to the role of first officer in the destroyer *Z34* so that, as Grand Admiral Raeder put it, 'he could re-learn some basic naval discipline.' Bartels was joined by Fritz Frauenheim, a U-boat commander extraordinary, and by Michael Obladen from the Army, who had been a businessman in Hamburg before the war. Since the Midget Weapons Unit came under the direct control of the Supreme Naval Command, without interference from the complicated naval administrative system, it was thought best for Heye to control everything except the actual

Grand Admiral Dr h.c. Erich Raeder wearing regulation coat with open cornflower-blue lapels. The other admiral with open lapels is Otto Schniewind, who was Fleet Commander. Ranks lower than admirals wore their coats buttoned up to the top, as can be seen in this picture.

operational missions. This meant that individual groups from the Midget Weapons Unit would be self-sufficient, so that they did not have to rely on others for any stage of their operations. Theoretically an operational commander in the field would only have to give them the location of a target plus the necessary intelligence details and the Midget Weapons detachments would do the rest for themselves. To this end, Heye collected a number of ships, trucks and even a few U-boats for transporting individuals to within striking distance of wherever they were needed.

The amazing point about the Midget Weapons Unit was that it started as just a collection of quick-thinking, unconventional men without weapons and in a few months it was organised and had a variety of ingenious devices. Some of these designs were modified from whatever could be found, while others were specially built from bits and pieces easily available during that period. For example, the *Neger* mentioned earlier, was constructed from a standard torpedo. Bartels, who had never been a submariner, even came up with a unique one-man U-boat called *Biber*. Complete with petrol engine and electric motor, it could dive and remain at sea for a little over a day before running out of fuel. Unfortunately a number of engines leaked exhaust slightly, poisoning their operators, and at least one such craft was recovered by the Royal Navy near to Dover after the occupant had been gassed. This boat is now in the Imperial War Museum in London. Many years ago, the museum's exhibits department gave the author permission to photograph the boat, but unfortunately this attempt was frustrated by the gentleman responsible for the area around the midget submarine. The images could not be procured because permission had been given to photograph the *Biber*, but not to stop with a camera in hand and stand on the floor surrounding it. Alas, I am still lacking the courage to apply for this permission.

Not only was the Midget Weapons Unit highly imaginative when it came to designing vehicles, but it was equally versatile when effective uses were found for them. For example, it was planned to carry two *Biber*s on top of a large submarine within striking distance of Murmansk with a view to sinking the battleship *Archangelsk* (ex-British *Royal Sovereign*). The undertaking was only defeated by faulty engines, although had the *Biber*s got under way, the cold water might well have frozen the operators. The Midget Weapons Unit also prepared a long-range Blohm und Voss flying boat to carry a *Biber* to Egypt. The idea was to launch it in a remote region of the Suez Canal so that the submarine could make its way to a narrow section and possibly sink a ship in such a way that it blocked the waterway. One wonders whether such a bold attempt could have worked.

THE MAIN MIDGET WEAPONS

SUBMARINES

Seehund (Seal – U-boat Type XXVIIB)
Developed from Type *Hecht* by making the hull some three tons heavier, adding a diesel engine and some more sophisticated equipment such as a small periscope and sound detection gear, this became quite a stable boat in seas up to about Force 4. (The majority of operational boats were probably never fitted with the sound detector.) The additional size allowed two torpedoes to be carried, although these usually had only half to three-quarters of the normal battery load. The diesel engine improved the performance, enabling the craft to remain at sea for almost three full days and giving it a maximum range of 500 km. However, under battle conditions, it was more practical to calculate a total range of about 250 km. Several successful hits were achieved by boats stationed in the English Channel. When British forces entered Kiel

they found considerable numbers under construction at the Howaldtswerke. Other boats were in the process of being built at Schichau in Elbing (near Danzig in East Prussia) and at Klöckner in Ulm (South Germany). After the war, a number of this type turned up during dredging operations in several European ports, suggesting that they had been positioned at likely places where sea-borne forces might have landed.

Biber (Beaver)

This one-man submarine was conceived by Korvkpt. Hans Bartels and developed by Flender Works in Lübeck. As has been mentioned, its major drawback had not been in the design but in the construction of the petrol engine, which had a tendency to leak, poisoning the operator with carbon monoxide fumes. The other major drawback lay in the incredible simplicity of the design. Although it

was capable of remaining at sea for almost a full day, the cold, dampness and the levels of concentration needed to pilot the boat defeated the majority of men. Again, as with Type *Seehund*, the *Biber* carried two torpedoes, but with half to three-quarters the usual battery load to save weight. Towards the end of 1944 a number of *Biber*s were engaged in the seas around Le Havre and in the approaches to Antwerp. From there the Channel tides carried a number of them back and forth, resulting in considerable losses from natural causes, although many also fell foul of aircraft.

Despite all the drawbacks, it became apparent that a two-man crew would offer considerably better performance because the men could recover some strength by sleeping, but the war ended before this slightly larger version (*Biber II*) went into production. There had also been a prototype called *Adam*, which did not go into mass production.

A one-man submarine of Type *Biber* at the Deutsches Museum in Munich, showing the conning tower and one of the two torpedoes.

The controls of the one-man U-boat of Type *Biber*.

VESSELS WITHOUT INTERNAL COMBUSTION ENGINES

Hecht (Pike – U-boat Type XXVIIA)

These were conceived and designed by the U-boat Office within the Supreme Naval Command, which was responsible for the building of submarines, and a number of contracts were issued to Germania Works in Kiel, Simmering in Graz (Austria) and Pauker in Vienna. Some sources state that about fifty units were completed, while others suggest that a number nearer three is more likely to be correct. It seems certain that the majority were never completed because production was switched to the superior Type XXVIIB (*Seehund*).

The initial idea for the *Hecht* design came from Italian midget submarines and from the early development plans for the all-electric *Molch* type. The crew of two carried either one standard torpedo slung underneath the hull or a detachable front section containing a specially made mine with time-delay fuse. This basic design gave the craft some interesting potential because the mine section could also accommodate additional batteries to increase the performance by almost 50 per cent, or it could be made into an accommodation area for two frogmen. The drawback with all this was that there were considerable differences in employing midget craft in the Mediterranean and trying the same idea in cold, cloudy northern waters. There was no means of charging batteries unless they were connected to an external power source, which meant that even during trials, the electricity supply frequently started sagging-off just when it was required. Once back by its mother ship, it was not a case of quickly pouring some fuel into a tank, but waiting for several hours before power could be restored. Although it was possible to keep running for just over 12 hours at about 4 kt, covering some 100–120 km, under battle conditions this would frequently have been reduced to an operating time of about 6 hours and 70 km.

Neger and *Marder* (Negro and Marten)

Although often classified as a submarine, it is questionable whether this is correct, since *Neger* had no way of diving. However, once under way at its fixed speed of just under 3 kt, water washed over the dome above the operator's head, obscuring his view and hiding the craft, though not the tell-tale bow wave. Although the German Navy usually claimed that none of these midget weapons had been conceived as suicide craft, the hatch with window dome could only be opened from the outside, meaning the operator was trapped until he returned to a friendly base. Since he had no way of communicating with the outside world, he could not announce his arrival anywhere nor surrender. The *Neger*'s range during its 10–15-hour-long operating period would have been somewhere between 60 and 70 km. For armament it carried another torpedo with half battery load underneath the hull. About 200 were built with a view to attacking ships bringing supplies into Anzio (in Italy) and to the Normandy beachheads after D-Day, but their incredibly high losses meant that operations were curtailed towards the late autumn of 1944. Yet, despite the casualties, a number of these craft were kept in readiness in case suitable opportunities for their engagement presented themselves.

Type *Neger* was further modified into the Type *Marder* and *Hai*. *Hai* was originally a pure suicide weapon, which did not progress far beyond an early experimental stage. The *Marder* differed from Type *Neger* by having a diving cell for going down to depths of about 10 m for brief periods, but it was necessary to return to the surface to release its torpedo. On photographs the two similar-looking types can be distinguished because the front of the *Marder* hull was noticeably longer than the torpedo slung underneath, while both the front of the weapon and the upper hull of the *Neger* are roughly the same length.

Molch (Newt/Salamander)

The *Molch* was also developed by the Torpedo Trials Centre at Eckernförde and built on the shores of the River Weser near Bremerhaven. It consisted of a tubular hull, almost 12 m long with room for one operator near the back. Two standard torpedoes with reduced battery capacity could be attached to the sides, and at about 11 tons, these craft could reach almost 5 kt. It was thought that they could maintain this speed better than the *Neger* Type because the boat could dive, thus eliminating the problems of turbulence caused by bow waves washing over the hull. Although almost 400 were completed, they turned out to be somewhat troublesome due to several design faults. Type *Molch* appeared in Italy and along the Belgian coast, but it seems highly likely that they did not inflict a great deal of damage on the enemy.

SURFACE CRAFT

Although the *Neger* was not fitted with diving tanks, this type of human torpedo craft was designed to travel through the water rather than on top of it. In contrast, the following group consisted of designs based on the motor torpedo boat concept, which tried lifting much of the craft clear of the water.

A rear view of the all-electric Type *Molch*, also at Deutsches Museum in Munich.

Linse (Lentil or Lens)

Linse or *Sprengboot* ('Explosive Boat') was developed from a concept advanced during the First World War. The idea was that the operator would ram the entire speedboat into the side of the target, triggering a minor explosion which would break off the front of the boat. The main explosive package in the rear section would sink and a time-delay fuse would then set off the main detonation. The scheme was that these boats would hunt in packs of three, with one of the trio being a control and rescue boat without explosives. This would pick up the operators after they had ejected before the final run-in. This third boat would also carry two radio operators who would take over remote control of the two explosive-carrying craft.

Type *Linse* could carry 300–400kg of explosives at speeds of up to 35 kt, while the cruising speed of 15 kt could be maintained for about 5 hours, covering some 150 km. However, although this speed was ideal at the moment of attack, the bow waves were an obvious give-away in calm waters meaning progress was often very much slower. The craft were too fragile for operations in rough conditions, which limited their employment to the English Channel. Yet, despite this, plans went ahead for an even faster catamaran, which was thought to be able to achieve over 45 kt. *Linsen* (plural of *Linse*) were employed around Anzio in Italy and from the Le Havre region in France, but it seems likely that they did not inflict a great deal of damage on the enemy.

It is rather interesting to add that these speedboats were not a naval creation at all, but a concept developed by the Army for the Brandenburg Regiment. Also, the youngest person to have been awarded a Knight's Cross of the Iron Cross was the 21-year-old Lt.z.S. Alfred Vetter, a commander of a *Linsen* Group, who received the award on 25 August 1944.

Hydra

This experimental type of torpedo boat functioned on a similar principle to the *Linse*, but it was about two tons heavier and carried a couple of operators with two aerial torpedoes as weapons. Although basically experimental, about forty were produced for employment in the approaches to Antwerp in Belgium.

EXPERIMENTAL CRAFT

Controlling midget craft during the hours of darkness was only part of the precarious operating procedure. Transporting them secretly to an embarkation port, hoisting them into the water or launching them down a slipway, charging the batteries and actually getting the operator inside were just as big problems. All this was only possible with Hitler's personal intervention because no other individual possessed the authority for mobilising so many supporting services. Take the early *Neger* operations at Anzio for example. The craft and their torpedoes were moved to Rome by rail. From there, Army low-loading tank carriers had to be requisitioned for carrying them to the launching point, where cranes were required. One advantage with this type of vessel was that the moving of manned torpedoes would not have aroused excessive interest in intelligence circles, as long as the operator's cabin could be kept hidden. The Midget Weapons Unit was also in the process of building special overland transporters, but in many cases development of the craft was so fast that they became operational before all the refinements could be added. Operations in Normandy were even more complicated. A convoy of about 100 lorries, made up of at least half-a-dozen different makes, carried the midget craft over a

period of several days to their launching area. The variation in the types of lorry was significant because repair facilities *en route* were so limited that it was thought best to carry spare parts. Obviously this meant carrying quite a store of duplicate essentials and it must be borne in mind that the lorries were no longer in prime condition. During this journey they had to fend off air attacks and cope with the appalling state of wartime European roads. (A good comparison is that it now takes eight hours to travel by car from Calais to the U-boat Archive in Cuxhaven. In 1962 before motorways, the journey took almost 20 hours.) Once at their destination, many operations were made more difficult because attacks on ports meant that the means of launching the craft had been made more difficult, while the cold winter weather did not make for ideal conditions once in the choppy seas.

Elefant or Seeteufel (Elephant or Sea Devil)

Of course, many operators were frustrated by too great a distance between their launching point and the target areas. Ideally the midget weapons had to be brought closer, but launching was always determined by port facilities. This problem was overcome by the production of the *Elefant* or *Seeteufel*, which was also known as Project Lödige. The craft consisted of a combination of submarine with tank tracks. It is not difficult to guess where the first mentioned name came from because this unstable-looking craft rolled slowly down any firm beach, waddled into the water and then dived to avoid detection. Although most clumsy on land with tracks far too narrow and a prototype engine a little on the weak side, the craft behaved exceptionally well in water, and once modified it would probably have been quite an asset for fending off invasions. However only a few experimental craft were completed before the end of the war and these were destroyed before the Allies reached them.

Schwertwal (Swordfish)

This tiny torpedo-looking craft with a two-man crew was conceived to fulfil a similar role to fighter aircraft. It was planned to carry a small radar set, a sound detector and one or perhaps even two of the new hydrogen-peroxide-fuelled torpedoes. Its own hydrogen peroxide turbine would have driven it up to a maximum of just over 30 kt, although the general cruising speed was nearer 10 kt. Trials were still under way when the war ended and because the experimental versions were thought to be too futuristic for destruction, they were scuttled in the larger of the lakes at Plön in Schleswig-Holstein with drawings and other essential documents stowed inside. Unfortunately the craft are no longer there. They were recovered by British forces after the war and then vanished into obscurity.

Delphin (Dolphin)

This was also an experimental high-speed submarine powered by a hydrogen peroxide turbine and designed to carry a torpedo underneath the hull or to tow a torpedo-shaped mine. Another possibility would have been for the operator to aim the entire craft at the target and then throw himself out, hoping a support craft would pick him up. The trials came to a premature end when a prototype collided with its tender. The few existing craft were destroyed shortly before British troops

arrived at the test site by the massive lagoon of the Trave Estuary near Lübeck.

KAMPFSCHWIMMER (BATTLE/COMBAT SWIMMERS OR FROGMEN)

By the middle of 1944, some three dozen men, many of them famous athletes, had completed training for a number of specialised missions. Originally such units, with each man carrying some 8 kg of explosives, were engaged against the Arnhem and Orne Bridges (the latter now known as Pegasus Bridge, which was made famous by Major Howard and the British glider troops who made the first landing on D-Day). Towards the end of the war Frogmen hatched a most ingenious plan to prevent Field Marshal Montgomery's forces from crossing the River Elbe near Hamburg. Lying hidden upstream with torpedoes painted brown to make them look like logs and fitted with light-sensitive detonators, they would have exploded them underneath a pontoon bridge. However, when it became clear that Hamburg was capitulating and that the British Army was crossing the main Elbe bridges, the unit packed its bags and brought their weapons back to Kiel. Both the Elbe road and rail bridges were too strong for the weapons and too high to make an appreciable difference in light for the photo-sensitive triggers.

THE NAVAL AIR ARM

Early attempts at using aircraft at sea appear to have been hindered by the euphoria created around the massive airships built by Ferdinand, Graf von Zeppelin. This enthusiastic wave flowed so strongly through Germany that the count was saved from bankruptcy by voluntary subscriptions donated by a supportive public. Even two early disasters with the Navy's L1 and L2 (L = *Luftschiff* – airship) did not dilute the excitement generated by these massive hydrogen-filled gas bags. Somehow airships inspired imaginations to such an extent that even the loss of seventeen of them during the First World War did not diminish their popularity. The fact that this resulted in aircraft development being sidelined to the extent that it lagged behind progress in other countries hardly mattered, because the Versailles Diktat decreed that all German flying machines had to be scrapped. Consequently some 2,500 aeroplanes taxied to the breakers' yards and the next generation had to start from scratch.

The Allies' lack of interest in the destruction of the basic aviation infrastructure meant that the well-equipped air stations at Holtenau (Kiel), near Wilhelmshaven and at several other locations along the coasts remained intact, and naval aircraft presented themselves as practical tools for beating the restrictions imposed by Versailles. As a result a number of 'civil' flying clubs quickly occupied some of the empty military premises to excite the nation's imagination. This mystique created by the still embryonic concept of naval aviation must also have stirred in the minds of the

British government because one of the first major bombing raids of the Second World War was against the naval air station on the Island of Sylt. Rather embarrassingly, the bombers missed their target and hit Denmark instead.

Although aircraft were prohibited by the Diktat of Versailles, the young Reichsmarine certainly did not lag behind with its thinking when it came to planning a naval air arm. A small core of flyers, headed by a number of enthusiastic admirals, made forceful suggestions for the Navy's likely requirements once the restricting shackles could be thrown off. The Naval High Command was firmly against the foundation of an autonomous air force, saying that a third branch of the armed forces should only be created once the needs of the Navy and Army had been satisfied. However, this option was hardly considered by Hitler's inner circle, where the First World War flying ace, Hermann Göring, held powerful and influential positions. In fact, it is quite likely that such forceful naval suggestions helped in distancing his mind from the sea.

Although maritime aviation made a terrific effort, it never developed far beyond the initial stages because the fledgling Luftwaffe, founded in 1935, kept pulling more and more aspects of naval flying under its wing. This became so deplorable that after a couple of years no one in the Navy was actually sure of what exactly came under their jurisdiction. Early in 1939, after Hitler had been asked to clarify the matter, things turned out to be even worse than expected. He decreed that virtually all aspects of

An Arado 196 with civilian registration letters, piloted by Heinfried Ahl of the 1936 Olympia Crew, attempting to land by the side of a warship. The ship, moving at considerable speed, was dragging a heavy rubber mat over the surface of the water with a view to calming the waves. It was found that it was far

easier to create a 'duck pond' of smooth water by sailing in a tight circle and the mat idea was later abandoned in favour of this technique.

A reconnaissance plane checking on the identity of *U48*. Operations with such flimsy aircraft were confined to good weather days.

An early Heinkel 114A without weapons. The Germans realised some time before Britain that double-decker wings were not necessary and by the beginning of the Second World War they had produced some very good aircraft. Unfortunately research was curtailed and it did not take long for them to be outperformed by superior British and American designs.

A Heinkel floatplane at sea.

A rare sight of a Heinkel floatplane far out in the Atlantic, having flown out to escort the blockade breaker *Anneliese Essberger* into Bordeaux. The aircraft acted primarily as a lookout to prevent the valuable cargo from running into enemy guns.

The front of *Prinz Eugen*'s aircraft catapult with a crane on the deck below. The black roof of the superstructure between the crane and funnel was used to store one of the ship's launches.

military aviation were to come under the jurisdiction of the Luftwaffe and that the Kriegsmarine would be left in charge of only two facets: marine reconnaissance flights and aircraft based aboard warships. Everything else was to belong to the Luftwaffe, including the administration of these two naval branches. The Luftwaffe was to be responsible for aerial attacks against ships at sea, bombing raids on naval bases, supporting naval operations and aerial mine-laying.

Not only did the Luftwaffe take control of naval flying, but it also failed to keep the Navy informed about changes in new developments. For example, work on long-range marine reconnaissance bombers was curtailed without the Navy being informed.

Another strange abnormality was that although Germany was building an aircraft carrier (the never-completed *Graf Zeppelin*), there was hardly any research into the types of planes suitable for such a vessel. While to some this was most frustrating, other points were far more detrimental. For example, after the beginning of the war the Luftwaffe presented Britain with one of the Navy's most closely guarded secrets: the magnetic mine. Naval commanders were under the strictest orders not to place these highly effective weapons where they might wash ashore or be discovered, but an aircraft dropped one into shallow water in front of observers near Southend in the Thames Estuary.

The fact that Hermann Göring (Supreme Commander-in-Chief of the Luftwaffe) was

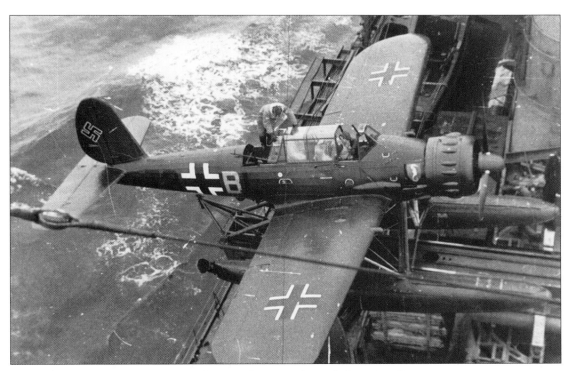

Prinz Eugen's Arado reconnaissance plane on the catapult, ready for take-off.

The Arado reconnaissance aircraft from the heavy cruiser *Prinz Eugen*. Although aircraft could be
launched relatively quickly, retrieving them was another problem. They had to land on water, to be
hoisted back on board by the nearby crane and this time-consuming procedure could only be carried out
in relatively calm weather.

As the war progressed, women started playing increasingly important roles. This shows a group of *Marinehelferinnen* tracking approaching enemy aircraft.

Marinehelferinnen, Germany's equivalent of the WRENs, in the aircraft tracking room at Wilhelmshaven. The board above the door is illuminating the various outlying districts under alarm for possible air attacks.

'playing' with the Navy without serious intention of cooperating for the good of the nation, is further supported by his incredible action of ordering marine aircraft divisions to create and to use a different chart system to ships at sea. Their radio codes and procedures were different as well, making liaison and cooperation incredibly difficult. In addition to this, the Luftwaffe concentrated on dropping bombs, despite the Navy having made the point that aerial torpedoes were far more likely to sink ships. In fact, aerial torpedoes were hardly developed and those which were built were often not powerful enough to bring a merchant ship to a halt, even when the explosion was right on target. Early failures and misjudgements were made worse by Erich Raeder's (Supreme Commander-in-Chief of the Navy) and Hermann Göring's highly contrasting characters. The sad point about this squabbling was that Germany had a number of excellent maritime aircraft at the beginning of the war, but even the

promising types such as the Dornier 18 and Heinkel 59 and 60 were not improved, meaning they quickly became obsolete simply because they were overtaken by progress.

Later in the war, when U-boats were in urgent need of air support, it became more than a joke that they were given a type of engineless kite, or autogyro, which was kept airborne by being towed. This ingenious device was indeed a novel little toy and one wonders why they have not yet appeared on modern holiday beaches. Combining the Focke Achgelis (FA300) with a speedboat would offer far better possibilities than paragliding because the device could be steered and made to go up and down without the boat altering speed. The operator usually carried a parachute so that he could descend rather quickly by jettisoning the rotors, but even this took too long if aircraft approached and the Bachstelze or Focke Achgelis was used only in out of the way locations.

NAVAL WEAPONRY

TORPEDOES

When Fregkpt. Blasius Luppis first suggested building torpedoes in 1860 the proposals were turned down. The importance of this new underwater weapon was not brought home until half a century later when the bitter conflict of the First World War clearly demonstrated its devastating results. The new Reichsmarine capitalised on the lessons by developing two basic torpedoes inside an almost identical shell.

The two torpedo types were known as G7a and G7e. 'G' stood for the diameter of 53.3cm; '7' for the length of 7 m; 'a' for the first design of this type. G7a was powered by an internal combustion engine with the fuel being injected by compressed air. G7e was

One of the administration blocks at the Torpedo Trials Centre (*Torpedo Versuchsanstalt*) at Eckernförde. Much of the site was demolished after the war and it is quite likely that the glass was blown out of the windows during this process rather than as a result of bombs during an air raid.

Cadets aboard the light cruiser *Karlsruhe* practising. Practice torpedoes had a red and white striped head, often with a lamp in the top so that progress could be observed at night.

powered by electric propulsion. The G7u appeared towards the end of the war as a universal identification for a variety of different experimental torpedoes with closed-circuit hydrogen peroxide turbines.

Although the size of the warhead of 300 kg and external dimensions were identical, the G7a offered slightly better performance than the electric version. At 30 kt it had a range of about 13 km, at 40 kt just over 7 km and at 44 kt 4–5 km. There were two ways of detonating the explosives inside the torpedo; either with a contact pistol hitting the target or with a magnetic detonator passing underneath it. The last mentioned had the advantage that it could literally break the average merchant ship in half. A torpedo exploding on the side very often failed to sink the ship.

The G7a had the disadvantage that it left a trail of bubbles and oil on the surface, making it easy to spot and to take evasive action. The G7e did not leave such tell-tale trails, but had the disadvantage that it required more maintenance. Part of the torpedo had to be withdrawn from the tube every three to four days for the batteries to be recharged.

During the war, these two basic torpedo designs were further modified to give rise to the T5, '*Zaunkönig*' (Wren), the FAT and the LUT. The first mentioned had a sound detector in the head so that it could home-in on propeller noises and was intended as a means of defence against fast warships. The idea that such torpedoes could be distracted by the target towing a loud sound-maker had occurred to the Germans and therefore the

It was common for men to take a souvenir when being drafted from one ship to another. Teddy Suhren (First Watch Officer) didn't mess about in this respect and took *U48*'s torpedo calculator together with a list of the ships he had sunk. The First Watch Officer was responsible for shooting torpedoes on the surface and by the time he left *U48*, Teddy Suhren had sunk more ships than anyone else in the Navy.

design incorporated a clever anti-foxer device. Once close to the target, the torpedo would abandon its straight run and turn to travel in a large circle around the sound source. At this moment the sound detector, at the end of a funnel-shaped depression in the nose, could not 'hear' the sound source. The torpedo's circle was too small for going around a ship and sooner or later it would pass under the hull, where a magnetic pistol detonated the explosives. (Unless, of course, the U-boat had selected the contact pistol.) However, if the torpedo was going around a sound-making device towed behind the

warship, then sooner or later the nose would point towards the real propellers and at that stage the torpedo would change direction and head for the new sound source to repeat the procedure. Such acoustic torpedoes were used for the first time during the autumn of 1943. Unfortunately for the Germans, they had a mechanical fault and only about 10 per cent of them actually sunk their target. Since many of these torpedoes were shot by submerged U-boats or boats which dived immediately after having shot one, Germany did not get to know about this disastrous state of affairs until after the war.

FAT stood officially for *Federapperat-Torpedo*, although many people also used the wrong name of *Flächenabsuch-Torpedo*. It was a sort of assurance attachment in an ordinary G7a for people who missed their target. The idea was that the torpedo could be aimed in the same way as existing types, but it would not continue running in a straight line past the target. At a pre-set range the FAT would start zigzagging, hopefully hitting a ship in a convoy. The first successes were reported towards the end of 1942 when *U406* (Kptlt. Horst Dieterichs) attacked convoy ONS154. However, the sinkings were not observed and the targets did not go down. The first observed hit took place in February of the following year when *U92* (Kptlt. Adolf Oelrich) used FATs against convoy ON166 and damaged the Norwegian freighter *N.T. Nielsen Alonso*. One feature of this anti-convoy torpedo was that it frequently only stopped the ship without sinking it, and *N.T. Nielsen Alonso* was later sent to the bottom by an escorting Polish destroyer after survivors had been taken off.

LUT or *Lagenunabhängigen-Torpedo* was a modification of the FAT principle inside a G7e body. This could be fired from depths of up to 50 m and then the torpedo would make it more difficult for observers in the target by running in loops rather than in the usual straight line. With a history of so many

A torpedo being launched. Up to the end of the First World War, the German Navy had experimented with a variety of underwater launching systems, but none of these could cope satisfactorily with ships moving at fast speeds. However, a few of these antiquated systems were installed in auxiliary cruisers during the Second World War.

torpedo failures, Germany conducted a saturation of tests with LUTs during November 1943. *U970* (Kptlt. Hans-Heinrich Ketels) fired about 100 of them during the hours of darkness. The reason for this was that a powerful lamp in the nose made it easy to observe progress. It was the middle of the following month before the torpedo was given the go-ahead for operational use, but it was another quarter of a year before they appeared at the front. Then they were plagued with the same problem as the FAT, damaging rather than sinking their targets.

The development of aerial torpedoes was somewhat neglected for a variety of reasons, the biggest being the almost total absence of a naval air arm. Then, when the Luftwaffe struck upon the idea of flying against naval targets, they were surprised to find that

aircraft development had progressed too far. By the time the war started, the majority of aircraft were already too fast for dropping torpedoes. The basic aerial torpedo, with a diameter of 45 cm and length of 5 m was also too small for inflicting significant damage on thin-skinned merchant ships and quite hopeless against armoured warships. In fact, although some of them exploded on target, they often failed to bring merchant ships to a halt. Their range of just over 3 km at about 30 kt was also somewhat on the meagre side.

THE TORPEDO CRISIS

The term 'Torpedo Crisis' usually refers to a series of diabolical torpedo failures towards the beginning of the war. During the Norwegian Campaign of spring 1940, thirty attacks out of a total of forty-two failed due to faulty torpedoes, showing quite clearly that Germany did not have an effective weapon for its submarine arm. While many of these breakdowns were deeply disappointing, they also led to the unnecessary loss of several U-boats. The first two boats went down, without damaging their targets, as a direct result of faulty torpedoes alerting escorts. (*U39* under Kptlt. Gerhard Glattes and *U27* under Kptlt. Hans Franz.) Contemporary reports are somewhat contradictory and many postwar authors have not fully understood the problems, thus adding even more confusion to the subject. The major problem was that the torpedoes were afflicted not by just one, but by three different and variable major faults. To make matters worse, not all of these applied all the time, hence it took a considerable time for them to recognised.

One of the first faults to be isolated was caused by a pressure sensitive depth-keeper, which could be adjusted while the torpedo was lying inside the tube ready for firing. During pre-war trials, torpedoes were shot either from tubes inside a building at Eckernförde or from a ship shortly after they had been loaded. During these tests, no one seems to have taken into account the fact that compressed air, used to eject torpedoes in submarines, is vented into the boat to prevent the bubbles from rising to the surface. This, of course, increases the pressure inside the U-boat. Torpedoes loaded under water started off with the pressure sensor already adjusted by this additional force acting upon it. Whence, additional settings made the depth control go even deeper. Consequently many torpedoes passed harmlessly underneath their targets.

Another problem was that too little was known about variations in the Earth's magnetic field and the type of magnetic forces created by ships, especially after these had been degaussed or demagnetised. This lack of knowledge was to have a detrimental effect upon the settings of the magnetic pistols. The idea was that the torpedo should run under the target to be detonated by the mass of iron on top of it. By the middle of the war it was thought that this problem had been overcome, but it cropped up again during the later months, when acoustic torpedoes were being used against fast-moving warships. Any fault in this magnetic system could, theoretically, be easily isolated by switching it off and using the contact pistol instead. This minor adjustment could also be carried out while the torpedo was lying in the tube with the outer door already open for ejection.

However, even this primitive contact trigger had an unrecognised fault. This was caused by a small propeller at the front which was rotated by the torpedo travelling through the water. It screwed two terminals inside the pistol together, enabling one side to touch the other and thus make the electrical contact to create the detonation. This safety mechanism prevented the torpedo from accidentally exploding at the wrong moment. The blades of this small propeller, which also acted as a trigger, could easily be unscrewed and they make ideal souvenirs, so they are often missing from museum displays where visitors can touch the exhibit. The mechanical fault lay in the fact that the blades were shorter than the radius of the torpedo. This meant the triggers were forced back once they hit a wall, such as the side of a deep-lying merchant ship or metal plates suspended in water as trial targets. However, when colliding with a curved hull of a small, shallow-draught warship, such as a destroyer, it was possible for the front of the torpedo to make contact without the trigger being touched. Obviously this had a similar result to two billiard balls hitting each other, and since the torpedo was very much lighter than the warship, it merely bounced under the target and continued its run.

Early in the war, the torpedo crisis appears to have been resolved, but one fault after another later hit back with powerful vengeance, especially when U-boats were using acoustic torpedoes against small fast-moving warships. Normally the submarine would have dived for a brief period or cut its engines to prevent the sound-sensitive head turning in a circle and then homing in on the boat which had fired it. The magnetic detonator had the built-in fault of going off before it reached the target. At times it blew off ships' propellers, but frequently failed to sink the target. The British propaganda system was intent on exploiting this weakness to its fullest, but the Admiralty objected on the grounds that it would be better for the Germans not to correct the fault. Consequently Germany did not become aware of the severity of the situation until after the war.

Putting a price on the financial cost of war is always difficult because exact figures were kept secret, and over the last fifty years there have been considerable changes in the value of money. However, in 1939 one torpedo cost about £4,000, which would also have purchased about a dozen houses in London. So the torpedoes shot during the attack on the battleship *Royal Oak* in Scapa Flow by *U47* (Kptlt. Günter Prien) cost about the same as about 120 London homes.

MINES

The basic mines were the EMA and EMB (*Einheitsmine* – Standard Mine Type A and B), which were further developed to produce the EMC and EMD. In addition to these, Germany produced an FM series meaning *Flußmine* or River Mine for inland waterways and also developed a variety for carrying in free flooding shafts aboard submarines. These had to be pressure resistant to cope with deep diving depths.

Mines carried inside the pressure hull of U-boats were ejected through specially modified torpedo tubes and prefixed with the letters TM (Torpedo Mine). The common types used during the war were the TMB and TMC. The first mentioned had a length of 2.31 m and the other a length of 3.39 m. There was another, rarer variety, the *Schachtmine* (Shaft mine), also for carrying in submarine minelayers.

Shortly after the beginning of the war, Britain was troubled by a number of unexpected and violent explosions in what was thought to be mine-free shipping lanes, making it obvious that Germany had introduced a new mechanism which could not be cleared by conventional sweeping techniques. Consequently this variety of magnetic mine created considerable havoc until the end of November 1939 when the Luftwaffe dropped one on the mudflats of the Thames Estuary. Not only did this aircraft deliver a most valuable present, but it also deposited it close to military workshops. A short time later when the tide had gone out, Lt Cdr J.G.D. Ouvry walked out to the spot, took rubbings of the various screws and bolts, and then returned the following day with a set of tools for dissecting the prize. Soon after this, the Royal Navy developed a means of detonating magnetic mines, rendering this most valuable weapon virtually useless.

The inside of this magnetic mine was quite sophisticated. It did not respond to just any old metal passing overhead. The magnetic mine was set off only by ships built in the northern hemisphere with a 'North Pole' acting downwards, and then it worked in a vertical, rather than horizontal plane. The idea was to change the polarity once Britain was suspected of having discovered this. However, by that time offensive mining in British waters had become too risky and the supreme advantage of closing down harbours had been lost.

After both world wars a vast number of mines continued to turn up in the most unexpected places, often torn from their anchors by severe storms. These photographs were taken in about 1933, which suggests that this is a specimen from the First World War.

There was obviously something of interest with this mine, otherwise it would not have been brought on board. The abundance of seaweed and barnacles indicates that the mine had been in the water for some time.

Usually it was far safer to stand well back and detonate old, unwanted mines.

It has been difficult to determine whether this is a smoke buoy (as seen on p. 44), a smoke marker or an old mine which is having some difficulty at going off the way it should.

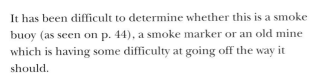

ROCKETS

Although there was some experimentation with naval rockets, only a few isolated models were employed against the enemy. The development, based on an Army smoke-making rocket, started in about 1944, with a view to supplementing anti-aircraft guns. A number of these rockets were shot from fixed tubes to detonate at heights of about 300–400 m. There were also a number of reasonably successful experiments with solid fuel rockets being fired from a submerged U-boat. These tests were carried out by *U511* under Kptlt. Friedrich Steinhoff, whose brother worked at the rocket research establishment at Peenemünde. There were also plans for towing a container holding a

V2 rocket to within range of New York. The idea was that it would then float upright, allowing the rocket to be launched. The major problems were maintaining depth while in tow and preventing water washing into the container at the moment of launching. None of this highly specialised machinery ever went into production, but one wonders what might have happened if the densely populated areas of New York had been bombed.

As a postscript it may be interesting to add that the general historical opinion has been that these rocket containers never progressed beyond the initial design stage. Yet recently some photos unearthed in the U-boat Archive show a U-boat towing a large cylindrical tank about the same size as a V2 rocket.

DISGUISE, CAMOUFLAGE AND COLOUR SCHEMES

The Reichsmarine used two basic colour schemes: small boats were usually painted black while large ships had a dark grey hull with light grey superstructure. However, on black and white photographs, light reflecting off ships frequently made light grey appear almost white. The first trials with alternative colours were not conducted until the late 1920s, when several torpedo boats received a bottle green coat. By the time the war started the Navy had created something of a record inasmuch as the rules regarding colours for warships were almost in single digits. They could certainly have been typed on a couple sheets of paper, and it was not until 1942 that the Naval High Command formulated some centralised thoughts on the subject of camouflage. This came about as a result of a memorandum by Korvkpt. Walther Dechend, from the heavy cruiser *Hipper*, who had been seconded to the Naval High Command as consultant on the subject. That is not to say that camouflage schemes had not been in use, but those which were had been created as the result of improvisation by individuals who looked for some ways of misleading the enemy. The designs were based on First World War concepts, and a number of them were so crude that they emphasised the bows and stern, making ships stand out even better than if they had been left in their pre-war greys. Other camouflage designs were based on one-off observations and in retrospect one wonders about their degree of effectiveness. Following Korvkpt. Dechend's memorandum, the Naval High Command set up a series of experiments where models were painted with a variety of different patterns to be viewed and photographed under a variety of different lighting conditions. These results then gave rise to an abundance of designs. The merchant navy had made a considerable headstart on the Kriegsmarine and many freighters were already under most ingenious painting schemes.

Although there have not been any international laws about the use of camouflage, the application of disguise is a different matter. This aspect of naval warfare was clarified at a conference in The Hague during 1907, which decreed that warships could sail under any flag and disguise as long as these were cast off before they started any aggressive action. Of course, the majority of genuine merchant ships were never in a position to start fights and auxiliary cruisers found ways of changing their disguise in a matter of seconds. The German war flag, for example, was pulled out of a tube on the masthead while the false one was still being hauled down. At the same time false names were covered up by dropping screens over them while concealed guns were uncovered for action. The whole process could be performed in a matter of seconds.

Some of the disguise worked exceptionally well by confusing the opposition during the war as well as naval historians after it. For example, photographs have been published of a boarding party from an unidentified British cruiser investigating a merchant ship at the beginning of the war. Closer examination of the Royal Navy ship shows it to be the pocket

Painting was one of the main occupations in the Navy, where men had to learn two totally different types of brushstrokes. The most important was the slow, leisurely up and down movement and the other a more erratic, faster action used only when supervisory eyes were in the vicinity.

battleship *Admiral Graf Spee* with a dummy gun turret built on top of the forward optical rangefinder. The illusion was enhanced by painting on extra large bow waves, giving the impression the ship was travelling at fast speed, and there was a makeshift camouflage pattern on top of the peace-time grey. Pictures have also been published showing the United States tanker *Prairie* refuelling U-boats on the high seas. Again, this is not a case of the Americans helping the wrong side, but the ship in question being the German supply ship *Nordmark*.

The establishment of a disguise for auxiliary cruisers was a long-winded and rather complicated business. First, men had to scour books to find ships with similar hulls because this was incredibly difficult to alter on the high seas. Then they had to find information about colour schemes and the fittings required to construct such alterations. This frequently involved storing quite large quantities of materials for building additional funnels, changing the superstructure and for adding the all-important tiny details. What's more, flimsy stage props were unsuitable because these additional features had to withstand ocean storms as well as scrutiny by aircraft passing close overhead.

Not all features of deception were created by the crew at sea. The Naval High Command had a dossier of confidential information about special devices to be incorporated into the design of auxiliary cruisers. In addition to the obvious, such as armaments, some ships were fitted with a means of jacking their funnels and masts up and down. In addition to this, many auxiliary cruiser masts could raise, and quickly lower, a crow's nest to the mast tip and, perhaps most cunning of all, a number of carefully positioned lights could be dimmed or brightened with a rheostat. The idea was to make the darkened ship resemble a warship's superior speed by increasing the intensity of light as it approached its quarry at night.

The amount of attention paid to details was immense, but despite this some apparently

Painting has probably been the scourge of all navies ever since iron replaced wood, but German raiders had the additional problem of having to disguise their ship in the colours of different shipping lines. This shows the final touches of disguise being added to *Anneliese Essberger* while north of the Falkland Islands, close to the area where Admiral Graf Spee lost his life. At this stage it was necessary to change from a Japanese disguise to resemble the Norwegian *Herstein*, belonging to Herlofson, Sigurd and Co. AS of Oslo.

insignificant point often gave the Germans away. For example *Pinguin*'s (Kpt.z.S. Ernst-Felix Krüder) disguise was rumbled because there were no coloured sailors waving at a passing reconnaissance plane. A rather ironic point because Krüder had several hundred men of various races in his prison rooms but he had ordered them to their quarters the moment the plane was first spotted.

A Norwegian flag has been laid on the deck of *Anneliese Essberger* to complete the disguise for the benefit of passing aircraft.

An incident between the men of *Michel* (Kpt.z.S. Hellmuth von Ruckteschell) and the 10,307-ton British turbine ship *Menelaos* provides another excellent example of how attention to detail made the difference between success and failure. Unable to catch its quarry, von Ruckteschell dispatched *Michel*'s light motor torpedo boat to bring the enemy to a halt. Flying the White Ensign and with the crew wearing Royal Navy duffle-coats with genuine British life-jackets over the top, they failed in their task because their adversaries had already been alerted by a signal where the word 'patrol' had been spelt with two 't's. On seeing the launch, people realised it was too warm for duffle-coats and the lifejackets were of a variety issued to the merchant navy rather than the Royal Navy. Being alert to a possible attack, the crew of *Menelaos* kept an extra keen lookout, making it possible to avoid the two torpedoes fired from the light motor torpedo boat in a last attempt to halt the merchant ship.

One of *Thor*'s guns hidden in what looked like a huge cable drum.

The naval scourge – painting auxiliary cruiser *Thor*.

Evading superior forces was the German Navy's strongest weapon and keeping vigilant lookout was an essential part of the continuously boring routine. This shows lookouts aboard the blockade breaker *Anneliese Essberger*. Some auxiliary cruisers went one stage further and had a specially built crow's nest with seat which could be lowered and hidden after ships had been sighted.

NAVAL TERRA FIRMA

BASES AND THE KIEL CANAL

A war between Prussia, the largest of the German speaking kingdoms, and Denmark during the middle of the nineteenth century, helped to focus attention on the Baltic coast. During this conflict the blockading Danish fleet was driven away from the Kiel approaches by the launching of Prussia's first submarine, the *Brandtaucher*, designed by Wilhelm Bauer, a Bavarian artillery officer. The Navy, or rather Prussia's collection of warships, was at that time under Army control and severely hampered by not being able to reach the North Sea without sailing all way around Skagen, the northern tip of Denmark. This made it clear that Prussia needed a base on the North Sea coast and also a means of moving sea-going ships over land. The concept of a sea connection between the Baltic and the North Sea during those early years was not as absurd as it may sound today. There were already a number of canalised river sections through the low North German plain, but many of these waterways were narrow enough to be jumped by an athlete and their winding courses did not take direct routes. The boats using these waterways were usually narrow punts, pushed along with poles.

The Grand Duke of Oldenburg, the ruler responsible for what is now the southern part of the German North Sea coast, could see the advantages of selling land to the Prussians for establishing a naval base because that would help put an end to the lawlessness in the shallow wadden sea. It seems that many small fishing communities supplemented their income with part-time piracy and wrecking, and on top of this there were constant intrusions from foreign sea robbers. The main problem with establishing a naval base on the North Sea was that the majority of officials could not determine exactly where the coast was actually located. This is not intended as a sarcastic remark, but as a reminder that the land there is very flat and the isolated marsh communities were indeed a long way from firm ground, with some completely inaccessible from the landward side for large parts of the year. Even today, where the coast is protected by high dykes, low tide still reveals up to about 10 km of sand flats. This vast flat area, interlaced with a myriad of deep, fast-flowing water channels, is not only Europe's last wild frontier but is still making ship access incredibly difficult. Apart from the Elbe, Weser, Ems, Eider and a few other river estuaries, there are only two places along the entire wadden sea coast where deep water touches firm mainland, and one of these, at Büsum, is too small for big ships. Therefore Prussia really had little choice when it came to selecting a location for its North Sea operations. A few small and extremely isolated fishing communities were amalgamated to form a new town, named Wilhelmshaven in honour of the Prussian King.

Around the same time as founding Wilhelmshaven, Prussia moved its main naval base from Danzig to Kiel. The Baltic coast was far more hospitable to accommodating warships because there are a number of deep estuary shaped coastal indentations which have some similarity with Norwegian fjords. Kiel was chosen for the same reason as Wilhelmshaven because deep water reached over 15 km inland, well out of artillery range of ships at sea. The building of Wilhelmshaven was by far a greater

A reception party assembled on the lock-side at the Baltic end of the Kiel Canal. The Navy usually referred to this quay as the main railway station platform.

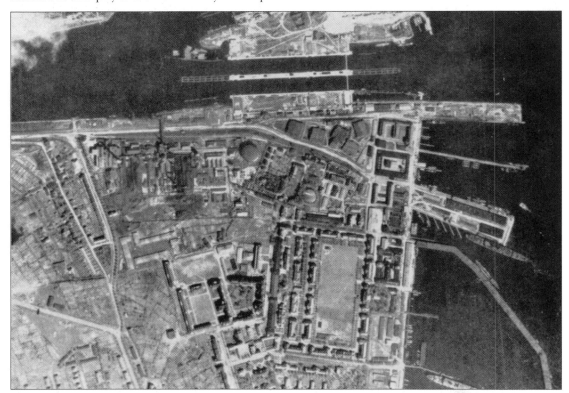

A wartime or pre-war view of Kiel. The locks of the Kiel Canal, together with road bridge can clearly be seen. The rectangular building pattern as well as the various jetties of the naval dockyard are also visible. The famous Tirpitz Mole is the somewhat wider pier, with its two corners which stretch downwards in the bottom right-hand corner.

U123 with Kptlt. Karl-Heinz Moehle sitting on the right. The magnetic sighting compass can be seen in the foreground and the signal tower in the background is of special interest. Until it was demolished, it provided the vantage point for numerous photographs of ships made fast at the Blücher Pier.

The main naval command offices at Quiberon in France. Any suitable building was commandeered and it was usually only the German signposts and guards that suggested there was some connection with the military.

Cuxhaven before the war when it was still a major minesweeping base.

problem than developing Kiel because, apart from the narrow deep water channel, there was nothing there for ships to float on at low tide. So a massive artificial or 'floating' harbour with sea locks had to be built by teams of men wielding shovels and pushing wheelbarrows. Over the years the facilities were gradually improved, and the wartime sea locks were the fourth set to serve the port.

During the Second World War, Wilhelms-haven had the great disadvantage that naval activities were concentrated around an artificial harbour with a relatively narrow tidal approach. Kiel had vast stretches of sheltered water, meaning shipping could be dispersed to make it a more difficult target for enemy bombers. At the same time there was enough shallow water to hide submarines, and many of them spent daylight hours resting on the sea bed with only a skeleton crew on board. Problems with the narrow North Sea channels were driven home in March 1940 when *U31* (Kptlt. Johannes Habekost) was bombed and sunk by an aircraft. A Friesian island ferry kept well clear of the trouble spot and it was a private individual, a soldier going home on leave, who reported the attack on an area of seemingly empty water. *U31* had its periscope marked with a flag for diving trials and another passing ship thought that the tiny bow wave around it was caused by the submarine travelling under the water. So the helmsman gave it a wide berth, not realising the bow wave was caused by the current. Nobody aboard the ship realised that the U-boat was lying on the bottom, with men gasping for their last breaths. Only when *U31* failed to return did the naval authorities make sense of the isolated reports and dispatch a search party. Everybody had died by the time divers reached the wreck.

U48 in Kiel with one of the bigger ships in the background. Identification is not easy at the best of times and can become quite difficult, especially when nets have been added to break up the outlines. There is an interesting album of photographs in the Imperial War Museum in London with the original ship identification crossed out and corrected. This, in turn, has then been crossed out and corrected, and later someone has added a third correction. Afterwards a fourth handwritten comment was added,'Does it matter? They have all been sunk anyway!'

Since the existing Eider Waterway between the Baltic and the North Sea was unsuitable for sea-going ships, work started on the Kiel Canal in 1887, around the same time as Wilhelmshaven and Kiel were being developed as naval bases. When it was finished, some eight years later, it too was named after Kaiser Wilhelm. Today it is known under the more modest name of Nord-Ostsee Kanal or internationally as Kiel Canal. It had hardly been completed when Germany responded to the development of the British *Dreadnought* battleship by increasing the size of another, newer type of warship. This new generation was too big for the canal, meaning the waterway had to be enlarged. This lengthy project was completed shortly before the beginning of the First World War. The new specifications gave it the same length of almost 99 km as before, but the narrowest width on the bed was increased from 22 to 44 m while the overall water-surface width was extended from 66 to 102 m with a good number of wider passing places. At the same time the water depth was increased from 9 to 11 m. Locks were necessary at both ends not only to compensate for the tide in the North Sea and the changing water levels in the Baltic, but also to allow the water in the canal to be raised a little above normal. Incidentally there is no tide as such in the Baltic, but changing winds make for a difference of a metre or so in water levels.

This pre-First World War waterway served Germany until further modifications were made in 1966. It was rather interesting that the large set of locks, completed in 1907, had never been completely drained until they were shut down for repairs in 1984. Then, as water was pumped out of the massive basins at the Kiel end, the concrete base threatened to disintegrate because groundwater below was forcing the foundations upwards. The problem was finally solved by filling the empty lock basins with heavy concrete blocks while the repairs were in hand.

During the Second World War, the canal was protected by barrage balloons, land-based anti-aircraft guns, at least one special Air Force fighter squadron, and anti-aircraft ships which would accompany convoys and other vulnerable targets. The passage was controlled from two stations, one at each end, and usually different pilots were required for the three stages, although a good number of naval commanders had the necessary qualifications for making the passage on their own.

Another frequently mentioned naval base, Gotenhafen, can hardly be found in atlases. The reason is that this German name for Gdynia was only used during the war years. It had been a tiny fishing village until the end of the First World War. Then, when that area was taken away from Germany to become part of Poland, it was developed into a seaport for both naval and merchant traffic. In 1939, Germany used the newly established naval facilities there for the benefit of the Kriegsmarine. Almost all of the facilities as well as the town were destroyed towards the end of the Second World War and have since been rebuilt.

Hamburg and Bremen have hardly been used as naval bases because both towns are located far inland with access along temperamental rivers where tides, currents, treacherous shallows and sandbanks play havoc with shipping. In wartime such passages could be made more difficult or even closed by block ships, mines and aerial attacks.

SHIPYARDS

Until not all that long ago the southern shores of the River Elbe in Hamburg were hidden behind a vast battery of floating drydocks, while the skyline was dominated by massive iron structures supporting a milliard of wires on which bogeys ran back and forth, feeding the constantly hungry slipways. The economic boom of the postwar years meant that these cable dominated cranes were replaced by modern, hydraulically operated equipment just a short time before the decline of European shipbuilding forced many of the dockyards to close. Although some corners have now been partly redeveloped, there remain some noticeable pockets of dereliction, some of which are filled with the most remarkable evidence of our turbulent past. Because the contrast between the old and modern is so obvious, the step back in history can be made with nothing more than a few photos from the abundance of books available.

Hamburg makes a good starting point for such a historic search because it is easily accessible and the remains of the old yards are not too difficult to locate. The last remaining large shipyard there, Blohm und Voss, lies on the southern shore, beside the old tunnel under the Elbe. At the turn of the twentieth century, the yard built up an excellent reputation for the construction of large merchant ships, especially fast liners, and these facilities were later tapped by the German government for building the heavy cruiser *Admiral Hipper* and battleship

The HDW yard in 1998. The scale is difficult to perceive, even when one stands immediately next to this massive crane. But that trolley at the top, holding the cables, is as high as a three-storey house.

This shows the slipways of the old Krupp Germania Works, which were at one time covered by huge glasshouses. This historic site has now been totally transformed to form a marvellous new ferry terminal.

Hamburg with a floating dry dock belonging to Blohm und Voss in the foreground and the bogey crane over Stülken Werft's slipways, photographed during the late 1960s. That mass of wires stretching over the slipways was the last of the massive cable-operated crane systems. The decline in European ship-building resulted in these structures being demolished and smaller cranes being replaced by hydraulically controlled systems.

The skyline of the Blohm und Voss yard in Hamburg with an array of more modern cranes.

Bismarck. Strangely enough, Blohm und Voss did not become involved with the construction of submarines until comparatively late in the war, but then, when a production line for the assembly of the large electro-Type XXI was introduced, the yard quickly became the most efficient builder in terms of man-hours for each boat.

The slipways in the Werfthafen, where the hub of this activity took place, can still be seen from the launches taking visitors around the port, and a multitude of excellent photos exist showing British soldiers exploring this hive of activity in 1945. At the end of the war, when the army of occupation moved into the premises, much of the workings were still intact, but there are also photos of the same U-boats with considerable damage, and the official captions state that the devastation had been caused by Allied bombing during the war. This is clearly false because bombing had ceased by the time British soldiers moved into the area. So one wonders why it was necessary for the armies of occupation to destroy cranes, water defences and other installations after the war, and then make out this wilful destruction had been caused before the cease-fire. It is also interesting to note that during the mid-1970s, when Blohm und Voss was approached for information about their participation in the building of U-boats, their public relations officer told the author that the yard had never built submarines. On being shown photos of such vessels lying on the firm's slipways, he declared them to be fakes.

Just a few hundred metres to the south of Blohm und Voss lies the site of the Howaldtswerke. The name of the basin, 'Vulkanhafen', is a fascinating throwback to earlier times when this yard was owned by the Vulcanwerke of Stettin. The Baltic port could no longer cope with the masses of orders flooding in, so Vulcan moved some of its production to Hamburg. In 1930, the works were taken over by Howaldt. After the war the concern was amalgamated with the Howaldtswerke in Kiel and with Deutsche Weft, but even this strong combination could not cope with the cheaper competition from far off countries and the site was abandoned in the mid-1990s for redevelopment, and the construction of new flood defences.

The U-boat building industry has left an interesting legacy in the corner of the Vulkanhafen in the form of a small fitting-out shelter. Three firms went bankrupt during the process of demolishing it, but the mass of concrete withstood all efforts to level it to the ground. Although a large part of the roof has been brought down, part of the centre support and the west wall have stood firm. The other, larger U-boat shelter in Hamburg was successfully destroyed with left-over stocks of old Luftwaffe bombs, but the army of occupation had run out of such vast quantities of explosives by the time it turned its attention to the smaller Elbe II bunker. In any case, surrounding buildings there would have been damaged had such a huge detonation taken place inside it. The remains of the bunker still stand, dominating the corner of the Europakai.

During the last days of the war, U-boats inside the western basin of the bunker were scuttled just a short while before the British Army arrived, and they are still lying there to this day and until recently they surfaced at every low tide. This somewhat unusual survival was largely due to the site having been inside the free port, which meant it was necessary to pass through customs to reach the area. In addition to this, the ruins were well hidden inside the shipyard's security area. This was so strict that visitors to the site had to leave identity cards or passports with the security staff at the main gate. Now, unfortunately, there is much easier access and the authorities have covered the submarines with sand to keep out the curious.

The sad point about this story is that these boats survived as late as the mid-1960s and it was a demolition firm's desperate attempt at fending off bankruptcy which resulted in two conning towers being removed. These were made from an expensive non-magnetic phosphor-bronze alloy. The engines were also salvaged, but the front sections of the two westerly boats and the entire hull of the third submarine remained intact. The snag was that the concrete roof was partly squashing the third boat. The boats have been identified as: *U3506*, lying virtually intact, although rather squashed by the roof, while the other two boats are *U3004* and *U2505*; all of them are large electro-boats of Type XXI. It seems a pity that these survivors of an incredible technology should be hidden away rather than serve as reminders of almost unbelievable innovation.

It could well be that a multitude of other relics are also still lying in the mud at the bottom of the dock basin. A Royal Navy report, compiled a few weeks after the end of the war, catalogues an abundance of gear all around the area, from large pieces such as engines and periscopes to smaller crates of supplies. Since virtually nothing was found close to the edge, one could assume that everything there was tossed into the water before the British forces arrived. During the early 1990s there were still a large number of cumbersome relics. Concrete blocks to protect the outside of basement windows from bomb blasts were used as road markers. (These are about 40 cm square in cross section and a metre or so long.) There was also quite a collection of portable armoured sentry boxes made of steel and concrete with tiny observation slits. One of the office blocks quite clearly has a wartime concrete extension and there is a circular personnel bunker with each door leading directly up to a different level. It was also quite amusing to spot a modern portable cabin being supported with what looked like an old anchor intended for a U-boat and no doubt anyone combing the area thoroughly will be rewarded with more evidence of an explosive history.

U-boat slipways belonging to the Stülkenwerft lie to the east of the old Elbe tunnel, just across the canal by the side of the southern entrance. Much of the machinery was demolished and removed while the buildings lay derelict for a considerable time. In the late 1980s further demolition took place with a view to redeveloping the land for use as a massive shopping centre, but the scheme seems to have foundered. The Stülkenwerft is of special interest because it specialised in the building of small ships and fishing boats, and in 1935 developed the highly successful minesweeper of Type 35, a design which was later copied by several other firms.

Deutsche Werft in Finkenwerder, which should not be confused with Deutsche Werke of Kiel, suffered considerably from bombing, from deliberate postwar destruction and later, in the early 1960s, it became one of the first victims of economic collapse. The U-boat bunker there, named Fink 2, was destroyed by detonating thousands of tons of old Luftwaffe bombs inside it. The remains were then levelled with the shoreline and tons of sand dumped on top. Since the postwar collapse of the shipyard, many installations have been demolished and much of the land has reverted to nature. Yet a few buildings remain and derelict railway lines with imposing but rusting gates point to the spot where the concrete U-boat bunker used to stand. Anyone visiting this site might like to acquire a wartime map because the filling-in of some dock basins has given rise to a different shore line to the one which can be seen in old wartime photos.

After the war numerous ship and U-boat wrecks from the Hamburg dock basins were cleared and dumped to the west of Finkenwerder, in an area where the Northern Elbe used to meet the Old Southern Elbe. The river there, just a trifle under 3 km wide, was dominated by a number of shallows with massive firm sandbanks exposed at low tide. During the early 1960s, a storm accompanied

Hamburg with the high Köhlbrand suspension bridge in the background, during the late 1980s. The quay on the right, where the floating crane has been made fast, was then occupied by Harms Ships Salvage and the area to the left was still occupied by HDW's ship repair yard. The ruins with crooked roof in the middle are the remains of Elbe II U-boat bunker. Inside it are still three Type XXI U-boats, which could be seen at low tide. Apparently these have now been covered with sand.

with rare tidal conditions resulted in the entire docks and the lower parts of the city being flooded. As a result the Finkenwerder water defences were strengthened and the river courses changed to prevent such a build-up of water in this area. This western tributary of the Southern Elbe has now been blocked off to become the Old Elbe and the currents have been diverted to flow under the huge suspension bridge in the port. It could well be that these changes have covered the wrecks, or the majority might have been salvaged at low tide to feed the ever-hungry blast furnaces in Hamburg long before the flooding disaster struck. The remains were visible at low tide until the late 1950s, but now there is no trace of them.

Like Hamburg, ship construction in Kiel was carried out exclusively on one side of the water, allowing sightseers easy access to the other shore for watching the hive of activity. Ferryboats will take passengers even closer. Despite the wartime bombing and although much of the production has been drastically changed in recent years, there are a large number of recognisable and rewarding relics still to be seen.

The furthest inland yard, now occupied by HDW, was the site of the famous Krupp Germania Works. Before the war, the slipways there were covered by a massive, four-gabled glasshouse. Most of the windows were blown out by bombing, but the huge lettering of 'Krupp' remained defiantly dominating the rusting wreckage. Krupp, the steel giant, which should not be confused with the electrical firm of Krupps, took over the Germania Works long before the beginning of the war. The glasshouses with their fittings were demolished, but the slips remained hidden until quite recently under a mixture of industrial dereliction, untidy heaps of scrap metal, and a tangle of wild plants. Today they have been covered with a modern ferry terminal. The shipbuilding parts of this site are still home to high technology, employing an army of steady handed Turkish workers for welding the most complicated secrets behind strategically placed screens. Since before the war, this area has been the hub of the U-boat industry, having been responsible for numerous innovations. The fact that this expertise is still being applied to modern submarines can easily be seen from across the water. Howaldtswerke took over the Krupp Yard after the Second World War and this, in turn, was recently amalgamated with Deutsche Werft to become HDW.

The area adjacent to the present-day HDW is now occupied by the Naval Arsenal. Part of this land was created by filling in old dock basins and burying several sunken ships, including the pocket battleship *Admiral Scheer*. A couple of kilometres northwards one cannot miss a tangle of concrete by the water's edge. These last remains of the old Kiel submarine bunker also mark the site of the wartime Howaldtswerke, where numerous U-boats were built. In fact, this is the site where Germany's first submarine, the *Brandtaucher* was pulled into the water in 1850, at an iron foundry belonging to Schweffel and Howaldt. The works there also hold the record for having cast the first large German ship propeller before the turn of the century, and it was the first German yard to build a salvage vessel with turbo-electric propulsion. The entire shipyard was sold to the Kriegsmarine just before the beginning of the war, but the subsequent management was not as efficient as the civil administration had been and three years later

naval authorities were pleased when it was taken over by Howaldtswerke of Hamburg.

Not long ago divers found a U-boat in reasonable condition entombed under the rubble of the submarine bunker and the subsequent hunt for information made people think the town council might be interested in considering a salvage operation. However, it transpired that the officials' curiosity focused on whether or not there was any ammunition on board. It appears that had there been, then the Federal German government would have been obliged to pay for the removal of the eyesore, but without explosives presenting a danger, the expensive clearing of the ruins would have to be paid for by the city council. The high cost of such an undertaking has ensured that the ruins will remain a semi-permanent feature of the Kiel waterline for some time to come.

The U-boat inside the ruins appears to be *U4708* (Oblt.z.S. Dietrich Schultz), a small coastal electro-boat of Type XXIII, which was sunk during an air raid on Kiel when a series of large bombs exploding in the water on the far shore caused a series of waves to wash through the open hatches.

Anyone viewing these ruins from the Kiel side of the water will probably also notice a number of cube-like concrete blocks by the western shore. The fact that these were the foundations for the famous Blücherbrücke is not hard to discover because the modern pier still displays this old name, although it is no longer the home pier for the sail training vessel *Gorch Fock*, which has been pushed further away into the naval dockyard.

Also located in Kiel was the Deutsche Werke, which was founded in the mid-1920s by combining the Reichsmarinewerft with the Kiel Torpedo Works. After the First World War the facility was down-graded by the Allies to a mere repair base, but the old expertise was quickly re-established to build a chain of large warships, including battleship

Gneisenau, heavy cruiser *Blücher* and pocket battleship *Deutschland*.

The dockyard in Wilhelmshaven was the only naval building yard to be allowed its full facilities after the First World War, although the Allies tried rendering it inoperative by confiscating much of the modern machinery. Known originally as the Kaiserlichewerft, then Reichsmarinewerft and later as Kriegsmarinewerft, this concern witnessed the consumption of an incredible amount of steel for warship construction. Battleships *Tirpitz* and *Scharnhorst*, pocket battleships *Admiral Scheer* and *Admiral Graf Spee*, light cruisers *Emden*, *Königsberg*, *Köln*, *Leipzig* and numerous smaller ships were built there.

The biggest German construction yard, Deschimag AG Weser, from Deutsche Schiff und Maschinenbau Aktiengesellschaft, was located on the banks of the River Weser between Bremen and Bremerhaven. Shortly after the First World War it constructed some most innovative ships, including the artillery training vessel and minelayer *Brummer*, with its set of prototype engines planned for installation in destroyers. Later the yard became a hub for submarine construction and just before the end of the Second World War almost 400 midget submarines of Type *Molch* were built there. A costly administrative mistake during the immediate post-First World War period could well have cost the firm a number of larger contracts, although Deschimag did build the heavy cruisers *Lützow* and *Seydlitz*. (This *Lützow* should not be confused with the renamed pocket battleship *Deutschland*. The cruiser built by Deschimag was sold to Russia for completion there. The other cruiser was converted into an aircraft carrier, but never made operational.) Deschimag's administrative problems came about as a result of its ambitions to become the most influential construction firm in Germany. A large number of older and less efficient yards were purchased shortly before orders dwindled during the 1920s. The economic collapse then left the firm with no alternative other than to scrap many of the facilities it had just acquired. At the height of its production in 1941, Deschimag AG Weser employed over 17,000 people with about 1,000 employees being located at the U-boat repair base in Brest on the French coast.

Deschimag was a major centre for assembling the large electro-boats of Type XXI. The sections for these were built in a variety of inland locations and then transported on pontoons for assembly at a major riverside location. Since this final stage was rather vulnerable, in 1943 it was decided to place the entire process under concrete. The large bunker Valentin, on the banks of the Weser near Farge, was big enough to accommodate the entire assembly line for this new generation of U-boats. The idea was that the sections could be brought in through thick steel doors on one side, and completed boats dispatched through a lock on the other.

Light cruiser *Köln*'s artillery in action.

Part of the engine control room aboard the light cruiser *Köln*.

Although this massive bunker was never completed, it seemed to have posed a considerable threat. The British Army was already within a short distance of Bremen when the House of Commons in London was told that this incomplete site could soon pose a major threat for convoys in the Atlantic and an intensive bombing raid was recommended. Consequently the Royal Air Force was given the go-ahead for a major offensive with newly developed, heavy bombs. These appear not to have inflicted too much damage on the concrete structure, although many of the U-boats on Deschimag's slipways and the yard's infrastructure and workshops were destroyed beyond repair.

The efficiently run Seebeck Werft was taken over by Deschimag AG Weser after the death of the founder, Dietrich Georg Seebeck. This smallish yard at Geestemünde in Bremerhaven was of special interest to the bigger giant because many of the tools and processes developed there were incredibly modern and organised along the most efficient production lines. Seebeck had started by building fishing boats and then went on to produce minesweepers for the Imperial Navy. The post-First World War boom then induced the management to enlarge facilities for the construction of larger merchant ships. These facilities were employed first for repairing U-boats, and

The U-boat bunkers in Bordeaux under construction. Although propaganda often states that these monstrosities were put up by slave labour, many of the workers were Spaniards and the prisoners of war who worked on the sites were also volunteers enjoying better living conditions than many of their counterparts in other camps.

later about six Type IXC and IXC42 boats were built from scratch each year.

The River Weser was also the home of Bremer Vulkan in Vegesack, which could easily be confused with the Vulcanwerke in Stettin. Facilities in Stettin and other yards in the eastern Baltic found themselves in a deplorable state after the First World War and the Depression of the 1920s was made even worse by the vast agricultural hinterland, which could not deliver the industrial support which kept the River Weser alive. Schichau Works in Elbing, Danzig and Königsberg virtually ceased to exist and it was only an intervention by the state and city authorities which kept the facilities alive to cope with future orders. This state of deep depression was short-lived because the area became a prime target for National Socialists' rejuvenation schemes, and by 1938 the three yards employed well over 10,000 people. Immediately after the beginning of the war, these facilities were tapped to supply the increasing demand for U-boats. They also provided repair facilities and built engines and other essentials for other firms. At the same time many smaller yards along the Baltic were drawn into war production and even factories such as the engineering works of Klöcker in Ulm, located far away from the coasts, was pulled into the submarine production sphere.

One of the new large electro-boats of Type XXI in Danzig towards the end of the war. It was planned that these should replace Type VII as the mainstay in the Battle of the Atlantic, but only a handful were ready by the time the war started.

Type XXIII, a small electro-boat, towards the end of the war. The inside was so cramped that torpedoes had to be loaded into the tubes from the outside and there was no room to carry spares.

MAJOR NAVAL MEMORIALS

There are three major naval memorials in Germany: the Naval Memorial at Laboe, the U-boat Memorial at Möltenort, both near Kiel, and the U-boat Archive in Cuxhaven. The first two are conventional types of memorials, although there is also a small, but fascinating museum display at Laboe. The U-boat Archive contains filed information, museum-type displays, a photo library and film archive, and is by far the biggest and most significant collection of U-boat information.

The proposal to build a naval memorial was voiced shortly after the First World War by Wilhelm Lammertz, a petty officer in the Imperial Navy, who felt that some place of remembrance was required for his dead colleagues. He was thinking about a focal point where people could meet and exchange ideas about facing the future, rather than creating a centre for joint mourning. Although this suggestion received favourable support from a wide spectrum of interest, the economic depression at the time meant there was no way that anyone could expect contributions from the Navy or from the taxpayer. Yet, the idea had hardly circulated when Franz Heinrich added to the proposal by suggesting that such a place could be built on a lonely spit of land overlooking the Baltic, close to where he lived in Laboe (Kiel). Lammertz, however, preferred Wilhelmshaven because that was the traditional home of the

The Naval Memorial in August 1935, just a few months after Hitler had made his famous military proclamation to repudiate the Diktat of Versailles and reintroduce national conscription.

The Naval Memorial in April 1998.

old Imperial Navy. Many other locations were also put forward, but the ruins of a demolished gun turret at Laboe were chosen, because the site was donated free of charge by the town council. The other advantages were that Laboe was easier to reach than places on the North Sea coast and the Kiel Canal was not too far away, meaning a good number of ships would pass it each day.

Following the decision to take the project one stage further, a number of eminent architects were asked to provide some basic designs during the autumn of 1926. The winner of this small informal competition, Gustav Munzer, had visited the ruined gun battery shortly after Christmas and came up with the simple design which stands there today. The organisers' stipulation had been that the memorial should serve as a focal point overlooking the sea and that it should be able to accommodate a large number of people. Munzer met these requirements by making a tall tower the dominating attraction. This was to give visitors an opportunity of seeing the sea as it appeared from a ship and, at the same time, to serve as a distinct landmark for passing sailors. The all-round view was emphasised with a circular assembly area at its base. Since there was already a large hole where the gun battery had been, the solemn commemoration hall was placed underground and an open space created on top of its roof. Later a third phase, the historic hall, was added on the opposite side of the circle to the tower.

Although it was known that the project had received favourable support, the organisers found themselves overwhelmed by the amount of popular interest. Over 5,000 people turned up on 8 August 1927 for the laying of the foundation stone by Admiral Reinhard Scheer. Special trains had to be laid on, ferries ran continuously from Kiel to Laboe and everybody present was rewarded with a splendid sunny summer's day. This enthusiastic support made it possible to start building the first phase, the 85 m high tower,

in June 1929. This in itself was no easy matter, because drilling was necessary to see whether the sandy ground could support such a tall building. The construction technique was also quite revolutionary inasmuch as the tower was cast from concrete with the lower part being pumped into place by a newly invented cement pump. Following this, the drab grey colour was hidden behind a cladding of red bricks and natural stones.

One interesting point about this column is that it later helped in the design of conning towers for submarines. This came about because the top of the tower lies in a wind-free eddy, even during gales when there is a strong wind on the lower platform. A young submarine designer, Christoph Aschmoneit, capitalised on this phenomenon by incorporating the responsible features onto submarines, and this gave rise to the two deflectors seen on the outside of World War Two conning towers.

The Naval Memorial complex was officially inaugurated on 30 May 1936. Although Hitler attended, he did not make a speech, but he did lay the first wreath in the Hall of Commemoration. Following this emotional beginning, the naval memorial survived the war with hardly any damage by enemy action, although much was destroyed by angry Germans just before the collapse of the Third Reich and later some items of value were apparently looted by British forces, who also proposed the demolition of the memorial. These reverberations of hate and revenge resounded as far as the House of Lords in London, who considered the proposal somewhat preposterous. In the end, sense prevailed and the Naval Memorial was closed to visitors instead of being totally destroyed.

On 30 May 1954, it was officially handed back to the German Naval Federation (Deutscher Marinebund), which is now responsible for its upkeep. It was received by the Naval Federation's President, Otto Kretschmer (the Second World War U-boat

In Germany it is customary on wreaths to attach ribbons with personal messages. These ribbons are on display at the Naval Memorial at Laboe (Kiel). The fourth from the left is from the East Prussian Ladies Group and the one next to it states, '1000 ships came. 33082 died. 2401367 survivors thank the biggest rescue operation in marine history.' These poignant reminders not only indicate that the two world wars were the worst episodes of European history but also warn the next generations of what could happen if they follow the same paths as their predecessors.

ace) and Hellmuth Heye (ex-Commander-in-Chief of the Midget Weapons Unit). Both of them made the strong point of saying, 'From now on this unique naval memorial is going to be dedicated to all people who lost their lives at sea – including the lives of our earlier adversaries.' The thoughts behind this wording were probably lost on many who attended and it might be of interest to emphasise that during the war the majority of U-boat men considered the other side to have been their adversaries or opponents, but not their enemies.

No doubt today many visitors make the effort of going to the Naval Memorial for the magnificent views from the top of the tower, but it is difficult not be caught up in the solemn atmosphere of remembrance created in the underground hall. Walking quietly through the dimly-lit room, one can brush shoulders with the famous whose names appear so frequently in history books. Those who have the time to relax can feel a multitude of emotions from Europe's horrific and totally unnecessary turbulent past. On emerging at the far side of the room, it is easy to realise how badly the famous national leaders had served their people. The Duke of Wellington was correct when he said that the most miserable

War losses have been engraved in a grey concrete wall at the Naval Memorial and painted black, as can be seen by this small section showing some of those lost in heavy cruisers.

The U-boat Memorial at Möltenort (Kiel) as seen from the water. The large bronze plates with names of the dead are sunk below ground level and much of the memorial can only be seen by entering the complex.

experience is losing a battle and the second most miserable experience is winning one.

Since 1954, there have been a number of modifications to the Naval Memorial. One of *Prinz Eugen*'s propellers lies near the entrance and as a result of this there is also a memorial for American sailors. Since official approval was difficult at the time, the propeller from *Prinz Eugen* was 'mysteriously' lifted and deposited on a quay near the Panama Canal where it was collected by a merchant ship and delivered to the Naval Arsenal in Kiel. From there it had to be moved at the dead of night because the low-loader carrying it would not fit underneath the electric cables for the trams. These had to be switched off and propped up with poles while the lorry transported the bronze coloured blades to their present resting place.

U995 has also been set up as a technical museum close to the base of the Naval Memorial's tower. After the war, the boat was commissioned in the Royal Norwegian Navy as *Kaura* and returned to Kiel when its practical life came to an end. After restoration, a channel was dredged from the Baltic, allowing two massive floating cranes access to the beach close to the road, where the submarine has been laid on concrete foundations. Although the interior has the feel of a real U-boat, many of the fittings are modern because the originals have been stolen since the museum was opened. It was thought that the dredged channel would quickly silt up again, but the experts were wrong and it has remained open, providing a pool of calm water for a small paddle-boat hire business.

The U-boat Memorial at Möltenort lies some 4 km (2.5 miles) inland from the Naval Memorial and can also be reached by passenger ferry from Kiel. These boats travel from the railway station quay past the Naval Arsenal, the Naval Dockyard and Holtenau to Möltenort, Laboe and then on as far as the Olympia Marina at Schilksee. The U-boat Memorial had originally also been a gun battery for an old muzzle-loader guarding a narrow section in the approaches to Kiel harbour. Much of the memorial has been constructed of red brick and the names of U-boat men lost during both wars are recorded on bronze plaques attached to the walls. When the peace is not disturbed by screaming children or by graffiti of the ignorant, the memorial stands guard over a unique atmosphere of silence and reverence, and it has formed a focal point for many U-boat reunions. Both here and in the Naval Memorial one will usually find an abundance of wreaths from and for the famous.

THE U-BOAT ARCHIVE

Being shot up at sea meant that Lt.z.S. Horst Bredow was admitted to hospital while his boat, *U288* under OL Willi Meyer, sailed without him. Just a few days later an aircraft attacked. There were no survivors. Shattered by fortune, Horst Bredow made it his duty to find out what had happened and then circulate the details to the next of kin of his dead comrades. This led to him being asked for news about someone else who had gone missing in a submarine. Collecting information during those turbulent postwar days was no easy matter because most of the German documents had been captured by the Allies and classified as secret. Obtaining even the simplest of facts was difficult. Researchers had to rely on people's memories or on a few scanty papers in private hands. As late as the 1970s, Britain continued with its determined efforts to suppress information about the war. While things had improved in the United States, people in England were prevented from gaining access to documents which were freely available in America. In this atmosphere of severe restrictions, Horst Bredow continued collecting information as a hobby for those who approached him for help. Slowly his efforts started snowballing.

During the early 1980s a unique opportunity presented itself to prevent Horst's collection

The U-boat Archive shortly after moving into this house in Altenbruch near Cuxhaven.

A display case in the U-boat Archive before it moved to Cuxhaven. In the middle is the naval ensign of the Third Reich and a U-boat 'tonnage sunk' pennant with the number '8000' at the bottom. The box on the shelf towards the right is an Enigma code writer.

from taking over his entire flat in Berlin. The heating system at the Naval Air School on the Island of Sylt was modernised to run automatically on oil, making the offices and living rooms of the heating engineer obsolete! Horst, who already had a small holiday flat on the island, was able to move his papers and give them more space. At the same time there was enough room for accommodating the occasional visitor. Although it was located in a restricted military area, far away from the rest of Germany, it was not long before ex-U-boat men and researchers trod a path to Germany's most northerly Friesian island. At the same time the archive grew until every available space was filled with something of interest. And this is not an exaggeration! People who knew the old Sylt Archive will know that every nook and cranny was filled with something.

The day came when a routine fire check concluded it was rather dangerous to have such a mass of paper stacked in the offices above huge boilers, and Horst was encouraged to look around for alternative accommodation. Surprisingly this was quickly found and, after a colossal effort, a fleet of lorries carried the archive to Cuxhaven, where the town council put a twenty-eight-roomed house at Horst's disposal and free of rent. The incredible point about this massive U-boat archive is that it has been created by one man supported by a small number of part-time volunteers. Anyone tempted to ask the question 'what is in the archive', should rephrase the request and ask 'what's missing'. It is the only place where I have always found answers to *all* my questions. The most significant thing missing is money! It is still run by Horst Bredow and supplemented with his pension, and he copes with well over 3,000 enquiries each year. This means answering hundreds of letters each week, in addition to dealing with the mass of new material flooding in.

For much of the year the archive is open for a few days each week to casual callers,

Horst and Annemie Bredow in the U-boat Archive before their move to Cuxhaven.

217

Horst Bredow, founder and director of U-Boot-Archiv in Cuxhaven. Behind him is the ensign of the old Imperial Navy. Although officially hauled down for the last time shortly after the First World War, it remained in use throughout the period of the Third Reich. A few ships were commissioned with it in preference to the ensign with swastika and this old flag flew officially to commemorate a number of First World War events, such as the Battle of Jutland. The jack in the top left hand corner was coloured black at the top, white and red at the bottom. The large cross was black on a white background.

many viewing hours for an individual to comprehend or look at. What is more there are facilities for examining a vast variety of different film formats. In 1990, the main library consisted of well over 50,000 published books and there must now be something in the region of 150,000 photographs. Virtually every U-boat log from the Second World War is there, as well as thick and comprehensive files on every German U-boat from *U1* in 1906 to the present day. All this is supported by a wealth of additional material such as letters, certificates, documents and other artefacts.

Unlike many archives, Horst Bredow actually allows visiting researchers access to everything in his care – but they will find only photocopies. This way, there is nothing valuable to steal and anyone who wants the information can press the button on the photocopier. It is rather sad that many items from museums' reserve collections have been decimated by researchers stealing items. Horst's approach makes a visit exceptionally interesting because nothing is hidden away. The archive really does make history come alive. Another reason for filling the accessible part of the archive with copies is that much of the material was borrowed, processed and then returned to the owners. That is not say the archive contains only copies. There is also a mass of guaranteed original relics safely locked away in display cases. In recent years this museum collection has become an ever increasing part of the Archive and has now resulted in the building of an extension.

The U-boat Archive is certainly an incredible place. Professor Michael Hadley, the prominent Canadian historian, said that any work about the war at sea which does not acknowledge the U-boat Archive is not worth considering. The place is certainly unique. Anyone wanting information should consider joining the FTU (Friends of Traditionsarchiv Unterseeboote), U-Boot-Archiv, Bahnhofstrasse 57, D-27478 Cuxhaven-Altenbruch. Please enclose some international postal reply coupons when writing.

except during the cold winter months when it is totally shut for everyone. However, anyone wishing to undertake serious research is best advised to make an appointment and to have plenty of time. The ground floor rooms contain a museum display of relics. There is a media room with too many films and too

THE SUPREME NAVAL COMMAND

Just a few months before the turn of the century, the Emperor (Kaiser Wilhelm II) appointed himself to the position of Supreme Commander-in-Chief of the Navy and thereby took ultimate control of the Admiralstab (Admiralty). Although this presented numerous administrative problems during the First World War, it was not until just a few months before the end that Admiral Reinhard Scheer succeeded in creating an autonomous Naval Command Office to be responsible for planning and conducting the war on the high seas. However, it looked as if

his plans would not last long. Just a few months later the Navy battled for its very survival to prevent ships from passing into Army control. The two admirals, Maximilian Rogge and Ernst Ritter von Mann und Edler Herr von Tiechler, maintained a grip on the reins of leadership until early in 1919 when Admiral Adolf von Trotha was appointed to head the small surviving core through the political chaos. Unfortunately this strong cornerstone of support for the Navy was unseated as a result of riots and Admiral William Michaelis took his place while things settled

Adolf Hitler followed by General Admiral Dr h.c. Erich Raeder, the Supreme Commander-in-Chief of the Navy, at the funeral of the victims from the air raid on *Deutschland* during the Spanish Civil War.

The number plate indicates that this car belongs to the navy: W for Wehrmacht (Armed Forces) and M stood for Marine. The Luftwaffe used the letter L and the Army H for Heer. The symbol painted on the mudguard is a command flag, indicating that the car is being used by an admiral. There are two admirals in the background with the tops of their coats open to reveal cornflower-blue lapels. Other ranks usually wore their coats buttoned right up to the neck. Note the officer with the 'Monkey's Swing' which indicates that he is an adjutant.

down. Then, towards the end of 1920, Admiral Paul Behncke became Supreme Commander-in-Chief for a stabilising period of four years. Although the Navy was not totally disbanded, the idea of re-creating an autonomous naval command for planning and conducting battles on the high seas did not materialise again until ten years later when the name *Seekriegsleitung* – SKL (Naval Command Office or Naval War Staff) resurfaced. The concept was then further developed by Admiral Erich Raeder, who decreed that the SKL should become responsible for the planning of naval warfare on the high seas. At the same time operational control of ships in coastal waters passed to two so-called 'Group Commands', one for the Baltic and the other for the North Sea. Later, during the war, the Group Commands were enlarged to include coastal waters of occupied countries, while the U-boat Command was added to take charge of all submarine operations.

In 1922, the German Navy was made up of the following two commands:

Baltic Command
Battleship *Hannover*, small cruisers *Medusa* and *Thetis*, the 1st Torpedo Boat Flotilla of eleven boats, and two tenders.

North Sea Command
Battleship *Braunschweig*, small cruisers *Hamburg* and *Arcona*, the 2nd Torpedo Boat Flotilla of seven boats, and two tenders.
Set aside for officer training: Small cruiser *Berlin* and sail training ship *Niobe*.
Also available, but temporarily out of commission were: *Schlesien*, *Schleswig-Holstein*, *Lothringen*, *Preussen*, *Nymphe* and not more than half a dozen torpedo boats.

THE NEW KRIEGSMARINE AFTER 1935

Although Hitler held the position of Supreme Commander-in-Chief of all the armed forces,

Admiral Karl Dönitz, the U-boat Chief and later Grand Admiral.

he very rarely interfered directly with naval operations. However, after the war the holding of this rank did result in him being blamed for unpalatable decisions made by other commanders. What is more, the power one would expect to be accompanied by such a grand standing was frequently missing and the projected image of Hitler as a dictator and ultimate Commander-in-Chief is somewhat misleading. The ramifications within the lower command chains meant that many of his wishes were frustrated by officials entrenched in powerful, closed-shop empires they themselves had created.

On 7 September 1939, four days after the British and French declaration of war, the exchange of information between Hitler and the Supreme Commander-in-Chief of the Navy took on a formal nature in the form of a conference. Minutes of these meetings were hardly ever taken, but shortly after each discussion both Raeder and Dönitz wrote down the main points. These have been preserved in the book *Fuehrer Conferences on Naval Affairs* recently published by Greenhill Books. Hitler's

The first page of the Navy's rank list showing the old version of the naval eagle, the emblem used before 1935.

The *Rangliste* with the eagle of the NSDAP, the emblem used from 1935–45.

main directives have been released by Professor H.R. Trevor-Roper with the title *Hitler's War Directives* (see Bibliography). Although these give an insight into the upper echelons of the naval command they hardly illustrate Hitler's incredible ability of amassing vast quantities of technical data. He carried details about the performance of major battleships in his head and often stunned experts during conversations by casually throwing out such vital information. Yet, this storehouse of facts lacked the ability of coordinating and analysing the affects such technology might have on the outcome of planned events. This was a field where Grand Admiral Erich Raeder, the Supreme Commander-in-Chief of the Navy, won Hitler's early admiration. Not only did he often come up with several alternatives for possible solutions to problems, but he always presented his

arguments by discussing the far-reaching implications each course of action might bring.

Erich Raeder was quite an extraordinary character and he had made quite a remarkable start in the Navy. During his last year at school, his family assumed that he would follow his parents to university before embarking upon an academic career, possibly in medicine. It was already well after the closing day for the 1884 intake of naval officer cadets, when he suddenly asked his father to write to the Naval Command to ask for his son to join the Navy. In those days, youngsters were considered too irresponsible to make such an application themselves. Less than two months later a perplexed seventeen-year-old was being chased through the initial training course with a naval infantry unit, wishing he had chosen some less strenuous career. This was the worst period of Raeder's life. The glamour in his childhood adventure books hadn't mentioned the hard training. Not only did he hate the hard physical effort but also the coarse language and rough treatment from the non-commissioned officers who served as instructors. Had it not been for the strong sense of duty instilled in him by parents and school, young Raeder would have cheerfully walked away from that harsh training arena. A few weeks later, this crude environment changed dramatically and Raeder found himself confronted by instructors aboard a sail training ship who led their charges not by watching them run around the barrack block, but by leading the way up the mast with the words, '*try* and follow me.'

By the time First World War started, Raeder had already held a number of challenging positions which led him to becoming the Chief of Staff for the famous cruiser pundit, Admiral Franz Ritter von Hipper. By the time he succeeded Admiral Hans Zenker as Commander-in-Chief of the Navy in October 1928, his exceptionally broad experience of commanding at sea was supported by a solid academic understanding of what was required. Unfortunately much of this was based on the impractical powerful battleship concept, and his strong religious character frequently clashed with the coarseness and flamboyance of the people around Hitler. Although Raeder respected Hitler, he despised the vulgarity of the high commanders he met in the

Grand Admiral Dr h.c. Erich Raeder, Supreme Commander-in-Chief of the Navy visiting U-boat headquarters near Lorient. It seems highly likely that this was not Raeder's official car, but one borrowed in France, since the grand admiral's emblem with crossed batons is missing from the car. Note that the man with the leather coat in the background is wearing an adjutant's lanyard. This is Kpt.z.S. Kurt Freiwald who served as adjutant to both grand admirals.

Führerhauptquartier. Consequently he called there only on official business and left the gathering of vital information for the day-to-day running to other men.

The name most commonly associated with this difficult task is that of the ex-destroyer commander, Kpt.z.S. Karl-Jesko von Puttkammer, who was appointed Hitler's Naval Adjutant and remained in that position until the end of the Third Reich. Another name frequently mentioned in the history books is that of Theodor Krancke, the Permanent Representative of the Navy's Supreme Commander-in-Chief, at Hitler's Headquarters. He was in office during that critical period towards the end of 1942 when Hitler's furious rages over wanting to throw the surface fleet into the dustbin resulted in Grand Admiral Raeder's resignation and the appointment of the U-boat Chief, Karl Dönitz, as his successor.

Many history books tell us that when he was asked to name a successor, Raeder suggested Admiral Carls, or Dönitz, but very little is

Grand Admiral Karl Dönitz in his old age. He became highly frustrated at not being able to hear properly and had to rely on a hearing aid for the last years of his life. Yet, despite this handicap, he continued to make a considerable effort to support his old colleagues, as well as historians and researchers.

known about the robustly quiet character who was rejected by Hitler. Rolf Carls had joined the Navy in 1903, just seven years before Dönitz. He also had been a U-boat commander during the First World War and during the mid-1930s became Fleet Commander. From that position he went on to command the German forces off Spain during the civil war. Once the Second World War started he held several positions which were considered more important than a sea-going command. He was killed in action just two weeks before the end of the war.

In January 1943, the 51-year-old Karl Dönitz brought with him a fresh approach to the naval leadership. He was already well known for leading from the front and being with his men. The fact that this policy worked is demonstrated by the high efficiency of the small U-boat force at the beginning of the war. He had welded the submarines into such an efficient fighting unit that the Allies considered his efforts to have been criminal and established a new law under which he was convicted at the Nuremberg Trials. This stated that soldiers should not prepare men for a war of aggression. Being unable to define the exact meaning of this harsh jurisdiction, the laws appear to have been abolished again immediately after the trials because no other leaders have ever been tried under them.

In January 1943, when he was appointed to the highest post in the Navy, Dönitz considered it most important to keep a pulse on Hitler's Headquarters and for that reason delegated his routine duties in running the U-boat Operations Room to his long-established deputy, Kpt.z.S. Eberhard Godt. In a way it is strange that these two highly contrasting characters should have worked so well together. Dönitz always exploited drama and excitement to drive his partly ruthless ambitions, while Godt was always quiet and calm. Code words used during the U-boat war such as 'Strike Dead' or 'Robber Count' almost certainly originated when Dönitz was on duty while 'Violet' and 'Daffodil' were probably conceived by Godt.

Admiral Karl Dönitz, the U-boat Chief and later Supreme Commander-in-Chief of the Navy, is sitting in his car while the Flag Officer for U-boats in the West, Kpt.z.S. Hans or 'Harro' Rösing is standing behind him, wearing a leather coat. Note that the blurred image of an officer with adjutant's lanyard can be made out in the background and the rank (*Maat* – petty officer) of the man next to Rösing can be recognised by the collar patch on his jacket.

RANKS AND INSIGNIA

Seamen

Men who had just joined the Navy held the rank of *Matrose* or *Heizer* (Sailor or Stoker). The ranks following this were:

–Gefreiter	Able Seaman
–Obergefreiter	Leading Seaman

–Hauptgefreiter Leading Seaman after 4½ years service

The dash prefix should be replaced by the man's trade. Hence the full title would have been *Matrosen-Gefreiter*, *Maschinen-Obergefreiter*, etc. Usually these ranks were written as

Friedrich Kiemle, the author's godfather, wearing a jacket over his shirt. The stripes of the large Nelson collar can just be seen. The cornflower-blue patch on the collar indicates the rank of *Matrose* or seaman. Note that this photograph was taken before the introduction of the eagle and swastika.

The cornflower-blue collar patch has one golden bar to indicate the rank of *Maat* or petty officer. The national eagle with swastika was introduced in 1935.

one word, but that makes the titles rather long and more difficult for non-German readers. Later, during the war, a more senior version of each rank was introduced and identified by the prefix '*Stabs*', whence ranks like *Stabsgefreiter* appeared. At the same time, some older naval language remained in use throughout the Second World War and it was not uncommon for a *Matrose* to be referred to by his trade suffixing the word '*gast*' to give *Signalgast* or *Funkgast*.

Unteroffiziere ohne Portepee (Junior NCOs – Petty Officers) *

There were two ranks:

–maat	Petty Officer
Ober–maat	Chief Petty Officer

The dash should be replaced with the man's trade:

Bootsmannsmaat, Funkmaat, Maschinenmaat
Obersteuermannsmaat, Obermaschinenmaat

Unteroffiziere mit Portepee (Senior NCOs – Warrant Officers)*

Initially there were two ranks:

Bootsmann	Boatswain
Oberbootsmann	Chief Boatswain

During the war a more senior rank of *Stabsoberbootsmann* was added.

Again, the term *Bootsmann* applied only to seamen and the men's trades were used to give:

The two golden stripes on the blue collar patch show that Fritz Kiemle now holds the rank of *Obermaat* or Chief Petty Officer. The anchor with cogwheel is a combination trade and rank badge for petty officers and the chevron shows that this is a Chief Petty Officer. The trade of engineer is shown by the cog superimposed over the anchor. Low down on his left breast is the National Sports Badge, which could also be gained by civilians. It was difficult to get early promotion in the Navy without this award.

Maschinist	*Obermaschinist*	*Stabsobermaschinist*
Funkmeister	*Oberfunkmeister*	*Stabsoberfunkmeister*
Steuermann	*Obersteuermann*	*Stabsobersteuermann*
Signalmeister	*Obersignalmeister*	*Stabsobersignalmeister*
Sanitätsfeldwebel	*Sanitätsoberfeldwebel*	——
Feuerwerker	*Oberfeuerwerker*	——
Torpedomechaniker	*Obertorpedomechaniker*	*Stabsobertorpedomechaniker*

* The *Portepee* was a small lanyard or sword knot with an acorn shaped end worn around the handle of the sword or dagger. Gold in colour for commissioned officers and silver for warrant officers.

Erna and Fritz Kiemle, the author's godparents. This shows Fritz wearing the uniform of a warrant officer. Both trade and rank were indicated on the shoulder straps. On the left breast is the Fleet War Badge and the ribbon of the Iron Cross Second Class can be seen threaded through the top button hole. The complete medal was usually only worn on the day of issue or for formal functions.

M18's *Schmarting* or senior boatswain showing that a variety of official naval gear could be worn.

Officer Candidates

Matrose (*Offiziersanwärter*)	Seaman (Officer Candidate)
Kadett	Cadet/Midshipman
Fähnrich zur See	Senior Cadet/Midshipman
Oberfähnrich zur See	Sub-Lieutenant

Commissioned Officers

Commissioned officers were divided into the following groups:

(The column on the right indicates the number of sleeve rings: s = standard width, n = narrow width, b = broad width.)

Leutnant zur See	(LT)	Lieutenant (Junior) 1s
Oberleutnant zur See	(OL)	Lieutenant (Senior) 2s

The *Leutnant zur See* on the left has a 'piston ring' on the sleeve of his coat, which indicates that he is wearing the official frock coat, not a greatcoat. Judging by the men's expressions, they are participating in some light-hearted venture.

Kapitänleutnant	(KL)	Lieutenant Commander 2s, 1n	Commissioned officer ranks were suffixed with the following:
Korvettenkapitän	(KK)	Commander 3s	Sea/Deck Officer: Nothing
Fregattenkapitän	(FK)	Captain (Junior) 4s	Engineering Officer: (Ing) = *Ingenieur*
Kapitän zur See	(KS)	Captain (Senior) 4s	Administration Officer: (V) = *Verwaltungsoffizier*
Konteradmiral	(KA)	Rear Admiral 1b, 1s	Weapons Officer: (W) = *Waffenoffizier*
Vizeadmiral	(VA)	Vice Admiral 1b, 2s	
Admiral		Admiral 1b, 3s	The ranks for doctors were: (in the same order as above)
Generaladmiral		No comparative British/US Rank (see below)*	*Marineassisstenarzt*: Equivalent to LT
			Marineoberassistenarzt: Equivalent to OL
Grossadmiral		Grand Admiral/Admiral of the Fleet 1b, 4s	*Marinestabarzt*: Equivalent to KL
			Marineoberstabarzt: Equivalent to KK
			Geschwaderarzt: Equivalent to FK
Kommodore		Commodore (a Kpt.z.S. in an admiral's position.)	*Flottenarzt*: Equivalent to KS
			Admiralarzt: Equivalent to KA
			Admiralstabarzt: Equivalent to VA

* When Raeder held this rank as Supreme Commander-in-Chief of the Navy he wore one broad and four standard rings. Later, other people with this rank wore the wide stripe with three standard rings.

The rank of *Generaladmiral* was introduced in 1936 as an equivalent to *Generaloberst* (Colonel General), which was then the highest rank in the Army, because the Commander-in-Chief of the Navy (Dr Erich Raeder) did not wish to have a higher position than his Army counterpart. At that time the Navy was not big enough to warrant a higher rank.

RANK BADGES

Seamen

Seamen's rank badges consisted of chevrons worn on the left sleeve. A trade badge was worn immediately above the chevron, giving the impression that it formed part of the rank insignia. The chevrons, all gold in colour, varied throughout the ten years of the Third Reich, but generally a *Gefreiter* wore a single plain chevron, an *Obergefreiter* a double chevron and a *Hautpgefreiter* a triple chevron. Later *Stabsgefreiter* and *Stabsobergefreiter* wore chevrons made from platted gold strips rather than plain gold braid and there was a pip inside the 'V' to make it look more elaborate. In addition to this, plain cornflower blue collar patches on pea jackets indicated the rank of seamen.

Unteroffiziere ohne Portepee

The rank of Petty and Chief Petty Officer was indicated by an oval badge, worn on the left sleeve. The basic design for *Bootsmannsmaat* (Petty Officer of the Seamen Trade) consisted of a plain anchor, but for every other profession a trade badge was superimposed on the top. *Obermaate* were distinguished by also having a chevron underneath the anchor. In addition to this, the cornflower blue patch on the collar of the pea jacket had a single gold stripe for Petty Officers and two stripes for Chief Petty Officers. Before the war these patches were attached to plain collars, but towards the end of 1939 a gold braid was added to the outside edge to make the jacket more elaborate.

Obermaat Padsun who later joined the U-boat Arm. The pea jacket with the gold braid around the outside of the collar is of the later, more elaborate variety for petty officers. The ribbon of the Iron Cross can be seen through the top buttonhole and on the left breast are the Fleet War Badge and the National Sports Badge. The oval badge with anchor and cogwheel is a combination rank and trade badge for *Maschinenmaat*. Below is an Electro-machinist special qualification. The fact that he held this qualification for more than three years is indicated by the chevrons.

Maschinen-obergefreiter Richard Klie of *U379* who was killed on 9 August 1942. A marksman's lanyard can be seen on his right shoulder. The acorn at the end indicates that proficiency had been achieved with a rifle. On the left breast are the U-boat Badge and below it the National Sports Badge.

Unteroffiziere mit Portepee

Warrant officers were identified by gold-coloured shoulder straps with a set of aluminium pips to denote rank and an additional emblem to indicate the man's trade. They also wore plain peaked caps instead of the traditional sailor's hats.

Commissioned Officers

In addition to the rings on their sleeves, commissioned officer ranks could be identified by their shoulder straps while their rank group was indicated by gold braid on the peaks of their caps. A scalloped edge for ranks up to *Kapitänleutnant*, a single row of oakleaves for *Korvettenkapitän* to *Kapitän zur See* and a double row of oakleaves for admirals.

The Main Trades

Bootsmann	Seaman/deck rating
Fernschreiber	Telex operator
Feuerwerker	Artificer
Funker	Radio operator
Kraftfahrer	Driver
Marineartillerist	Gunner
Maschinist	Machinist
Minenmechaniker	Mine mechanic
Musikmeister	Musician/bandsman
Sanitäter	Medical orderly
Schreiber	Yeoman/secretary
Signalmeister	Signalman
Steuermann	Navigator/helmsman
Torpedomechaniker	Torpedo mechanic
Verwaltung	Administrator
Zimmermann	Carpenter

Later a badge was added for men working with an admiral's staff and in 1944 the trade of radar mechanic was introduced.

TRADE BADGES

Seamen wore circular navy blue trade badges with an emblem in gold-coloured machine embroidery above their rank chevrons. Similar emblems were used for petty officers and chief petty officers, but here the emblem was superimposed over the anchor of the rank badge and the one badge served for two functions. Petty officer badges can be distinguished from seamen's because they were oval in shape. Warrant officers' trades were indicated on their shoulder straps and commissioned officers wore a small badge above the 'piston rings' on their sleeves.

SPECIAL QUALIFICATIONS

In addition to trade badges, there were also badges for special qualifications. These were machine embroidered with red thread on a navy blue background, oval in shape and also worn on the left sleeve. The badges covered the following special qualifications:

Light anti-aircraft gunner
Light anti-aircraft leader
Heavy anti-aircraft gunner
Gunner
Gunner with 3 years experience
Gunner with 6 years experience
Gunner specialising in shooting torpedoes
Gunner specialising in shooting torpedoes with 3 years experience
Gunner specialising in shooting torpedoes with 6 years experience
Gunner for coastal artillery
Range finder
Range finder for anti-aircraft guns
Diver
Torpedo diver
Mine foreman
Torpedo teacher
Torpedo control leader
Sports teacher
Electro mechanic in three grades
Engine mechanic in three grades

NAVAL WAR BADGES

A number of badges were re-created during the war years with the view that every man should

Steering the ship. Below the man's hands are buttons for controlling the electric motor which moves the rudder. In front of him is a speaking tube, a rudder position indicator and gyrocompass. The hood with porthole houses a magnetic compass. The chevron on the man's sleeve indicates his rank of *Matrosengefreiter* and the star shows that he is a seaman by trade.

A naval driver with rank and trade badge on the left sleeve. Note that he is also wearing a pistol, despite a number of books having stated that ordinary sailors did not carry such side arms.

Two naval artillery mechanics adjusting the sights of a 37-mm AA gun. The man on the right is a *Maat* or petty officer with a distinctive combined rank and trade badge on the left sleeve.

The *Steuermann*, which is often wrongly translated as helmsman, was responsible for navigation not for steering the ship. The two crossed anchors on the sleeve indicate that the man is a seaman by trade and *Maat* (Petty Officer) by rank. In the background is a sailor working the engine telegraph.

be eligible for some type of combat award. The majority of these were worn on the left breast below the Iron Cross First Class (if awarded), but as with so many things, the Navy seems to have incorporated a good many exceptions. In this case the Midget Weapons badges not only differed by being awarded in seven grades, but were also worn on the sleeve. As with other medals, the supply of possible rewards was exhausted long before the war ended and the naval administration was forced to come up with solutions to keep up morale. First, the officials considered easing the requirements for more prestigious awards, such as the Knight Cross, but finally a two-stage award system was introduced. To this end the U-boat Badge had a bronze-coloured clasp introduced and later a silver version was added. Similarly a naval clasp was also introduced in 1944.

Originally these badges were made from a good type of bronze, but later the quality deteriorated and some incredibly crude versions, looking almost like home-made reproductions, appeared towards the end of the war. The introduction of a cloth version was not so much for economic reasons, but because in certain situations men preferred something softer in the tender region of their

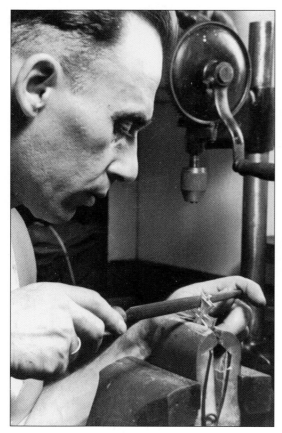 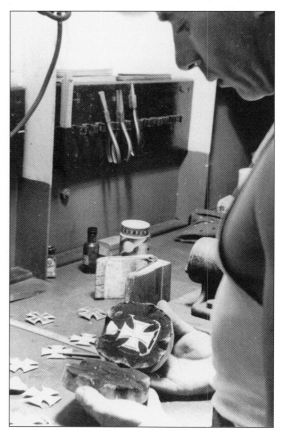

Both these photographs, taken aboard the auxiliary cruiser *Orion*, show stages in the production of iron crosses. Men sometimes received ship-made medals long before they were handed the official awards, and often valued the originals more than the factory produced items.

Part of the display in one of the rooms at the German U-boat Archive. The large rectangular emblems are reproductions of naval war badges. It is against the law to display swastikas in Germany, except for educational purposes, therefore the national emblem at the top has been replaced by a modern Iron Cross. The badges are: top left, Badge for Blockade Breakers; bottom left, Destroyers; centre, E-boats or S-boats; bottom right, Minesweepers; top right, the Fleet War Badge.

stomach, especially when having to frequently work in cramped conditions. In addition to the variable quality, there was also considerable diversity in the detail of the general appearance as well as size. This was largely due to an ever-increasing number manufacturers being used as suppliers. However, generally, those badges produced in foreign countries towards the end of the war were of better quality than the home-produced efforts.

As with the majority of other things, Germany kept tabs on the property it handed out to its servicemen, and being awarded any badge was recorded in his Pay Book. In addition to this, award certificates were often presented as additional documentation.

These varied from elaborate works of art to typing on poor war-quality paper, and this field has probably seen more convincing forgeries than the reproduction medal market. Some of these imitations have been good enough to deceive some highly respected authorities, sometimes making the collection of such items a real headache.

The majority of badges were oval in shape with the longest diameter lying vertically. The exceptions were the U-boat Badge, which was oval with the longest diameter lying horizontally, and the Blockade Breakers Badge which was round. The Midget Weapons Badges were also different and variable in shape, with a swordfish incorporated in the design. The somewhat rare Clasp for the Roll of Honour of the Navy was also round and consisted of a large swastika in front of a vertically standing anchor.

The oval war badges were designed as follows:
Fleet War Badge: a head-on view of a battleship.
Auxiliary Cruiser Badge: a Viking ship sailing over part of the globe.
Naval Artillery Badge: side view of a large gun.
Destroyer Badge: side view of a destroyer speeding through water.
Minesweeper and Submarine Hunters: a plume of water exploding upwards. This could, no doubt, be taken to be a detonating depth charge or mine.
Motor Torpedo Boat Badge: originally a side view of an earlier type of MTB speeding through water, but this was later replaced with a more modern-looking craft.
Air Sea Rescue Badge: a front-on view of a boat with smoking funnel and rigging on the mast. This usually had an Air Force eagle above the swastika on the top, whereas the other badges had a naval or national type of eagle.

The conditions for being awarded one of these badges varied considerably. For example a U-boat Badge could be gained after a couple of operational cruises or for being wounded during the first voyage. For the Destroyers Badge men had to have participated in three operations against the enemy or been wounded or taken part in twelve voyages. Generally war badges were also awarded for especially meritorious conduct and for some of the badges there are more detailed criteria.

UNIFORMS

The wearing of naval uniform was obligatory, even during free time when sailors went ashore. Each man carried a *Soldbuch* (Pay Book) which included a passport-type photograph and personal details, including a complete printed list of all the gear which could be issued. Items were ticked off and signed by the issuing authority. In 1935, following new defence laws, the Kriegsmarine published its first set of uniform regulations. These were officially modified in 1937 and the rules changed again throughout the war. One significant feature of these rules was that there were probably more exceptions to the rules than rules themselves, making any clear-cut statements about uniforms somewhat difficult. To list all of these exceptions now would probably produce a more complicated chapter than the original and the following should only be taken as a rough guide.

ITEMS OF CLOTHING

	Officers	*Non-officers*
1	Blue cap with peak	Blue cap without peak
2	White cap with peak	White cap without peak
3	Blue and white reefer jacket	Blue monkey jacket
4	Coat	Pea jacket
5	Blue trousers	Blue trousers
6	White trousers	White trousers
7	White shirt	Underpants
8	Stand-up collar	Vest
9	Black tie	
10	Scarf (white or blue)	Shirt collar
11	Woollen head protector	Silk scarf
12	Sidearm, dagger and sword	Woollen scarf
13	*Portepee* (sword knot)	Woollen head protector
14	Socks	
15	Frock coat (Jacket for cadets)	
16	Cloak – Spanier	Duffel bag
17	Ship's coat	Polish box
18	Mess jacket	Provisions bag
19	Boot bag	
20	Parade/brocade belt	Linen bag
21	Blue gloves	
22	White gloves	
23	Black lace-up boots	
24	Woollen vest	
25	Sport gear, vest, shorts, running shoes, swimming trunks	
26	Black leather gaiters	
27	Waterproofs	Waterproofs
28	Knee-length boots	Boots
29	Hat	
30	Epaulettes	
31	Dress trousers (usually only worn abroad or for one's own wedding)	
32	Gold-coloured buttons	Gold-coloured buttons
33	Plimsolls	Plimsolls
34	Sport shirt	
35	Sport belt	
36	Work jacket	
37	Blue riding trousers	Work trousers

In addition to the personal clothing listed above, men could be issued with the following:
Clogs for wearing in boiler rooms
Iceland jackets and head protectors for cold weather

Waterproof clothing for sentries and men working on deck
Denim work clothing for exceptionally dirty work
Leather gear
Heavy coats for non-officer grades

Footwear
Plimsolls could be worn off duty or on duty when specified by a senior officer.

Black shoes, without fancy decorations, could be worn by commissioned officers and warrant officers at times when the crew was wearing plimsolls. Brown shoes were also permissible.

White shoes could also be worn by commissioned officers and warrant officers.

Black high dress boots could be worn on board and on land by commissioned and warrant officers.

Highly polished dress shoes could be worn with formal dress uniforms.

Rubber boots were allowed on board by all ranks during bad weather.

Rubber over-boots, worn on top of ordinary footwear, could be worn on board during exceptionally wet or very cold weather. These could also be worn on land when going off-road.

CLOTHING COMBINATIONS

Although the Navy had firm rules about the wearing of uniforms, once the war started necessity dictated that these should be relaxed. For example, some survivors from the sinking of the heavy cruiser *Blücher* arrived back in Kiel almost before their clothes had dried and it took a while before quartermasters issued new gear. As a result men wore whatever they could borrow or steal. Shortages during the war meant some items such as officers' cloaks were appropriated by wives for making into dresses. After the war tablecloths and bed

linen from the naval base in Wilhelmshaven (and probably other places as well) were thrown out to prevent them from being looted by the enemy and also from being fashioned into ladies' wear. The reason this had not been done during the war was because such naval items had most distinctive patterns to make them unattractive. Stealing naval clothing for alternative uses was discouraged by often branding items with the name 'Kriegsmarine' and an eagle with swastika. In addition to this many naval jumpers were trimmed along the edges so that when they were unravelled one ended up with numerous short pieces of wool rather than one longer piece for re-knitting.

According to the regulations, the items of clothing listed above could be worn in the following combinations:

Full dress uniform
The full dress uniform (consisting of hat, frock coat, trousers with gold bands running down the outside seams, golden epaulettes, stand-up collar and white gloves) was usually worn only to one's own wedding or for official visits in foreign countries.

Dress or parade uniform
Officers wore a frock coat, blue trousers, peaked cap, brocade belt with dagger or sword, and grey gloves. Other ranks wore a monkey jacket, blue shirt with Nelson collar and silk scarf, blue trousers, hat and grey gloves. This gear came in two varieties: it could be worn with full medals or with the small medals ribbon bar. The first mentioned was worn for parades, official functions such as commissioning and launching ceremonies, court martials, church parades or when ordered by a senior officer. The less official gear was worn when dignitaries visited the ship or for official visits on land or when attending functions in other ships.

This photograph has been included for the benefit of a couple of clever collectors who assured the author that warrant officers *never* wore swords! The medals are commemorative awards made between 1935 and 1939 and the absence of war badges would suggest that this picture was taken between 1938 and 1940. The badge on the lower left breast is the National Sports Badge.

The hatband reads '*Schiffsstammdivision der Nordsee*'. These units were responsible for taking new recruits through the initial training. The man here is wearing the blue naval uniform with Nelson-type collar.

Small dress uniform

The small dress uniform consisted of a blue jacket, trousers, peaked cap, stand-up or ordinary collar, dagger, and grey gloves. The crew usually wore work trousers and work shirt with silk scarf and blue cap. This gear was worn when off-duty and for the daily routine, unless more formal clothing had been ordered. When engaged in infantry duties a sword could be ordered for officers instead of the dagger. In tropical regions or between 1 May and 30 September the blue colour was replaced by the white version of the blue naval uniform.

Walking-out uniform

Officers wore a frock coat, blue trousers, blue peaked cap, shirt with ordinary or stand-up collar, dagger and grey gloves while cadets, warrant officers and petty officers wore a jacket instead of the frock coat. There was no special walking-out uniform for the lower ranks.

Full formal dress uniform

This served as formal evening dress and consisted of frock coat with brocade belt and dagger, the usual peaked cap and stand-up collar. A full medals bar and white gloves usually accompanied the outfit. It was worn for celebrations including family functions such as weddings, christenings and funerals. However full medals were usually not worn to private functions.

Formal dress uniform

This was very similar to the full formal dress uniform, except that ribbons were worn instead of the medal bar.

Tropical and summer uniform

Officers wore a white jacket with epaulettes, white trousers, white peaked cap or pith helmet, stand-up collar, dagger, and white gloves. Other ranks could wear a white jacket or just a white shirt with white trousers and white cap. This white version of the blue naval uniform was worn for daily work in the tropics or between 1 May and 30 September. During exceptionally hot weather senior officers could allow this light gear to be worn when walking out and while off-duty. To complicate matters, there was also a light khaki-coloured uniform for the tropics which was worn while working on land. Senior officers could determine whether daggers or swords were to be carried or whether full medals or just a ribbon bar was to be worn with the tropical uniform.

Sports uniform

This was similar for all ranks and consisted of a sports shirt with military sports badge and either

A warrant officer wearing the formal shirt with stand-up collar and showing the shoulder strap of an *Obermaschinist*.

Maschinen-obergefreiter Striegl of *U351* in November 1943, wearing sailors' formal uniform. On his left breast is the oval U-boat Badge and Iron Cross Second Class. His trade is indicated by a cogwheel on the top of this sleeve. Below this is his rank badge and below that are two specialists' badges for Electromechanic and Bosun for handling small boats.

At first glance this may look like the tropical or white summer uniform, but the men are wearing working denims. The star on the man's sleeve indicates his trade: he is a seaman; the chevron indicates his rank of *Obermatrose* and the badge at the bottom shows that he has a special qualification as operator of anti-aircraft rangefinders. The photograph was taken on the bridge of a minesweeper.

blue or white lightweight shorts. Running shoes were also worn and all this could be replaced by just swimming trunks. Swimming in sports shorts was definitely prohibited.

Apropos of not being allowed to swim in sports shorts or in other uniform clothing, there was an amusing incident shortly before the First World War when some nuns complained to Kaiser Wilhelm II about the dreadful attire of sailors seen bathing on a secluded beach. When

questioned about this, their commanding officer (Admiral Wilhelm Souchon) replied that his majesty had been misinformed by the nuns about the men's inappropriate attire for swimming. The sailors in question obeyed the uniform regulations – they didn't have any attire.

Lanyards

Lanyards were worn for three basic different functions: as a marksman's award, to identify officers serving as adjutant or by naval attachés.

The marksmanship lanyard was worn from the right lapel with the other end fastened to the top button of the jacket. At the lower end there would have been one or more of the following: an acorn if shooting proficiency had been achieved with a handgun, a winged shell for anti-aircraft guns, a shell for heavier artillery or a torpedo. The minimum standards for each award were laid down by regulations and it was a case of scoring a certain number of points on a target in a given period of time. The fact that one sees relatively few of these lanyards on photos suggests that the standards were not easy.

When the lanyard was awarded for the first time it was made from blue woollen thread, but men could also buy a more elaborate version made from silk. Should the test be passed on more than one occasion, then a blue aluminium thread would be added for the second and third occasions. The rosette

This shows the author's father in 1939 while he was training to become a warrant officer. The white tropical or summer shirt is worn with blue naval trousers.

The naval sports' shirt with national eagle printed on the front.

The two lower grades of hat embroidery can be seen in this photograph. On the left is Kpt.z.S. Kurt Freiwald with adjutant's lanyard or '*Affenschaukel*' (Monkey's Swing), who had the distinction of serving as adjutant for both Grand Admirals of the Third Reich.

at the shoulder end was also slightly more elaborate by having a gold-coloured badge incorporated in the knot. The second award had a silver instead of a black-coloured miniature at the lower end. For the third award there would have been a gold-coloured miniature while the fourth also had a more elaborate knot with golden anchor at the top.

An adjutant's lanyard looked similar to the marksmanship award, except that it would have been worn by a commissioned officer instead of a seaman and it was gold in colour. If a commanding officer had more than one adjutant then this lanyard would have been worn only by the most senior officer who dealt with commander's personal matters.

During gatherings where several adjutants might be present, only the adjutant of the most senior commanding officer would have worn the lanyard.

Naval attaché's lanyards were much rarer, obviously because there were far fewer people holding such posts. It consisted of a double lanyard made from gold wire thread and was only worn during formal functions.

THE FIELD GREY NAVAL UNIFORM

The field grey naval uniform was worn by naval units based mainly on land and its appearance was controlled by Army regulations. There were fewer items than for the blue naval uniform and it generally consisted of everyday work gear. In photographs one is more likely to confuse this uniform with Army clothing, although the presence of naval badges gives some indication that the wearers were sailors. There was a basic frock coat or long jacket which could be worn with a full length great coat; both had a bright red belt. Trade badges and special qualification badges were not worn and there were no piston rings on the sleeves for officers.

SIDEARMS

Firearms

Rifles and pistols were usually issued only when ordered by a commanding officer, and they would usually have come from the ship's stores to be handed back after use. Officers and men of other ranks who might find themselves on land in particularly dangerous situations were allowed to carry pistols if permitted by a senior officer. However, personal firearms in general were not carried. Yet, despite this rule, a number of men carried personal weapons.

Bayonets

A bayonet formed part of the man's personal equipment and was accounted for in the

Wearing field grey naval uniforms at a rifle range near Glücksburg.

Two naval instructors at an initial training course before the war and before the introduction of the swastika. The regulations regarding the wearing of this naval field grey uniform were very much based on Army patterns and it is difficult to identify the clothing as being naval.

The inscription on this rifle target reads, '100 m standing freehand, W.haven 17 August 1933.' Heizer Mallmann refers to the author's father just after he had joined the Navy.

Initial training with a naval infantry unit near Wilhelmshaven during the early 1930s. Every recruit went through one of these introductory courses and many men have said that the good pre-war grounding they received contributed to their survival during the war. The training was roughly the same for officers and men.

Soldbuch (Pay Book). There were a variety of basic designs, with men usually being issued with black leather frogs and officers with brown leather frogs. The leather belt holding the bayonet usually also contained a number of pouches for ammunition.

Daggers

Throughout the time of the Third Reich, three different naval daggers were in use: the old-fashioned type with an imperial crown at the hilt, the Reichsmarine dagger with a flame, and the version with eagle and swastika. The reason for this variation was that a basic type was issued from naval stores, but men could buy more elaborate versions themselves and some of these could be incredibly expensive. Grand Admiral Erich Raeder also introduced a 'Dagger of Honour' which was only awarded about half a dozen times. Daggers were worn by warrant officers with *Portepee* and by commissioned officers. Cadets wore daggers without a sword knot.

Swords

Naval swords differed from those issued to the Army and Air Force by the lion's head on the hilt. The Navy lion always had one red and one green eye, denoting the colours for port and starboard. It would appear that swords could be worn by the same ranks who were allowed to carry daggers, but the occasions when warrant officers were seen with swords seem to have been few and far between. Although the dagger was usually not carried in the hand on official functions, there were elaborate rules about when and how the sword should be carried. One of the reasons for this was that the long straps holding the scabbard easily tripped up the wearer.

New recruits were introduced to a variety of weapons and skills needed for survival in situations where they had to react quickly because things happened too fast for detailed evaluation.

A naval sword on display at the International U-boat Archive in Germany showing the method of attachment to the belt. To the right is a shield with a naval officer's silver brocade belt.

Dönitz's baton.

The Grand Admiral's Baton

At the turn of the century the German Emperor created a tradition of presenting his high military officials with a baton as symbol of their office, and to ease the burden of their having to stand at a full salute for long periods. On parades they could acknowledge the troops by merely holding their staff at shoulder height. The baton was not a military award 'loaned' to the recipient through the armed forces, but a personal gift. Whilst the difference of this wording may sound academic, it has rather an important bearing because the baton became the property of the individual official, it never belonged to the state. Bearing in mind that some of these batons were made from precious metals with embedded diamonds, their melt-down value was somewhere in the region of £20,000–£50,000 by modern standards. So, it was indeed a most valuable gift.

What is more, it was also a very rare gift Dr Erich Raeder was only the fourth, perhaps fifth head of the Navy to have been presented with such an honour. The first baton was presented to Hans von Koester in 1905, the second to Prince Heinrich of Prussia in 1909, and another to Hennig von Holtzendorf just before the end of the war in July 1918. It seems highly likely that the great torpedo pundit, Grand Admiral Alfred von Tirpitz, did not receive a baton. The presentation of a baton in 1939 and Raeder's promotion to Grand Admiral took place on the same day as the launching of the battleship *Tirpitz* in Wilhelmshaven. Raeder had been Supreme Commander-in-Chief of the Navy since October 1928, but first with the rank of Admiral and then General Admiral, a position specially created at a time when the Navy was too small to warrant an Admiral of the Fleet.

The production of Raeder's baton was quite a complicated process, made more difficult by the fact that its construction and the materials involved were a closely-guarded secret. The specifications and drawings of earlier admiral batons had vanished after the end of the First World War and Dr Ottfried Neubecker, who had been entrusted with the production, had to research his subject without giving away the reasons for his interest. In addition to this, he was working to a set of most stringent specifications as far as size and appearance went. In the end he created a magnificent piece, consisting of a silver rod covered in blue velvet with delicate decorations on top and with stunning golden ends. Silver embellishment used on Army and Air Force batons was thought to oxidise too quickly in the damp sea air and platinum was used to provide a contrasting colour. This was important because some of the decorations were sitting directly on velvet, making it impossible to clean or polish them without spoiling the backcloth.

The drama around the creation of Dönitz's baton started during the summer of 1942, long before his appointment as Commander-in-Chief was even contemplated (January 1943). An ordinary, low-ranking gunner in a flak regiment received a personal telegram from Hitler's Headquarters ordering him to report immediately to Berlin. On setting foot inside the firm where he had worked before being called up, Helmut Scheuermann was told that his skills as a jeweller were required for the production of a number of Army batons. Until he had been conscripted, Scheuermann had worked as a goldsmith with the well-established firm of H.J. Wilm, who had served Germany's nobility since 1767. In a way Scheuermann found himself thrown into a most ridiculous situation because the German High Command not only required a large number of impressive batons, but wanted them completed in period of about three weeks. Having fulfilled these assignments, Scheuermann was then

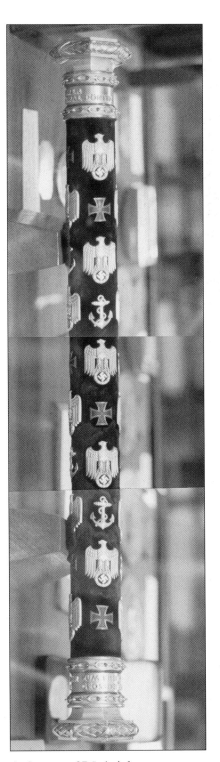

A close-up of Dönitz's baton.

Dönitz making a speech at Wilhelmshaven, holding the baton, 1943.

entrusted with the design and production of a baton for Grand Admiral Karl Dönitz.

Both Raeder and Dönitz were officially presented with two batons. The grand, golden staff for official parades and a so-called *Interimstab* for everyday functions. Raeder's less formal version doubled up as a telescope, with modern precision optics inside, while Dönitz carried a plainer staff, resembling a short walking stick with heavy silver head. Photographic evidence suggests that he also had a third version, with a smaller silver head.

When the Red Army approached the outskirts of Berlin, Raeder set about burying a case containing valuables near his home in Potsdam-Babelsberg. It appears that a workman helping with this task was later forced to reveal the location to the Russians. Following this, Raeder's grand baton vanished into obscurity. Since it had a high scrap metal value, it could well be that it has long since been melted down. On the other hand, with the improving East–West relations there is always a remote possibility that it might reappear one day. Raeder's *Interimstab* and his medals were confiscated by Russian troops when he was arrested, and they have also vanished into obscurity. That is, all except his Golden Party Badge. When Raeder heard about some of the atrocities committed in the name of the Third Reich, he destroyed the badge by hacking it to pieces with an axe.

Dönitz's grand baton and other personal items were stolen from his luggage shortly after the war, when his government was arrested at the Naval Officers' School in Mürwik. It appears that British soldiers rifled through unattended bags while the men were being questioned. Some German officers were also robbed of personal items in their pockets, and wedding rings were stolen as well. Even buttons were cut off their uniforms by soldiers desperate for souvenirs. Despite a complaint to the British authorities, the Germans received only a written apology, but the treasured items were not recovered. The whereabouts of some personal items still remain a mystery, but in 1982 the author stumbled across the grand baton at the regimental museum of the Shropshire Light Infantry in Shrewsbury (England). It had been presented by Maj Gen J.B. Churcher, who apparently participated in the arrest of the Dönitz government.

Just a few weeks after this most amazing find, there appeared a brief article in German newspapers saying that the Naval Federation (Deutscher Marinebund) had started legal proceedings against the jeweller W.J. Wilm in Hamburg because the firm was reputedly in the wrongful possession of Dönitz's baton. Although Dönitz had never ascertained what had happened to his baton and he had not seen it since it was stolen in 1945, his will and last testament stated that it should pass on to the Marinebund, so that it might be displayed at the Naval Memorial near Kiel. W.J. Wilm claimed that the baton in the firm's possession never belonged to Grand Admiral Dönitz, but that it was the model made for Hitler's approval before work started on the real thing.

The news of another baton in Shrewsbury brought the court proceedings to an adjournment while matters were clarified. There was no doubt about the original owner of the baton in Shrewsbury because Dönitz's name is engraved in bold letters on the golden collar at one end. Disassembling their batons, Wilm could also show that their model had an aluminium core instead of a silver rod and that the inscription had a spelling mistake. In addition to this, the delicate decorations on the model were made from silver and gold-plated silver instead of gold and platinum, making it nowhere near as valuable.

Despite considerable legal wrangling in Germany and in Britain, the real baton is still in the regimental museum in Shrewsbury Castle, but instead of lying behind a sheet of ordinary window glass it is now resting in a double armoured glass safe. Somehow it seems strange that officialdom is allowed to keep private property stolen from an individual. Just to add a further footnote to illustrate German law, when Wilm's model appeared in court and when it was photographed by the press in 1983 with the 74-year-old Helmut Scheuermann, the swastikas on its decoration had to be hidden behind sticky paper because it is illegal to display them in Germany. The only exception to this law is that swastikas may be displayed for educational purposes.

MAPS

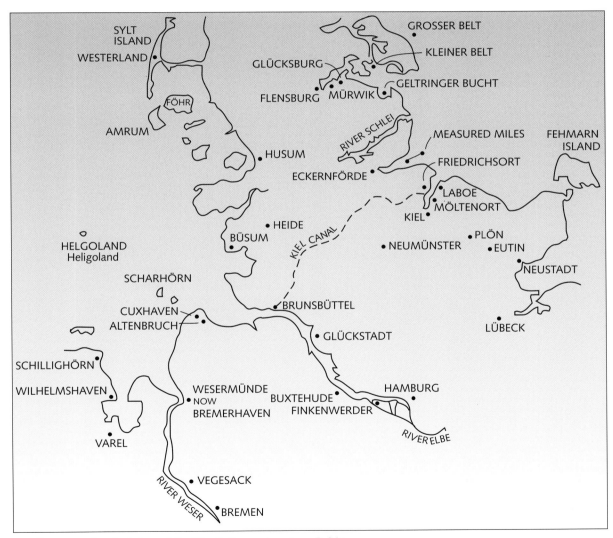

Germany: detailed view of the North Sea and western Baltic.

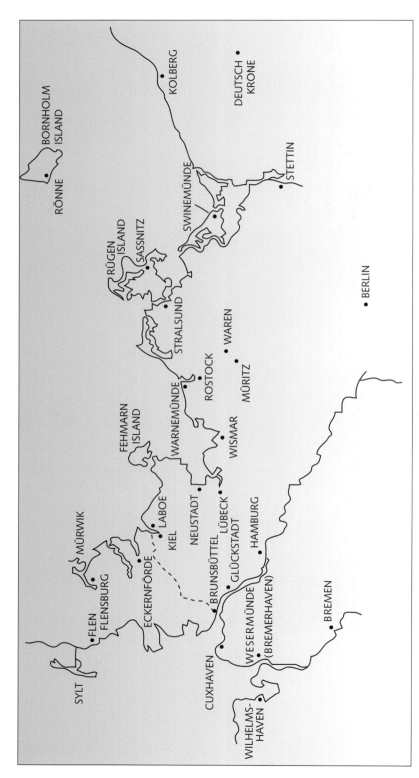

Germany: the North Sea and western Baltic coasts.

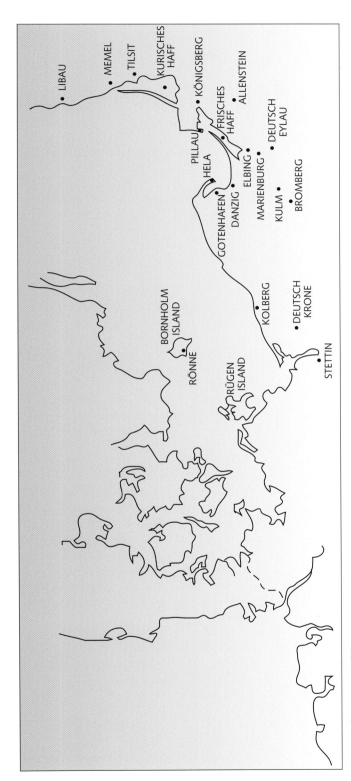

Germany's eastern Baltic coast.

GLOSSARY

Admiralinspekteur

An honorary rank awarded to Grand Admiral Erich Raeder after his retirement in January 1943.

Agru-Front

A name derived from *Ausbildungsgruppe für Frontboote*, a command for testing new U-boats and their crews before they became fully operational.

'Alberich Skin'

A code-name for a rubber-like coating applied to U-boats for absorbing Asdic impulses with a view to making submerged boats more difficult to detect **with Asdic**.

Allies

Originally the powers of the Triple Entente: Great Britain, France and Russia. Also included other nations fighting on their side.

'Aphrodite'

A code name for a type of radar foxer (decoy) which consisted of a hydrogen-filled balloon holding aloft a number of metal foils for reflecting radar impulses. A weight floating on the water prevented the device from flying too high.

Arctic Smoke

A natural fog created when cold winds blow over warmer water.

Asdic

A name derived from the initials of Allied Submarine Detection Investigation Committee and now known as Sonar. Apparatus for detecting submerged objects by listening for the echoes from audible pings sent out by its transmitter.

Asto

A term derived from *Admiralstaboffizier* meaning Admiral's staff officer.

Auxiliary cruiser

A merchant ship which has been fitted with armaments and engaged as a warship. Also known as 'ghost' cruiser or raider, although the last mentioned also applied to purpose-built warships.

Aviso *Grille*

Aviso was originally a small fast warship, but the term was later used to describe Hitler's state yacht named *Grille*.

Axis Powers

The alliance of Germany, Italy and Japan formed shortly before the beginning of the Second World War.

Bali

A device for detecting radar impulses used towards the end of the war.

'Barbarossa'

Code-name for Germany's attack against the Soviet Union in June 1941.

Battlecruiser

A warship of battleship size but with smaller armament and usually faster speed.

B-Dienst

Short for *Funkbeobachtungsdienst*. Germany's radio monitoring service under command of Heinz Bonatz.

Befehlshaber

Commander-in-Chief.

Biscay Cross

An improvised radar detector used by U-boats mainly in the Bay of Biscay area towards the end of the war. It consisted of a wooden cross with wires strung around the outside and plugged into a receiver in the radio room. The device had to be dismantled before diving. Soon after its introduction, it was quickly replaced by more permanent and retractable aerials on the outside of the conning tower.

Blockade breaker

A merchant ship with non-military crew running into Germany or France during the war. Not to be confused with *Sperrbrecher* which were merchant ships for detonating mines.

Bold

An Asdic foxer.

Bundesmarine

Federal Navy, a name for the German Navy used before 1852 and after 1954.

Carno von Kastel

A German misunderstanding, refers to the British auxiliary cruiser *Carnavon Castle*.

Checkmate

A British system for helping identify suspicious ships at sea by calling for information from land-based control centres.

Coastal Command

A Royal Air Force Command which specialised in flying over sea areas. If translated from the German, it could refer to land-based coastal artillery units.

Corvette

Originally a sailing ship. During the Second World War it was used to describe an ocean-going warship, slightly smaller than a frigate and employed mainly as anti-submarine convoy escort.

Crew

A German term for the annual intake of officer cadets.

Cruiser War

The employment of warships against merchant interests, in areas where the raiders could not easily be caught by superior enemy forces.

Dead Man

A German term for a faulty torpedo.

'Deadlight', Operation

The code-name for the Allied operation to scuttle U-boats after the war.

Destroyer

A small to medium-sized fast warship. The Germans tended to refer to all convoy escorts as destroyers, although some commanders insisted the word 'fast boat' should be used instead to prevent unnecessary alarm among the crew.

DeTe or D/T Apparatus

Officially the abbreviation for *Dezimeter Telefonie Apparatus* but unofficially also called *Drehturm Apparatus* meaning 'revolving turret apparatus'. An early type of efficient radar for ranging guns after targets had been visually sighted, but could also be used as a search device. In 1938 it helped ships find their way in and out of harbours in thick fog by indicating the position of buoys on the sides of the deep water channel.

Dreadnought

Originally the name of a new, large British battleship and later used to describe any powerful battleship of over 20,000 tons. Britain had hoped to dominate rival nations with this powerful weapon because it was thought it would give its navy considerable superiority for some time. Although the locks at the naval base in Wilhelmshaven and at both ends of the Kiel Canal were too small for such vessels, Germany responded to the *Dreadnought* threat by building equally large ships and by enlarging its waterways. At the same time *Dreadnought* sparked off a extensive arms race with other countries.

Duck Pond (*Ententeich*)

The introduction of marine aircraft raised the problem of landing on fairly rough seas. At first, a huge rubber mat was suspended from a crane over the side of the ship, and dragged over the surface to smooth the waves. The boffins had just fitted this in the pocket battleship *Deutschland* when the ship went into a tight turn at fast speed. It was quickly realised that the water within the circular wake was much calmer than the surrounding seas. So the mat was removed and commanders instructed to smooth waves by turning in a circle at a fairly fast speed. This area of calm water was called 'Duck Pond'.

E-boat

Enemy boat; a motor torpedo boat known as *S-Boot* in Germany.

Electro-U-boats

Originally Types XXI and XXIII designed from 1943 onwards. Fast underwater speeds were achieved quite simply by enlarging the hull and adding additional batteries. These types later gave rise to the postwar patrol or hunter-killer submarines of the Cold War era.

Engelmann Boat

An unsuccessful experimental high speed boat produced during the war.

Enigma

Enigma, the impenetrable puzzle, was the name of a German code writer which was adopted for use by all the armed forces. The naval version was known as *Schlüsselmaschine* M (Code Machine – 'M': for Marine). Today it is well known that Britain's success at breaking the codes was a major contributing factor in winning the war.

Escort Carrier

Small aircraft carrier used mainly for convoy escort duties.

Escort Group
A group of small, fast warships used for protecting convoys against U-boats.

Etmal
The distance a vessel travelled in twenty-four hours.

Eto
Abbreviation derived from Electric Torpedo.

Falke
Forerunner of the German acoustic torpedo which came into service under the name of *Zaunkönig* (Wren) or T5.

FAT
An anti-convoy torpedo.

'Felix', Operation
Code-name for the planned invasion of Gibraltar.

Finland
In 1941, following long-standing border disputes with Russia, Finland joined the war against the Soviet Union on the German side until a cease-fire was agreed in September 1944.

Fog-making Apparatus
Most German warships could generate artificial fog or smoke in three different ways. Fog-making plants could be activated from a variety of positions aboard the ship to force out dense white fog forced by compressed air. Fog buoys or cylindrical drums of about 120 kg in weight and just over a metre long, could be thrown overboard to emit white smoke for about twenty minutes, while non-diesel ships could produce black smoke by adjusting the air flow to the boilers.

Frigate
A small to medium-sized warship of moderate speed used for anti-submarine convoy escort duties.

Frogmen
A group of swimmers officially known as *Kampfschwimmer* (Battle or Combat Swimmers).

FuMB* and *FuMO
Funkmessbeobachtung and *Funkmessortung* meaning radar detection and radio ranging or radar.
German Mine-Sweeping Administration (GM-SA)
Founded after the Second World War because one of the conditions of the cease-fire stated that Germany should be responsible for clearing mines in the Baltic and parts of the North Sea. Although only volunteers were accepted, who could live as free men in Germany, they were forced to live as prisoners of war in other countries. This was a

direct contravention of the Geneva Convention which prohibited prisoners of war from being employed in life-threatening occupations. At first there were two main mine-sweeping divisions. One in Kiel and the other in Cuxhaven. Later facilities were expanded and there were active units in Bremerhaven, Holland, Belgium, Denmark and in Norway. In 1946 the Administration was reduced from about 28,000 men to 15,000 and further reductions continued until it was disbanded in 1948. However a small number of mine clearing vessels remained operational and were later taken over by the Bundesmarine.

'Ghost' cruiser
See auxiliary cruiser.

Goldbutt
An experimental type of torpedo with closed-circuit Walter turbine.

Goldfish
Similar to Goldbutt.

Goliath
A powerful radio transmitter near Magdeburg which was capable of reaching submerged U-boats in the Caribbean. There were some twenty masts covering an area of over 4 sq km with aerials consuming up to 200,000 volts. The installation was dismantled after the war and moved to the Soviet Union.

Group attacks
Used by U-boats to attack convoys in groups on the surface at night, at a time when there were not enough boats for forming patrol lines. Also called Wolf Pack Attacks.

Group Commands
Two localised commands for the east and west, the Baltic and the North Sea, ranking between the Naval War Staff (*Seekriegsleitung* – SKL) in Berlin and the Fleet Command at sea. The Commander-in-Chief of these Group Commands was responsible for controlling naval action in his area and the defence of the appropriate coastal waters.

Grundhai
A submarine lifeboat planned towards the end of the war for rescuing men from sunken U-boats. It had a diving depth of up to about 1,000 m, but was never built.

Gruppenhorchgerät (Group Listening Apparatus)
A passive listening device which consisted of a group of underwater microphones for detecting

sound. The receiving head could be rotated until maximum volume had been achieved and then the direction of the sound was read off a scale in the radio room. Now often called Passive Sonar.

Handelsschutzkreuzer
Auxiliary cruiser for the protection of merchant ships.

Handelsstörkreuzer
Auxiliary cruiser for the harassment of merchant ships. Also known as *Hilfskreuzer*.

'Haunebu'
Haunebu is a code-name for a disc-shaped flying object built by the SS during the 1930s. Although a number of realistic photos exist and there are numerous reported sightings from near a testing site, there is some dispute as to whether or not such devices existed. The story that an experimental version met the auxiliary cruiser *Atlantis* in the South Atlantic seems to be false.

h.c. – *honoris causa* (Latin)
An honorary title.

Heligoland
An island in the North Sea dominated by red sandstone cliffs. Originally British. Acquired by Germany in 1890 when swapped for the East African island of Zanzibar. Became a strategic defence centre for the German Bight with accommodation for almost twenty submarines during the First World War. The Diktat of Versailles demanded the removal of all military defences, but the island was re-fortified from 1935 onwards, although by the beginning of the Second World War it had lost much of its strategic importance and was used only as a minor base. After the war, Britain forced the civilian population away and totally destroyed all the houses as well as much of the wildlife, reducing the island to a barren, rocky desert. It was handed back to Germany, totally wrecked, on 1 March 1952.

High Seas Fleet
The term 'High Seas Fleet' was abolished shortly after the First World War and replaced with just 'The Fleet' under control of the Fleet Command. Following this there were considerable changes in administration and names, giving the impression that the Navy didn't know how to organise itself. None of this had a great deal of bearing on ships

at sea because once away from port, commanders were given a free hand to follow their basic directives. The Fleet Command or its representatives very often went to sea with the big ships, thus the higher officers issuing orders had their hands directly on the pulse of battle. The Fleet Commanders throughout the war were: Admiral Hermann Boehm; Admiral Wilhelm Marschall; Admiral Günter Lütjens, who went down with battleship *Bismarck*; General Admiral Otto Schniewind and Vizeadmiral Wilhelm Meendsen-Bohlken.

Hilfskreuzer
Auxiliary cruiser.

Hohentwiel
Radar equipment used aboard U-boats.

Hütte
Could mean hut, but in a ship-building context it is more likely to mean 'iron foundry'.

IIWO and IIIWO
2nd and 3rd Watch Officer, see also IWO.

Imperial Navy
Translation for *Kaiserliche Marine*, but could also refer to the Imperial Japanese Navy.

Ingenieurbüro (Engineering Bureau) *Glückauf*
Founded in 1943 to develop the new U-boat types.

Ingenieurskantoor voor Scheepsbouw
The cover name for a German submarine development bureau in Holland, used to keep abreast with new developments at a time when the Versailles Diktat prevented Germany from owning or building submarines.

Ingolin
Originally a cover name for hydrogen peroxide as used for fuel in high speed Walter turbines. Named after his son 'Ingo'.

International Military Tribunal
See Nuremberg Trials.

IWO
1st Watch Officer, pronounced *Eins-W-O* or One-W-O.

Kaiser
Emperor.

Kaiser Wilhelm Canal
The name for the Kiel Canal until the end of the First World War.

Kaiserliche Marine
Imperial Navy. Name used by the German Navy from 1871 until the end of the First World War.

Kaleu

Although included as the name of a U-boat commander by some authors, there was no officer with such a surname. It is a corruption of *Kapitänleutnant* and was usually preceded by the title 'Herr' – Mr Kaleu.

Kampfgruppe

Fighting or battle unit.

Kampfgruppe Thiele

Founded in July 1944 as a stop-gap measure when the advancing Red Army was threatening bases in the far eastern Baltic. Remained operational until April 1945. Named after its commander, Vizeadmiral August Thiele who had earlier been commander of the heavy cruiser *Lützow* (ex-pocket battleship *Deutschland*). First the unit supported the Army by directing the fire from heavy ships against land targets, but later training groups were employed in a vast variety of tasks from land-based attacks to escorting refugee transports.

Kampfschwimmer

Frogmen.

Kommandant

Commanding officer of a sea-going unit.

Kommandeur

Commanding officer of a land-based unit.

Kriegsmarine

The name of the German Navy from 1935 until the end of the Second World War.

KTB

Kriegstagebuch – War diary.

Kurzsignal

See short radio signal.

L

Abbreviation for *Luftschiff* (airship).

Laboe

Originally a small fishing village on the Baltic near Kiel where the Naval Memorial was built and where *U995* is now resting as technical museum.

Lerche

An acoustic torpedo which could be steered via a wire connecting it to an operator. Developed towards the end of the war but not made operational.

'Lessing'

A code name for radar apparatus capable of detecting aircraft at ranges of up to about 40 km.

Linse

See LS Boot.

LMA

Luft (Air) Mine Type A. A mine developed for dropping from aircraft by parachute and filled with about 500 kg of explosives. Later modified into a more powerful LMB (Air Mine Type B) and a moored mine known as LMF.

LS Boot

Leichtes-Schnellboot (Light Speedboat) employed in the Mediterranean and carried by some auxiliary cruisers.

LT

Lufttorpedo (aerial torpedo).

Luftschiff

Airship.

LUT

Anti-convoy torpedo.

M – Marine

Navy. The Kriegsmarine tended to use the abbreviation 'M' rather than 'K'.

M-Boot

Minensuchboot (Minesweeper)

Metox

A device developed in France for detecting the presence of radar signals and used successfully by U-boats. The first aerial was a rough wooden cross with wires strung around the outside, known as the Biscay Cross. This was soon replaced by more permanent aerials.

Milchkuh

Nickname for supply U-boats of Type XIV.

Möltenort

Originally a small fishing village near Kiel where the U-boat Memorial is located.

Mondfisch

An experimental torpedo with high speed Walter turbine which did not go into production.

Monsoon Boats

Name for long-range U-boats which voyage to the Far East.

Naxos

A radar detector.

NSDAP

Nationalsozialistische Deutsche Arbeiter Partei, the Nazi Party. When it was founded, the Socialists were nicknamed 'Sozis', hence members of the NSDAP became 'Nazis'.

Nuremberg Trials

The first International Military Tribunal for men accused of war crimes started in November 1945.

The main counts were: waging wars of aggression by preparing men for battle; violating the laws and customs of warfare and crimes against humanity. Both Grand Admirals Erich Raeder and Karl Dönitz were found guilty of several counts and sentenced to jail at Spandau in Berlin. However, some of the laws under which they were found guilty had been formulated just before the trial and they were abolished again shortly afterwards. No other leaders have been charged with such 'crimes'. It has recently become known that Allied commanders who wanted to support the two grand admirals were prevented from giving evidence.

Ob.d.M./*Oberbefehlshaber der Marine*
Supreme Commander-in-Chief of the Navy.

OKM
Oberkommando der Marine (Supreme Naval Command).

OKW
Oberkommando der Wehrmacht (High Command of the Armed Forces).

Panzerschiff
Pocket battleship.

Paukenschlag
A roll on the kettledrums, the code-name for Germany's first attack against the United States with five U-boats in January 1942.

Pearl Harbor
An American naval base and anchorage in Hawaii, attacked by Japanese forces on 7 December 1941.

Pour le merite
Prussia's highest decoration awarded during the First World War and worn around the neck.

Prussia
The largest of the Germanic kingdoms. In 1871, following the unification of the German states, the King of Prussia became Emperor of Germany.

Radar
A word derived from Radio Detection and Ranging.

Räumboot **or** *R-boot*
A small minesweeper.

'*Regenbogen*', Operation
German code-word ordering the scuttling of U-boats at the end of the war.

Reichsmarine
Name of the German Navy between 1920 and 1935.

Samos
Name for a radar detector used by the German Navy.

Schlitten **(Sledge)**
A tiny speed boat designed for the Midget Weapons Unit.

Schnellboot **(S-Boot)**
Motor Torpedo Boat or MTB. Also called 'E-boat' meaning Enemy Boat.

Schnorkel
(American: Snorkel) The original word, '*Schnorchel*', was invented by Grand Admiral Karl Dönitz to describe a ventilation mast for running diesel engines inside a submerged submarine.

Schwertwal
An experimental midget submarine.

'Sealion'
Code-name for the planned invasion of Great Britain.

Seekriegsleitung/**SKL**
Naval War Staff.

Short signal
The 'short signal' enabled fairly lengthy messages to be transmitted by sending only a few letters of Morse. The source of these signals was thought not to be detectable by Allied radio direction-finders, but Britain's new invention of High Frequency Direction-Finders proved capable of determining the direction of such signals. This played a major role in the Battle of the Atlantic because U-boats usually told the U-boat Command when they were starting their attack and from this the convoy escorts were able to determine the direction of an impending onslaught. Radar could then be used to locate the U-boat on the surface.

Sloop
A small, long-range warship used for anti-submarine escort duties.

Spanish Civil War, 1936–8
A number of warships of various nationalities were stationed off Spain, ostensibly to protect their nationals. Several German ships came under attack and suffered some losses.

Sperrbrecher
Barrage breaker or mine clearing ship.

Steinbutt
An experimental torpedo with high speed Walter turbine.

Steinfisch
A forerunner of *Steinbutt.*

T5 (*Zaunkönig*)
Acoustic torpedo known as *Zaunkönig*.

'Thetis'
A code-name for a radar foxer used successfully in the Bay of Biscay to fool aircraft.

Third Reich
(Third Kingdom or Empire) The first having been the Charlemagne Empire, the Second was founded in 1871 and headed by the German Emperor. Hitler then claimed to have formed the Third Empire.

Toter Mann
(Dead Man) A torpedo that didn't work.

TVA
Torpedoversuchsanstalt – Torpedo Trails Centre based in Eckernförde.

UA
From *U-Ausland* meaning U-Foreign. A large U-boat built for Turkey before the war which was commissioned into the Kriegsmarine on 21 September 1939.

UB
German identification for HM Submarine *Seal* which was captured early in the war.

UC
Former Norwegian submarines.

UD
Former Dutch submarines.

UF
Former French submarines.

UIT
Former Italian submarines.

Volksmarine
The name of the East German (German Democratic Republic) Navy after the Second World War.

Walter Propulsion
A high speed turbine using highly volatile and concentrated hydrogen peroxide as fuel. The idea was that it could be used in submarines without air being required to run the engines.

Weserübung
The code-name for the invasion of Denmark and Norway in the spring of 1940.

Westwall
Not to be confused with Germany's western land defences. This was a mine barrage in the North Sea.

'Wolf Pack'
Translated from the German '*Rudel*' meaning troop, bunch, swarm, herd or pack and used to refer to a group of U-boats operating together. The term 'sea wolf' and 'sea dog' then gave rise to 'wolf pack', so U-boats were referred to as wolves and groups as wolf packs.

'*Wunderland*', Operation
A sortie into Arctic waters by pocket battleship *Admiral Scheer*.

BIBLIOGRAPHY

Ailsby, Christopher. *Combat Medals of the Third Reich*, Patrick Stephens, Wellingborough, 1987. (Well illustrated, but some of the text is somewhat dubious.)

Angolia, John R. and Schlicht, Adolf. *Die Kriegsmarine Volume 1 and 2*, R. James Bender, San Jose, 1991. (An excellent and well-illustrated work about German naval uniforms of the Third Reich.)

Baasch, H. *Handelsschiffe im Kriegseinsatz*, Gerhard Stalling, Oldenburg and Hamburg, 1975. (A pictorial work of merchant ships used for war service.)

Beaver, Paul. *German Capital Ships*, Patrick Stephens, Cambridge, 1980. (A collection of good photographs from the Bundesarchiv, although a good number of captions are wrong and others are somewhat inadequate.)

——. *E-boats and Coastal Craft*, Patrick Stephens, Cambridge, 1980. (Excellent Bundesarchiv photographs but rather inadequate captions.)

Beesley, Patrick. *Very Special Intelligence*, Hamish Hamilton, London, 1977 and Doubleday, New York, 1978. (An interesting book dealing with Admiralty Intelligence.)

Bekker, Cajus. *Das grosse Bildbuch der deutschen Kriegsmarine 1939–1945*, Stalling, Oldenburg and Hamburg, 1973. (An excellent pictorial record.)

Bensel, Rolf. *Die deutsche Flottenpolitik von 1933 bis 1939*, E.S. Mittler, Frankfurt, 1958.

Bidlingmayer, G. *Einsatz der schweren Kriegsmarineeinheiten im ozeanischen Zufuhrkrieg*, K. Vowinkel, Neckargemünd. (Details about the engagements of the larger ships.)

Blundel, W.D.G. *German Navy Warships 1939–1945*, Almark Publishing Co., New Malden, Surrey, 1972. (An excellent little book with very good photographs.)

Bonatz, Heinz. *Seekrieg im Äther*, E.S. Mittler, Herford, 1981. (The author was Commander-in-Chief of the German Radio Monitoring Service and has written this account about the role played by radio during the war. There are interesting short sections on each of the raiders.)

Bracke, Gerhard. *Die Einzelkämpfer der Kriegsmarine*, Motorbuch, Stuttgart, 1981. (An interesting account of the Midget Weapons Units.)

Bredemeier, Heinrich. *Schlachtschiff Scharnhorst*, Koehlers, Herford, 1978. (Written by one of *Scharnhorst*'s officers in conjunction with the commander, Kurt Caesar Hoffmann and the navigation officer, Helmuth Giessler.)

Brennecke, Jochen. *Die deutschen Hilfskreuzer im zweiten Weltkrieg*, Koehlers, Herford, 1958. (Originally called '*Das grosse Abendteuer*', it is a chatty account of the auxiliary cruisers, with technical details and information of ships sunk.)

——. *Ghost Cruiser HK33*, William Kimber, London, 1954 and Crowell, New York, 1955. (The story of auxiliary cruiser *Pinguin*.)

——. *Schwarze Schiffe, weite See*, Gerhard Stalling, Oldenburg, 1958. (An account of German blockade breakers during the Second World War.)

——. *Hilfskreuzer Thor*, Koehlers, Herford, 1967. (The story of auxiliary cruiser *Thor*.)

——. *Die Wende im U-Bootkrieg*, Koehlers, Herford, 1987.

Breyer, Siegfried. *Handbuch für U-Bootkommandanten 1935–1945*, Podzun-Pallas, Wölfersheim-Berstadt.

——. *Flottenparaden und Repräsentationen der Marine 1925–1940*, Podzun-Pallas, Wölfersheim-Berstadt.

——. *Stapelläufe auf deutschen Schiffswerften*, Podzun-Pallas, Wölfersheim-Berstadt.

Brice, Martin. *Axis Blockade Runners*, Batsford, London, 1981.

Brown, David. *Tirpitz the Floating Fortress*, Arms and Armour Press, London, 1978. (Many good photographs, although their reproduction could be better.)

Brustat-Naval, Fritz. *Ali Cremer U333 Ullstein*, Frankfurt, 1983.

—— and Suhren, Teddy. *Nasses Eichenlaub*, Koehlers, Herford, 1983.

Buchheim, Lothar-Günther. *U-boot Krieg*, R. Piper, Munich, 1976. (A pictorial work about the U-boat war.)

Busch, F.O. *Konteradmiral Robert Eyssen*, Pabel, Rastatt.

——. *Kosaren des Seekrieges*, Pabel, Rastatt. (A chatty account of the second voyages of auxiliary cruisers *Thor* and *Michel*.)

Busch, Rainer and Röll, Hans-Joachim. *Der U-Boot-Krieg 1939 bis 1945*. Vol 1, *Die deutschen U-Boot-Kommandanten*, Koehler/Mittler, Hamburg, Berlin, Bonn 1996. (Brief biographies produced from the records of the German U-boat Archive.)

Chapman, John W.M. *The Price of Admiralty*, University of Sussex Printing Press, Lewes, 1982. (A three volume work with an annotated translation of the war diary of the German Naval Attaché in Japan from 1939 to 1943.)

Childers, Erskine. *The Riddle of the Sands*, Sidgwick and Jackson, London, 1972. (A novel set in German coastal waters before the First World War. There probably is no better description of those waters.)

Dau, Heinrich. *Unentdeckt über die Meere*, Berlin, 1940. (The story of the blockade breaker and supply ship *Altmark*, written by her last commander.)

Davis, Brian Leigh. *German Uniforms of the Third Reich*, Blandford, Poole, 1980.

——. *Badges and Insignia of the Third Reich 1933–1945*, Blandford, Poole, 1983.

Dechow, F.L. *Geisterschiff 28*, Ernst Gerdes, Preest/Holstein, 1962. (The story of auxiliary cruiser *Michel*.)

Detmers, T. and Brennecke, J. *Hilfskreuzer Kormoran*, Koehlers, Herford, 1959. (The story of the auxiliary cruiser by her commander. Translated from the original English language edition: *The Raider Kormoran*, William Kimber, London, 1959.)

Deutsches Marineinstitut. *Marineschule Mürwik*, E.S. Mittler & Sohn, Herford.

Dollinger, Hans. *The Decline and Fall of Nazi Germany and Imperial Japan*, Odhams, London, 1965. (Excellent photographs.)

Dönitz, Karl. *Ten Years and Twenty Days*, Weidenfeld & Nicolson, London, 1959.

——. *Deutsche Strategie zur See im Zweiten Weltkrieg*, Bernard & Graefe, Frankfurt, 1972.

——. *Mein wechselvolles Leben*, Musterschmidt, Göttingen, 1968.

——. *Deutsche Strategie zur See im Zweiten Weltkrieg*, Bernard & Graefe, Frankfurt, 1970.

Elfrath, U. & Herzog B. *Schlachtschiff Bismarck*, Podzun, Dorheim, 1975. (A collection of interesting photographs depicting the life of the battleship.)

Elfrath, Ulrich. *Die Deutsche Kriegsmarine 1935–1945*, Podzun Pallas, Friedberg, 1985. (With extensive photo captions in English, published in five volumes.)

Ellenbeck, Major Dr Hans. *Die Verantwortung des deutschen Offiziers*, Tornisterschrift des Oberkommando der Wehrmacht, 1941.

Enders, Gerd. *Auch kleine Igel haben Stacheln*, Koehlers, Herford, 1987. (The story about U-boats in the Black Sea.)

Evers, H. *Kriegsschiffbau*, Springer, Berlin 1931 and 1943. (Contains some interesting technical details of warship construction.)

Eyssen, Robert. *Hilfskreuzer Komet*, Koehlers, Herford, 1960. (An edited version of auxiliary cruiser *Komet*'s log-book by her commander.)

—— et al. *Hilfskreuzer Komet*, Oberkommando der Kriegsmarine, 1942. (A souvenir album of *Komet*'s voyage with interesting photographs, most of them taken by Gerhard Julius, though the captions are poor for security reasons. Limited distribution and now very rare.)

FTU. *Das Archiv*, U-boat Archive, Cuxhaven. (A journal published twice a year for members of FTU, U-Boot-Archiv, D-27478 Cuxhaven-Altenbruch. Please enclose two International Postal Reply Coupons if asking for details.)

Gander, Terry and Chamberlain, Peter. *Small Arms, Artillery and Special Weapons of the Third Reich*, Macdonald and Jane's, London, 1978. (Although it does not deal directly with the Navy, this book is jolly useful. It is well illustrated and filled with useful data.)

Garrett, Richard. *Scharnhorst and Gneisenau*, David & Charles, Newton Abbot, 1978. (An interesting account of the two elusive sisters.)

Gibson, Charles. *Das Schiff mit fünf Namen*, Wilhelm Heyne, Munich, 1966. (The story of *Speybank/Doggerbank*.)

Giese, Fritz. *Die Deutsche Marine 1920–45*, Bernard & Graefe, Frankfurt, 1956.

Giese, Otto and Wise, James. *Shooting the War*, Naval Institute Press, Annapolis, 1994. (Otto Giese was an officer in the merchant navy when he ran the blockade to Europe at the beginning of the war and then went on to become a U-boat officer. An interesting account with good photos.)

Gröner, Erich. *Die deutschen Kriegsschiffe 1815–1945*, J.F. Lehmanns, Munich, 1968. (This is the standard book on the technical data of German warships. Much of the information is tabulated, making it relatively easy for non-German readers. However the section dealing with U-boat losses contains a good proportion of questionable information.)

——. *Die Schiffe der deutschen Kriegsmarine und Luftwaffe und ihr Verbleib*, J.F. Lehmanns, Munich, 1976. (A condensed version of the previous title.)

——. *Die Handelsflotten der Welt*, 1942, J.F. Lehmanns, Munich, reprinted 1976. (Includes details of ships sunk up to 1942. This valuable publication was originally a confidential document and contains a complete list of ships, in similar style to Lloyd's Register. There is also a lengthy section containing Gröner's line drawings.)

—— and Mickel, Peter. *German Warships 1815–1945*, Vol. II 'U-boats and Mine Warfare Vessels', Conway, London, 1991. (Some of the information about U-boat losses is terribly out of date and needs revision.)

Groos, Otto. *Seekriegslehren*, E.S. Mittler, Berlin, 1929. (An account of the lessons learned during the First World War, written by a captain in the Imperial Navy.)

Güth, Rolf. *Die Marine des Deutschen Reiches 1919–1939*, Bernard & Graefe, Frankfurt, 1972. (A most interesting account of naval developments between the wars, written by a naval captain.)

Hadley, Michael. *U-boats against Canada*, McGill-Queen's University Press, Kingston and Montreal, 1985.

——. *Count not the Dead*, McGill-Queen's University Press, Montreal, Kingston and London, 1995.

Hahn, F. *Guidebook to the Military Historical Training Centre Exhibition of the Marineschule Mürwik*, Marineschule Press, Flensburg, 1978.

Hansen, Hans Jürgen. *Die Schiffe der deutschen Flotten 1848–1945*, Stalling, Oldenburg, 1973. (Contains excellent illustrations.)

Harlinghausen, C. Harald. *Ein Junge geht zur Kriegsmarine*, Wilhelm Köhler, Minden, 1942.

Harnack, Wolfgang. *Zerstörer unter deutscher Flagge*, Koehler, Herford, 1978.

Has, Ludwig and Evers, August-Ludwig. *Wilhelmshaven 1853–1945*, Lohse-Eissing, Wilhelmshaven, 1961. (A collection of most interesting and good quality photographs.)

Hering, Robert. *Chronik der Crew 37A 1937–1987*, produced for limited distribution by the author. (An excellent account of how naval officers were trained.)

Herlin, Hans. *Der letzte Mann von der Doggerbank*, Wilhelm Heyne, Munich, 1979. (About Fritz Kuert, the only survivor of *Doggerbank* [ex-*Speybank*]. He joined the ship in mid-ocean from the *Charlotte Schliemann*, after the mine-laying operation off South Africa. Most of the book deals with his survival, rather than with *Doggerbank*'s role in the cruiser war.)

Herzog, Bodo. *60 Jahre deutsche Uboote 1906–1966*, J.F. Lehmanns, Munich, 1968. (A useful book with much tabulated information.)

——. *U-boats in Action*, Ian Allan, Shepperton and Podzun, Dorheim. (A pictorial book with captions in English.)

Hirschfeld, Wolfgang. *Feindfahrten*, Neff, Vienna, 1982. (The secret diary of a U-boat radio operator compiled in the radio rooms of operational submarines. A most invaluable insight into the war and probably one of the most significant accounts of the war at sea.)

——. *Das Letzte Boot – Atlantik Farewell*, Universitas, Munich, 1989. (The last journey of *U234*, surrender in the United States and life in prisoner of war camps.)

—— and Brooks, Geoffrey. *Hirschfeld – The Story of a U-boat NCO 1940–46*, Leo Cooper, London, 1996. (A fascinating English language edition of Hirschfeld's life in U-boats.)

Hoffmann, Rudolf. *50 Jahre Olympia-Crew*, Hoffmann, Hamburg, 1986. (An excellent history of Crew 1936. Well illustrated.)

Högel, Georg. *Embleme Wappen Malings Deutscher Uboote 1939–1945*, Koehlers, Hamburg, Berlin, Bonn, 1997. (An excellent work dealing with U-boat emblems, especially those which were painted on conning towers. Very well illustrated with drawings by the author who served in U-boats during the war.)

Hümmelchen, Gerhard. *Handesstörer*, Mercator, Munich, 1960. (Although rather old, this is still the standard reference work on cruiser warfare. It has never been bettered and is invaluable, covering a wide aspect of the raiders' operations.)

——. *Die deutschen Seeflieger*, J.F. Lehmanns, Munich, 1976.

——. *Die deutschen Schnellboote*, Koehler/Mittler, Hamburg, Berlin, Bonn, 1997.

Hurd, Sir Archibald. *Britain's Merchant Navy*, Odhams, London. (Written during the war, it contains a fair volume of propaganda and wartime inaccuracies, but it provides an excellent insight into the British Merchant Navy.)

Hutson, Harry C. *Grimsby's Fighting Fleet,* Hutton Press, Beverley, 1990. (An interesting account of fishing boats' war service.)

Janssen, Jens. *Die Einsamen der Weltmeere*, Pabel, Rastatt. (An account of the last voyage of the blockade-breaker *Ermland* and of *Passat*'s minelaying operations. Janssen is a pen name of Jochen Brennecke.)

——. *Schiff 23 – Hilfskreuzer Stier*, SOS Heft No 197, Munich, 1956.

Jones, Geoffrey. *Under Three Flags*, William Kimber, London, 1973. (The story of the *Nordmark* and other armed supply ships of the German Navy during the Second World War. The author served aboard her after the war.)

Jones, W.A. *Prisoner of the Kormoran*, Australian Publishing Co., Sydney, 1944. (Cruiser warfare from a prisoner's point of view.)

Jung, D., Maass, M. and Wenzel, B. *Tanker und Versorger der deutschen Flotte 1900–1980*, Motorbuch, Stuttgart, 1981. (This excellent book is the standard reference work on the German supply system. Well illustrated with interesting photographs.)

——, Adneroth, Arno and Kelling, Norbert. *Anstriche und Tarnanstriche der deutschen Kriegsmarine*, Bernard & Graefe, Munich, 1977. (With English captions.)

Kähler, Wolfgang. *Schlachtschiff Gneisenau*, Koehlers, Herford, 1979. (A detailed account by the ship's First Gunnery Officer.)

Kahn, David. *Seizing the Enigma: The Race to Break the German U-boat Codes, 1939–45*, Houghton Mifflin, Boston, 1991. (A good comprehensive account.)

Kannapin, Norbert. *Die Feldpostnummern der deutschen Kriegsmarine 1939–1945*, Kannapin, Itzehoe, 1974. (A reprint of an original Kriegsmarine booklet giving the field post numbers of sea-going units.)

Kaplan, Philip and Currie, Jack. *Wolfpack*, Aurum, London, 1997.

Keatts, Henry and Farr, George. *Dive into History*, American Merchant Marine Museum Press, New York, 1986. (Well researched with excellent illustrations giving a deep insight into U-boat activity on America's eastern seaboard.)

Kemp, Paul. *The Admiralty Regrets*, Sutton Publishing, Stroud, 1998. (British warship losses of the twentieth century.)

——. *U-boats Destroyed*, Arms and Armour, London, 1997. (An excellent book containing a great deal of recent research and useful explanations.)

Klietmann, Kurt-G. *Auszeichnungen des deutschen Reiches 1936–1945*, Motorbuch, Stuttgart, 1982. (A well-illustrated account of awards and medals.)

Koop, Gerhard and Mulitze, Erich. *Die Marine in Wilhelmshaven*, Bernard & Graefe, Koblenz, 1987. (Contains a large number of interesting photopraphs.)

——. and Schmolke, Klaus-Peter. *Battleships of the Bismarck Class*, Greenhill, London, 1998.

Krancke, Theodor and Brennecke, Jochen. *RRR Das glückhafte Schiff*, Koehlers, Biberach, 1955. (The story of *Admiral Scheer* written by the ship's commander.)

Kroschel, Günther and Evers, August-Ludwig. *Die deutsche Flotte 1848–1945*, Lohse-Eissing, Wilhelmshaven, 1974. (A collection of interesting photographs from Foto-Drüppel – now WZ Bilddienst. Most useful when identifying pictures.)

Kühn, Volkmar. *Torpedoboote und Zerstörer im Einsatz 1939–1945*, Motorbuch, Stuttgart, 1983.

——. *Schnellboote im Einsatz 1939–1945*, Motorbuch, Stuttgart, 1986.

Lakowski, Richard. *Deutsche U-Boote Geheim 1939–1945*, Brandenburgisches Verlagshaus, Berlin, 1991.

Ledebur, Gerhard. *Freiherr von Die Seemine*, J.F. Lehmanns, Munich, 1977.

Lohmann, W. and Hildebrand, H.H. *Die Deutsche Kriegsmarine 1939–1945*, Podzun, Dorheim, 1956–64. (This multi-volume work is the standard reference document on the German Navy, giving details of ships, organisation and personnel.)

Lumsden, R. A. *Collector's Guide to Third Reich Militaria*, Ian Allan, London, 1987.

Mattes, Klaus. *Die Seehunde*, Koehler/Mittler, Hamburg, Berlin, Bonn, 1997.

Meister, Jürg. *Der Seekrieg in den osteuropäischen Gewässern 1941–1945*, J.F. Lehmanns, Munich, 1958. (Includes details of cruiser warfare in Arctic waters.)

Mewissen, P. *Blockadebrecher*, Pabel, Rastatt.

Millington Drake, Sir Eugene. *The Drama of the Graf Spee and the Battle of the Plate*, Peter Davis, London, 1964.

Mohr, Ulrich. *Atlantis, Oberkommando der Kriegsmarine, 1942*. (Souvenir photograph album of *Atlantis*'s cruise produced for private distribution and now very rare.)

—— and Sellwood, A.V. *Atlantis*, Werner Laurie, London, 1955. (Dr Mohr was the commander's adjutant.)

Mollo, Andrew. *Naval, Marine and Air Force Uniforms of World War 2*, Blandford, Poole, 1975.

Moore, Captain Arthur R. *A Careless Word . . . A Needless Sinking*, American Merchant Marine Museum, Maine, 1983. (A detailed and well-illustrated account of ships lost during the war.)

Morison, Samuel Eliot. *History of United States Naval Operations in World War II*, Little, Brown and Company, Boston. (A multi-volume official history of the war at sea. Some of the information is rather one-sided and also somewhat dubious.)

Muggenthaler, August Karl. *German Raiders of World War II*, Robert Hale, London, 1978 and Prentice Hall, New York, 1978. (A detailed account dealing with auxiliary cruisers.)

Müllenheim-Rechberg, Baron Burkhard von. *Battleship Bismarck*, Bodley Head, London, 1981 and The United States Naval Institute, 1980. (A most detailed account by *Bismarck*'s senior surviving officer.)

Mulligan, Timothy P. *Lone Wolf: The Life and Death of U-boat Ace Werner Henke*, Praeger, Connecticut and London, 1993. (A well-researched book.)

OKM (Supreme Naval Command). *Bekleidungs und Anzugsbestimmungen für die Kriegsmarine*, Berlin, 1935; reprinted Jak P. Mallmann Showell, 1979. (The official dress regulations of the German Navy.)

——. *Rangliste der Deutschen Kriegsmarine*, Mittler & Sohn, published annually, Berlin.

Ostertag, Reinhard. *Deutsche Minensucher: 80 Jahre Seeminenabwehr*, Koehlers, Herford, 1987.

Pargeter, C.J. *'Hipper' Class Heavy Cruisers*, Ian Allan, London, 1982. (An excellent and well-illustrated book.)

Philpott, Bryan. *German Marine Aircraft*, Patrick Stephens, Cambridge, 1981. (An album of Bundesarchiv photographs.)

Plottke, Herbert. *Fächer Loos*, Podzun-Pallas, Wölfersheim-Berstadt. (The story of *U172*.)

Pope, Dudley. *73 North*, Weidenfeld & Nicolson, London, 1958. (About the Battle of the Barents Sea.)

Porten, Edward P. von der. *The German Navy in World War II*, Arthur Baker, London, 1970.

——. *Pictorial History of the German Navy in World War II*, Thomas Y. Crowell, New York, 1976. (An excellent book spoilt by poor reproduction of photographs.)

Powell, Michael. *Die Schicksalsfahrt der Graf Spee*, Heyne, Munich, 1976.

Prager Hans-Georg. *Panzerschiff Deutschland / Schwerer Kreuzer Lützow*, Koehlers, Herford, 1981. (A detailed account of the ship, her operations and her crew. Well illustrated with many interesting photographs, diagrams and maps. The author served aboard her.)

Preston, Anthony. *U-boats*, Arms and Armour Press, London, 1978. (Excellent photographs.)

Price, Alfred. *Aircraft versus Submarine*, William Kimber, London, 1973.

Raeder, Erich. *Struggle for the Sea*, William Kimber, London, 1959.

——. *My Life*, United States Naval Institute, 1960; translation of *Mein Leben*, F. Schlichtenmayer, Tübingen, 1956.

Rasenack, F.W. *Panzerschiff Admiral Graf Spee*, Wilhelm Heyne, Munich, 1981.

Rogge, Bernhard and Frank, Wolfgang. *Under Ten Flags*, Weidenfeld & Nicolson, London, 1957; translation of *Schiff 16*, Stalling, Oldenburg and Hamburg, 1955. (Rogge was commander of auxiliary cruiser *Atlantis*.)

Rohwer, J. *Der Krieg zur See 1939–1945*, Urbes, Munich, 1992. (Excellent photographs about the war at sea, but there are no captions and it is necessary to read through the text to understand their meaning.)

——. *Axis Submarine Successes of World War II 1939–45*, Patrick Stephens, Cambridge, 1983. (To be republished by Greenhill, London, 1998.)

—— and Hümmelchen, G. *Chronology of the War at Sea 1939–1945*, Greenhill, London, 1992. (A good, solid and informative work. Well indexed and most useful for anyone studying the war at sea.)

Rosignoli, Guido. *Naval and Marine Badges and Insignia*, Blandford, Poole, 1980.

Roskill, Captain S.W. *The War at Sea*, 4 vols, HMSO, London, 1954, reprinted 1976. (The official history of the war at sea, 1939 to 1945. Somewhat one-sided.)

Rössler, Eberhard. *Die deutschen Uboote und ihre Werften*, Bernard & Graefe, Koblenz, 1979.

——. *Die Torpedoes der deutschen U-Boote*, Koehlers, Herford, 1984.

——. *Geschichte des deutschen Ubootbaus*, Bernard & Graefe, Koblenz, 1986.

Ruge, Friedrich. *Sea Warfare 1939–45: A German Viewpoint*, Cassell, London, 1957; translation of *Der Seekrieg 1939–1945*, Koehler, Stuttgart, 1962 and published in the United States as *Der Seekrieg* (*The German Navy's Story, 1939–45*), Naval Institute Press, Annapolis, 1957. (Ruge was an officer in the Kriegsmarine.)

Schmalenbach, Paul. *Die deutschen Hilfskreuzer*, Stalling, Oldenburg and Hamburg, 1977. (This is a pictorial record of German auxiliary cruisers from 1895 to 1945, the best photographs being from the two world wars.)

——. *Kreuzer Prinz Eugen unter drei Flaggen*, Koehlers, Herford, 1978.

Schmeelke, Michael. *Alarm Küste*, Podzun-Pallas, Wölfersheim-Berstadt.

Schmelzkopf, Reinhard. *Die deutsche Handelsschiffahrt 1919–1939*, Stalling, Oldenburg and Hamburg. (A two-volume chronology about the development of the German merchant navy between the two wars.)

Schmoeckel, Helmut. *Menchlichkeit im Seekrieg?* Mittler und Sohn, Herford, 1987.

Schultz, Willy. *Kreuzer Leipzig*, Motorbuch Verlag, Stuttgart.

Schwandtke, Karl-Heinz. *Deutschlands Handelsschiffe*, Stalling, Oldenburg and Hamburg. (Details of German merchant ships at the start of the war, with information about ships captured during the conflict. Also included are vessels that were not completed, and detailed line drawings.)

Showell, Jak P. Mallmann. *The German Navy in World War Two*, Arms and Armour Press, London, 1979; Naval Institute Press, Annapolis 1979 and translated as *Das Buch der deutschen Kriegsmarine*, Motorbuch Verlag, Stuttgart, 1982. (Covers history, organisation, the ships, code writers, naval charts and a section on ranks, uniforms, awards and insignias by Gordon Williamson. Named by the United States Naval Institute as 'One of the Outstanding Naval Books of the Year'.)

——. *U-boats under the Swastika*, Ian Allan, Shepperton, 1973; Arco, New York, 1973 and translated as *Uboote gegen England*, Motorbuch, Stuttgart, 1974. (A well-illustrated introduction to the German U-boat service, which is now one of the longest selling naval books in Germany.)

——. *U-boats under the Swastika*, Ian Allan, London, 1987. (A second edition with different photos and new text of the above-mentioned title.)

——. *U-boat Command and the Battle of the Atlantic*, Conway Maritime Press, London, 1989; Vanwell, New York, 1989. (A detailed history based on the U-boat Command's war diary.)

——. *Germania International*, Journal of the German Navy Study Group. Now out of print.

——. *U-boat Commanders and their Crews*, Crowood Press, Marlborough, 1998.

Smith, Constance Babington. *Evidence in Camera*, David & Charles, Newton Abbot, 1974. (The story of the Royal Air Force's Photographic Reconnaissance Unit, with an interesting insight into how the major German warships were tracked and consequently attacked.)

Sorge, Siegfried. *Der Marineoffizier als Führer und Erzieher*, E.S. Mittler, Berlin, 1937.

Stahl, Peter. *Kriegsmarine Uniforms, Insignia, Daggers & Medals of the German Navy 1935–1945*, Die Wehrmacht, Stanford (California), 1972. (A well-illustrated book.)

Stärk, Hans. *Marineunteroffizierschule*, Naval Officers' School, Plön, 1974.

Stern, Robert C. *Kriegsmarine: A Pictorial History of the German Navy 1939–1945*, Arms and Armour Press, London. (Very good photographs.)

Syrett, David. *The Defeat of the Wolf Packs*, South Carolina Press, Columbia, 1994.

Tarrant, V.E. *The U-boat Offensive 1914–1945*, Arms and Armour Press, London, 1989.

Terraine, John. *Business in Great Waters*, Leo Cooper, London, 1989.

Thomas, David A. *The Atlantic Star 1939–45*, W.H. Allen, London, 1990.

Trevor-Roper. *Hitler's War Directives 1939–1945*, Sidgwick & Jackson, London, 1964. (One would think that the name 'Hitler' in the title would not require the years at the end! But still a good book, giving an insight into the higher command.)

US Naval Intelligence. *German Naval Vessels of World War Two*, Greenhill, London, 1993. (An excellent book for identifying warships. It was originally carried on board ships at sea for identifying vessels they might meet.)

Vat, Dan van der. *The Atlantic Campaign*, Hodder & Stoughton, 1988. (A well-researched and interesting book.)

Verband Deutscher Ubootsfahrer. *Schaltung Küste* (Journal of the German Submariners' Association).

Wagner, Gerhard (ed.). *Lagevorträge des Oberbefehlshabers der Kriegsmarine vor Hitler*, J.F. Lehmanns, Munich, 1972. (Translated as *Fuehrer Conferences on Naval Affairs*, Greenhill, London, reprinted with new introduction 1990, but originally the English language edition was published before the German version.)

Watts, A.J. *The Loss of the Scharnhorst*, Ian Allan, Shepperton, 1970.

——. *The U-boat Hunters*, Macdonald and Jane's, London, 1976.

Welham, Michael. *Kampfschwimmer*, Motorbuch, Stuttgart, 1997.

Werner, Herbert. *Iron Coffins*, Arthur Baker, London, 1969.

Weyher, Kurt and Ehrlich, Hans-Jürgen. *Vagabunden auf See*, Katzmann, Tübingen, 1953. (The story of the auxiliary cruiser *Orion* by her commander.)

Whitley, M.J. *Destroyer! German Destroyers in World War II*, Arms and Armour Press, London, 1983.

——. *German Cruisers of World War Two*, Arms and Armour Press, London, 1985. (An excellent account, well-illustrated with plans and photographs.)

Williamson, Gordon. *The Iron Cross*, Blandford, Poole, 1984. (An excellent and well-illustrated account.)

——. *Knights of the Iron Cross*, Blandford, Poole, 1987. (An excellent follow-on from the above title.)

—— and Pavlovik, Darko. *U-boat Crews 1914–45*, Osprey, London, 1995. (A most interesting book with excellent colour drawings and black and white photographs.)

Winton, John. *Ultra at Sea*, Leo Cooper, London, 1988. (About breaking the U-boat radio codes.)

Witthöft, Hans Jürgen. *Lexikon zur deutschen Marinegeschichte*, Koehler, Herford, 1977. (An excellent two-volume encyclopedia.)

Woodward, David. *The Secret Raiders*, William Kimber, London, 1955. (An account of German auxiliary cruisers.)

Zienert, J. *Unsere Marineuniform*, Helmut Gerhard Schulz, Hamburg, 1970. (An excellent record of German naval uniforms.)

INDEX

Where entries run over more than one page, only the first page has been indexed.